NAKED HEART

Talking on Poetry, Mysticism, and the Erotic

WILLIAM EVERSON

An AMERICAN POETRY *Book*
Albuquerque, New Mexico

Cover and text design by Amy Evans
Cover portrait by Kathryn Tousaint

Published by the College of Arts and Sciences,
University of New Mexico

First printing.

LIBRARY OF CONGRESS CATALOGING-IN-PUBLICATION
Everson, William, 1912–
    Naked heart : talking on poetry, mysticism, and
erotic / William Everson.
        p.   cm. — (American poetry studies in
twentieth century poetry and poetics)
    "An American poetry book."
    Includes index.
    ISBN 0-9629172-4-9
    1. Everson, William, 1912–   —Interviews.
2. Poets, American—20th century—Interviews.
3. Mysticism in literature.   4. Sex in
literature.   5. Poetry.   I. Title.   II. Series.
PS3509.V65Z466   1992
811'.52—dc20   92-8016
                                          CIP

Contents

Preface

For the poet, the ongoing preoccupation with the interview as a literary form endows it with something like the status of a mainstay. The practice of poetry is so demanding that only the most profound of subjects succeeds with it; and it goes without saying that the poet has much more to offer. His passion and intelligence between them constitute a wide parameter. No matter how much he talks he feels he has not quite had his say.

The virtue of the interview lies in its immediacy. Compared to it the essay emerges as formalistic and even stilted, dismissed as dry unless it also happens to be very good. An essay has to have style; not so the interview. All it consists of is the speech of people conversing. It is true that some writers possess spectacular conversational skills, among whom may be counted many poets. But it is also true that such skills are not acquirable by the verbally unendowed, and in any case are in short supply. But the interview is so rudimentary that it can redeem those with valuable ideas or experience but who lack the means to express them. For a skilled interviewer can take an intelligent but inarticulate candidate, and by the force and subtlety of acute questioning can produce a comprehensive verbal artifact. So it should come as no surprise that the poet, however gifted with a golden tongue, finds it easier and more direct, touching on expository matters, to speak through the interview.

This brings us to our title, *Naked Heart*, chosen to body forth the point just noted: that the most pervasive literary form of immediacy is, after poetry itself, the interview. Each invites, nay, demands, candor. Naked heart is the last stage before bleeding heart—excess is that fatal to the form. But candor is its own reward, and the interview shares it with the poem. The affinity between the two modes is not contrived but subsistent. Poetry of itself is more palpable, and concurrently more evocative, but the interview is right behind it, in the shimmer of its insights, its rapidity of turn and counterpoint, its verve and changing pace.

Take for instance the work of William Carlos Williams. Although he published some traditional verse, his contribution, and his prestige, lay in his advocacy of open form. He reads like the flow of prose, or, better, like a fervent interview, in that significance springs like telepathic promptings from the weft of words, guided by the genius of the poet to the measure of objective tenets.

Before him, Ezra Pound, writing in 1912, had confirmed open form as the fundamental American poetic idiom, following the lead of Whitman, defining thereby the quintessence of the inceptive Modernist movement, and the reflex took. Its properties of brilliant improvisation, as well as its scrupulously acute attention to the factor of aesthetic distance, became its hallmark.

This made for brevity of form in the interest of precision, but open form is still open, and with the passing of Modernism, Whitman's "buffalo strength," typified by his long line, is emerging into favor. It will be none too soon. If the poet's function is to translate the terrors of the past, through the exigence of aesthetic form, into the resolution that the properties of wholeness confer, he will need all the certitude of his charismatic calling to carry him through, from the unspeakable horror of this century into the empty womb of the next. Nothing less will serve for a torch through the night of the pitiless stars.

> For the naked heart of the poet
> Glides ever away, returning
> To the dim swamp lands of the soul
> Where Good and Evil, ancient antagonists
> Like rutting dinosaurs in the freezing sloughs,
> Savagely disembowel each other
> As they copulate to the death.

NAKED
HEART

The Artist And Religious Life

QUESTION: Brother Antoninus, what are your views in regard to a creative artist in a religious community? The first problem that comes to mind is that creativity requires a certain amount of freedom. But in religious life there must be a regimen and people tend sometimes to get into a rut, or they tend toward mediocrity; they also find life monotonous. This seems to be just the opposite of the spontaneous creativity typical of an artist. Do these two problems really fit together, or not?

BROTHER ANTONINUS:[1] Strictly speaking, they do not go together. The problem of the artist in religious life is to try to bring them together, but that point of union is a cross because, strictly speaking, they do not go together. This reflects the basic conflict of the Church itself between its charismatic and its institutional life. By conflict, I do not mean an irreconcilable opposition, but creative tension. This is the situation of the artist in religious life. He is definitely on the charismatic side but he finds that the life he lives is very institutionalized. Between these two factors, this problem emerges.

The basic question is, why does an artist go into a religious community at all? The artist is an imaginative man, and the whole mode of an artist is freedom. The imagination, strictly speaking, knows no laws. It operates on the correspondence it sees in its inner vision, and this has no restrictions. It is an amoral phenomenon; it has no pejorative commitments to make; it has nothing but its own power of synthesis and its projection into the possible. Memory contains the past; imagination presents or projects the possible; and after this the intellect

Originally appearing in *The American Benedictine Review*, XI, 3–4 (Sept.–Dec., 1960), pp. 223–238, this interview was conducted by Colman Barry as part of a symposium, "The Catholic and Creativity."

makes the judgment. To overcome the *vis cogitativa* which already predetermines the action anyhow, is the problem of the spiritual man. But at least for the artist, whose domain is imagination rather than the intellectual realm of the philosopher, this is the problem which he brings into the realm of institutional life. It is the problem of any highly imaginative man. The problem for the spiritual man, the man seeking perfection, is to curb the sensibility; for the artist, to liberate the sensibility. I do not think there is any solution to it except that he knows, when he comes in, that the reason he comes in, is because he is willing to put his art second. If he is not willing to do this, then he is not an artist meant for a religious institution. He should remain a secular artist in the world. When he comes to religious life, it is because he is probably drawn by the fact that there is so great an imbalance in himself between imagination and intellect. Now I am not equating institutional life with the intellect by a long shot, but it is the conventional life and it has taken a long history to establish itself. The conventional, while often not very intelligent, does relate to man's rational life. The artist however, is attuned to the irrational unconscious. He may be drawn to religious life because he hopes that the charismatic element in its conventions will help solve his difficulties with the institutional world.

QUESTION: You were a creative artist before you came to the Dominicans. Dominican life, the contemplative life, should bear some fruit in terms of creative art. Some young people coming to religious life could develop into creative artists; they have been and will be an inevitable part of the community. Superiors look at religious life somewhat differently, and it is possible that they might be worried by the individuality that attaches itself to an artist; if there are a number of them, there are possibilities of clashes in the community. It is the kind of conflict that is almost inevitable. Do you have any helpful or hopeful suggestions in this matter?

ANTONINUS: I think that the conflict is inevitable. The artist himself will find himself on the cross in society. This is part of his fate there, and it is the fate that he encounters very directly in religious life, because in that tension between the institutional and the charismatic, the institutional mentality is, by nature, by virtue of its position, not necessarily maliciously suspicious of any charismatic phenomenon. If you are a mystic today, you get hauled off to a hospital for observation. Any real breakthrough from the unconscious side into the ego is a highly suspect phenomenon to the institutional mind. St. Paul himself outside of Damascus would not last a minute today. They would have him in a hospital under observation very shortly. This is the institutional side of all cultures.[2]

Any religion can only develop by refining the tension between its charismatic and institutional elements. This tension finally breaks through, and I think the prophets in the Old Testament demonstrate the history of this tension between institutional and charismatic lives. When the charismatic finally breaks through an institutional matrix, and makes its pronouncement, it brings down upon itself the whole wrath of an almost unconscious terror from the opposite side. But for the religious artist himself, you see, the problem is complex because he bears these two things within himself. Before there is a censor from without there is a censor from within. It is this censor within, the institutional man within himself, fearful of his charismatic side which is his great individual problem. It is a situation of the real Dionysian artist over against the Apollonian who fits fairly well. The Apollonian artist will go to college, he will take writing courses, he will pass them all, do competent work, good work; then he will become an instructor and constantly adapt himself to the institutional side. But your Dionysians, charismatic people, cannot do this. They are drawn to college at first because they find no understanding outside in the practical world. The only place they can see any consolation at all is in the universities. So they go there but they don't find themselves very happy there. The reduction of the charismatic thing to the formula of the teaching method becomes intolerable to them. Either that happens, or they come into an ego conflict with their mentor. Or, more fatally, they will become assimilated or lost in the personality of a stronger man. That sometimes happens.

Usually, however, the Dionysian will make a break after a semester or two and then go out and go it alone on the outside. This is what happened to me. It was a semester or two at college for me, and that was the end of it. I had no more to gain there.[3] I went back to the practical world, and I had nothing there. So I became a solitary and projected over against the world, and had no real mode of communication with it, until, actually, my conversion, when I, as I put it to *Time* magazine,[4] began my road back to the world and the "squares." That is true, I think, because the institutional world is the world of the "squares," in the modern "Beat" parlance. It is the structured, solid, safe world. The function of institutions is to make for security. The function of the charismatic is to break that down,[5] to see beyond it into a new illumination. Otherwise the very of the formative phase becomes sterile.[6] I think that this reverses back to the problem of the division in the human intellect which St. Thomas treats of, the fact that there cannot be a third type of life. There is only the active life of the institutional, or the contemplative life of the charismatic, this fatal oscillation between the two.[7] The Dominicans try to solve it by adopting a third form of life which is, as St. Thomas says, under the active, although it is an overflow from the contemplative side. Strictly speaking it is an active life. Dominicans like to call it the apostolic life. This is to distinguish it from the straight works of mercy of the active life.[8]

The artist himself is directly involved in this problem of the human intellect. He, being over on the contemplative or charismatic side, and very strongly over there, then finds himself at odds. I think the mystic goes through this same problem in his religious life. In fact the history of the mystic proves it. They are often at odds with the institutional framework. In this sense the pattern of the artist is very old, although you will not find many of the true artists in religious life. There is John of the Cross, and Gerard Manley Hopkins, Fra Angelico, and people like that. The first two suffered but the last, Fra Angelico, apparently did not because they had an institutional need for him. But there is no institutional need for poets. St. Thomas could write a poem on commission for the liturgy, and it could be a great poem. How he could do that I do not know. But John of the Cross had to put away his gift. Hopkins had to really make a sacrifice of his gift. There again the censor was within Hopkins. I do not think this point is brought out sufficiently in the life of Hopkins, namely that he censored himself out of the picture.[9] He did not do it in the way John of the Cross did.

He did not die the saintly death of John of the Cross because he had not met the matter within himself. He was snowed under by the situation, whereas John of the Cross was not.

QUESTION: There is obviously some problem about the spontaneity of the artist and the regimen of communal living. There is some conflict between the creative artist that normally emerges in a contemplative life and the administration of the superiors in charge of the institution. From the superior's point of view, the artist is going to have various interests. Would you think that he should confine his indulgence to an interest in sacred art? Is there relatively little room in a religious community for a man, a creative artist, whose interests are not religious, that is, his artistic interests are not religious?

ANTONINUS: I think that a man who comes to the religious life will have interests that are religious. Otherwise, he will not stay very long. Every once in a while a religious artist himself will be compelled to take up a secular theme. As a matter of fact, a man might come to the religious life for a year or two; he might even become 'trapped' in the religious life, say he took vows rather early before he matured, or he matured late and then finds himself stuck with his situation, and constantly nurses this nostalgia for secular life, and treats of it in his secular poems. I do not think even in a case like that there is any real disparity between the religious life *per se* and work. It might become a problem if he came to publish, as far as the reaction it will cause. I do not think the artist's case is worse than any other. There will not be any more of a problem, for an artist than any other secular vocation that a religious might have, such as teaching secular history. A religious would naturally be interested in that, or in any of the other interest that a religious might have. I think that the problem falls more or less in line, except for the one of publication, which I really do not think in modern life would be much of a problem either.[10] The participation in secular affairs by a religious is so broad now that one could even be a golf champion.

The amount of freedom an artist needs in order to do what I do comes into conflict from the point of view of superiors. The problem

as I have encountered it myself has opened a tremendous insight into
the tolerance on the part of superiors who do not know quite how to
make an exception in a community where they have the problems of
corporate living to deal with. In other words, when you make an
exception for a man and give him freedom from other responsibilities,
it sets up a special situation which takes a very committed superior to
be able to ignore objections, and just go ahead, saying, "We have a
genius in our midst and we are going to protect him." I have never
heard it done to that extent.[11]

QUESTION: A superior might be quite sympathetic to the complex
situation facing a member of the community who is a creative artist.
However, there are some active artists who are genuine, and there are
some who are escapists. Are there any suggestions you could make?
How is the wheat separated from the chaff?

ANTONINUS: We must see how it works out practically, and that is the
only way we can operate because a hypothesis always breaks down in
actual experience. If a man comes to religious life he has to be reformed.
That is the reason be comes in the first place. The reason that an artist
comes to the religious life is the same reason that anyone else comes.
He wants a reformation of the inner man, and he is going to have to
be forced to give up a lot of things he would otherwise want to do.
Maybe there will have to be an abandonment of a very considerable
part of his talent for a while. In fact, if he were a great artist, the
world might even lose some great masterpieces in that period of time.
I myself have lost some poems which I knew would have been fine
things if I could have gotten to them. But it was not possible under
those circumstances. It was better for me that I had to live the full
regimen in order to keep the thing I came for than if I had total
freedom of expression. For it was my sense of lack of perfection that
brought me to the religious life, and the need for perfection that
brought me to the religious life, and the need for perfection that comes
before the overflow. Unless the contemplative part of religious life can
be purified, the overflow itself will not be pure. It is this need to get
rid of impurities in the ego that brings a man and bears him through.
Under the inevitable testing, the reality of human life is so great that

what you are becomes apparent to others. The reason why a man like Hopkins, although he must have been loved in his community, was not taken seriously as an artist was that he censored himself out on the inside. The problem in himself was never met, and historically his time was unfortunate in religious life, because in late nineteenth century Victorian England the whole concept of obedience was pretty much oversimplified. I do not know what a whole Thomistic penetration into that matter would yield. Often one of the problems is that he throws away or does not have the interior freedom to be, to measure to the wholeness of his gifts because he has not measured up to the inner problem. That is a broad generalization to imply in Hopkins, and I do not know if I will regret these candid observations that are coming out of me. But I do know that I must believe them because I have thought about him a good deal, and I have not liked at all his solution to the problem, his failure to meet the problem. But this does not have anything to do at all with his ability as an artist.[12]

I prefer the solution of John of the Cross because he made it a renunciation.[13] I have never renounced. John of the Cross was a priest, and a superior. My problem has not been that well-defined and as a result my instinct, to put it that way, has never told me that there is an incompatibility between the most extreme penetration of my imagination and my state in life as a religious. My Dominican background has cancelled out that problem. I might have brought it in with me, but what I could pick up form the Order by osmosis and by consultation with the Fathers, but more by living the life, was that there is not any problem here. It is a pseudo-problem.[14] You simply go to the extreme of creative intuition, and that is the end of it. If there are fears that rise up against that, it is an imperfection within myself that has also to be met and overcome. The form of the art will carry that imperfection forward into itself and will register itself there. That is where the tension comes from, this cleavage within the person, and this is the thing that spiritualizes you, and it is a meeting of these inner problems. The cross of the artist is both interior as well as exterior.

QUESTION: As far as external appearances go, you have adjusted to the life. There must have been within you, as with all of us, a certain amount of internal struggle. There must be a certain number of men who are, by God's gift, creative artists who also feel the need of some of the benefits that are provided by religious life. Would you tend to encourage those men, would you tend to discourage them, or would you be willing to talk on the subject of that type of vocation?

ANTONINUS: It seems to me that without doubt the isolation and the alienation of the artist leaves a great emptiness in his heart for assimilation into some form of the institutional life. It might well be that his only mode would be under the religious aspect. This is certainly true of myself. I would never be able to teach at a college or to fit into any mode of the institutional world except as a religious. This was my solution when I entered the Church. It became inevitable to me before very long that I was going to gravitate into religious life. It was the healing of this alienation on one side of my personality that was part of the motivation, but it was not the primary thing. The first thing about a vocation is that there is a need for perfection. This is what impels a man to come. If he is confused about his motives when be comes, they will soon be clarified in the religious life because its pressures force him very soon to come to terms with that problem. You can get along, as you know, in the novitiate on a variety of impulses. But before long the realities of the situation will clarify themselves strongly, especially if a man is mature. To be no more than a farmer, to be no more than a philosopher or a teacher, no more than any one of things can a man enter religious life and expect to find a haven for the practice of his gifts. I wish that were so, but if that is all he wants, he should build another kind of community. Just because there is not an adequate art community does not mean that one is not possible. But they never seem very successful.

If you come to the religious life, you come to do sacrifice. This is imperative. If this is not understood, woe to the man who comes; if his inner search, his grasp of reality, does not exceed his other concerns, even his art becomes a trifling thing. There is a difference between an authentic artist and the pseudos. There is the pseudo artist who is a man not willing to carry his art to the point where the art drops away and a superior principle subsumes it. To be able to do that heroically, to be able to carry your art to that point and then to be able to cancel it out, and know your search is for that life beyond art—this is the thing that makes an artist great. I have no fear of this problem. I once had a fear of it. During the years of holocaust in the religious life, the first seven, I feared losing the only thing I had which I had placed a priority of human value upon, and that was my art. A young man who comes into the religious life before his talents are developed does not have a problem that is so acute. He hardly knows what he can do. But I had fifteen years of a developed career as a poet and was, in fact, just coming into my own on a national scene when my conversion occurred and I was drawn to the religious life. Suddenly I found myself confronted with a problem and its ego-demand on me was very great because usually one's sensibility has found its anchor someplace in the world. Until the transformation, the spiritual crossover is attained in the inner soul, the whole impulsion of the will is going to be that earthly anchorage. In the introduction to *The Crooked Lines of God*, I spoke about a great talent dried up in 1954. This was the problem at the bottom of it all, namely that I had come to this impasse. I had exhausted my capacity to create in the confines of the religious life as it had been, as I had experienced it. I had to go through a whole transformation of attitude towards the religious life, and to break through my restrictive notions on literal observance and the terrible attempt to be the most monastic of monks when the interior thing had been stifled. I had attempted exterior observance and I had no inner freedom. In the years that followed, and the real breakthrough came, I was forced either to leave the life or to go abandoning the creative urge as St. John of the Cross was able to do. I was torn from it. I mean it dried up on me, and I could very easily have left the Order in those years. It was only by the grace of God I did not, because I do not know why.

QUESTION: You have written poetry, both profane and sacred, and have been successful in both fields. Do you have any ideas about sacred art? What is it? What is its function?

ANTONINUS: The latitude of art is so great that it is able to serve many aspects of the human community and the individual psyche. Most of sacred art as it has come down to us due to the historical conditions of Christianity has been a kind of collective art. The major instances of sacred art which are commonly listed—Gregorian chant, mosaics, cathedrals[15]—these three examples are all collective art. They reveal the ability of a religious movement or community to consolidate itself in terms of collective performances, probably over against the secular world in order to insure the permanency of registration of it values. It was in modern times when that collective mould was broken at the Renaissance. Out of this new order emerged the individual ego freed from the collective. The problem became different. It is not possible for us to revive at this time anything like a liturgical art of collective authenticity. The various attempts to do it in Europe produce an art which is monkish. Some people have even felt in the revival of Gregorian chant a stiltedness that, due to its pedantic character, they hold, would not obtain in more creative centuries when that art itself was vibrant, young, and useful. I do not know. To me the epitome of the modern sacred artist is Rouault. I look to him as the sign and archetype of what an individual artist confronted with the problems of his relation to society is capable of producing. He was a solitary by nature and never did engage in events.[16] He was, therefore, charismatic and on the contemplative side. This solitude he preserved religiously, so he was able to plumb into the depths of his soul and to emerge with the most powerful expression of Christian art that the contemporary world has produced; his art is more powerful than any other sphere—literature, music, or painting.[17]

As a printer I am able to engage in this too, because as a printer I am able to contribute and participate with my aesthetic sense in the collective, more as a medieval monk might have done than I am able to as a poet. A printer's work is essentially functional. Therefore, you can subsume the aesthetic; I do not say embellish. That is a mistaken notion. But you can subsume the aesthetic sufficiently into the functional that a work of genuine validity, deep earnestness, and real creativity emerges. This is possible. But this is not the same thing as with the fine arts. I doubt if it is any longer possible for an artist to take a commission, for instance, to do a sculpture in a church and out of that have emerge art of the greatness, the unconscious greatness, of Rouault, in his private individual revelations.[18] I think the unconscious bond of the collective that produced great sculpture that we see in medieval cathedrals is lost. You could get a high degree of proficiency and of aesthetic satisfaction in that art; in fact, we see it everywhere, but you do not get the terminal point. You do not get in our contemporary liturgical art what could rival the great collective periods themselves. I think, however, that in a Rouault you do get the thing that rivals them. We can posit the achievement of a Rouault and say that the individual artist in his creative vision achieves in this time that same depth. Possibly it is even higher, because he bears it on his back as he subsumes it into himself,[19] and projects beyond it, and gets the new dimension of the creative.

This is what I believe the poet himself must strive for, and what I myself strive for. The functional falls a way for the modern artist in a way it did not for the collective artist. He stood on his functionalism and blessed it with his effort. Because of the unconscious need to achieve collective wholeness he transcended himself in that achievement. The artist moved out of his collective side into the naked exposure, which is the depths of creative illumination. He approached very close to the mystics with this charismatic insight.[20] Maybe the artists will be for our day the modern mystics in the true sense of the word.

Those are my feelings about art, not because of theory, but because of the direction within myself, as I have been forced to overcome the merely super-ego aspects to do good monastic work, and to be real always to the creative vision. It has carried me to a situation of great exposure within myself, and sometimes it is very terrifying because the ego wants to deny this. The ego wants to censor it out, wants to deny its truth. To be truer and truer to that vision is the whole function of what the artist is and must be. In this he is like the prophet. We have heard a great deal about this problem of art and contemplation, but I am not very happy with some of the solutions that have been posited to it. Their hypotheses of that seem good. You have practical activity, then you have aesthetic activity, and then above that you have transcendent activity where these two fall away, namely, illumination of mystical infusion. No one can quarrel with the scale, but in practice something else happens. It was not until I read Father White's book *God and the Unconscious*[21] that I realized that, when he was talking about the prophet, he was actually talking about how the prophet sees the same field of vision as everyone else, but he sees it under a different aspect, in a different modality. It is this difference of perspective of the prophet from the collective around him which gives him his prophetic character. I saw that is essentially what the artist does. I saw that there are actually two kinds of contemplatives—the contemplative as we generally understand him, and another aspect which is the prophetic. It is very well and good on the ascent to contemplation, but there is also a descent. It is wrong to put the artist on the ascent. There is the practical, the aesthetic, and then the mystical infusion, because there is an aestheticism by which we behold the beauty of nature and perceive beauty. But when you make art you are on the other side. You are coming down.[22] As the religious artist comes down from contemplative intuition and infusion, his art partakes of that infusion. So his art is in a sense a step beyond contemplation, in the very way that the prophetic gift[23] is greater than contemplation, because it is an overflow of the act of contemplation, and therefore higher. In some such way the art is greater than the artist, if his theme is the theme of the highest things, and shares the prophet's preeminence in the domain of religious intuition. A Rouault does this. His tremendous range and impact of chromatic intensity, infused in his paintings into the Christian mystery, are prophecies, in the same way that through the sentient medium they reveal; and communicate. I should not say they communicate, because art is not a communication, really. They reveal. It is a connaturality that transcends the media of communication. I believe that a fusion of the aesthetic and the illuminative truth becomes truly prophetic. The poet shares this, too, if he has reached within himself those depths where his vision is fused together and his ego is transcended in the exalted contemplative illumination that mystical infusion is capable of.[24]

Notes

1. There are two types of verbal communication. One is oral, spoken; the other is literary, written. I practice both, but I am usually disconcerted to see the one transliterated into the other. The spoken work is often art; it is rarely literature. Literary style is precisely the art of bringing to writing the meaningful inflections which are lost when speech is stenographically recorded. The following interview, which was tape recorded and should be heard to be completely understood, dismayed me with its diffuseness on the written page. I had no idea my speech was so loosely formulated. But the customary recourse

to editorial correction seems to result in a hybrid product, possessing neither the directness of speech nor the structure of literature. I have, therefore, let the script stand as it comes to me from the editor and will rely on footnotes to amplify my meaning rather than modifying for matters of style. I am somewhat reassured in this by the practice of the more reliable news magazines, who report the words of, say, the president, exactly as caught by the tape recorder, even to the suggestive hemming and hawing of a man searching for the right word; which somehow, in spite of the disconcerting shapelessness, communicates the gist of the man's thinking, especially as to relative emphasis, more than the literary but sometimes totally misapplied renditions of the fancier reporters. Men in public life are constantly appalled to see in the press words attributed to them which in phrasing do violence to their meanings. What follows then should be heard, and since this is not possible, the reader should bear with the diffuseness, the gangling awkwardness, the almost painful incoherence of these groping phrases. I must have said them, but on the naked page I do not recognize them as children of mine. My real meaning, which is my attitude, was lost with the sound of my voice. You might say it never got off the tape.

2. This could have been stated more circumspectly, but the identity of the mystic and the madman is historic, if not to say classic, so I shall let these pungencies stand without fear of contradiction. Exceptions apart, their truth seems obvious.

3. That is, I *felt* I had no more to gain. Actually, I had a great deal to gain, but the unconscious imbalance in my nature would not tolerate it.

4. *Time*, 25 May 1959. The sensational, inaccurate way in which my conversion was reported in this magazine stands, for me, as an object lesson in journalistic practice. I refer to the difference between the story as read back to me by a sympathetic reporter, and the text which finally issued from the editor's desk in New York.

5. Not in the destructive, but rather in the transforming sense. From the institutional point of view, the problem is always one of determining between regressive (destructive) and transforming (charismatic) effects. It is an egoistic identification with the institutional world which makes the pharisee, so that he condemns the charismatic truth as potentially dangerous: "He stirreth up the people . . . ." But more poignantly there is an archetypal mystery that renders each inexplicable to the other. The charismatic man, the mystic, is bound to adhere to the truth envisioned, and that truth is innocent of harm. The institutional man, in responsibility to his charge, is bound to proscribe and even persecute the charismatic man until the actual state of affairs is clarified. This is the tragic apotheosis by which the Church is purged, and through which she develops her inner life.

6. If the defects of the institutional man are blindness and aridity (pride), those of the charismatic man are indiscipline and excess (enthusiasm). The liabilities of pseudo-charismatic excess have been brilliantly exposited by the late Monsignor Ronald Knox in his masterpiece, *Enthusiasm*. But who will write its companion piece (entitled, say, *Sterility*), in which the horrible inertial of a monumental institutionalism is delineated and laid bare? It is indicative of our time that the one task has been accomplished with such brilliance and dispatch, while the other is quite undreamed of, or left to the malice of the Church's enemies.

7. I say fatal oscillation because, due to the division in the human intellect, it is not possible for there to be a true stasis, a true synthesis. One or the other must dominate. The question arises, which one should it be? There is no doubt in the minds of the institutionalists, and history does not gainsay them. But that at the time of Christ the institutional element dominated the charismatic to the deficity of the latter seems undeniable; that Christ came to redress the balance in favor of the charismatic seems unquestionable; that in his own lifetime he was content to leave the institutional side of his temporal creation at a loose, unformulated level, is scripturally obvious; that the Church herself maintained the charismatic emphasis until the time of Constantine is generally accepted. These facts seem to argue a preponderance of divine favor on behalf of the charismatic. But that the social exigencies confronting the Church since Constantine have continued to require her to emphasize the institutional is, apparently, historically irrefutable, and given the facts of human nature, virtually inevitable, though one could argue the same for the Pharisees, whom Christ did not excuse. At any rate, however it be argued, what is historically inevitable is not thereby from the charismatic point of view ideal. When times are confused the people demand security, and they find it only too often not in charismatic infusion, but in the material fact of institutional identification. Such a Church, inevitable or no, is only temporary; when we find her in such straits we say of her that she is not herself.

8. This digression began principally as an example, as one tends to do in conversation. Since it could not be developed, it should properly have been struck out, but I let it stand as a clue for anyone who might wish to pursue it further. The germ of my thought is that the tension between the charismatic and institutional aspects of religious life is sourced in the division of the human intellect itself, as St. Thomas developed it after Aristotle. Hence the problem is personal before it is social, the secondary theme running throughout this interview.

9. Martin D'Arcy, S.J., hints at it: "Quite possibly the fact that he was a convert and that he had been brought up in the atmosphere of rectitude which belongs especially to Victorian religion, may help to account for some of the

puzzles of his character . . . . Other converts have exhibited the same un-resolved tension. They have startled and still startle the traditional Catholic by their inability to unbend," in Claude C. H. Williamson, O.S.C. (ed.), *Great Catholics* (New York: Macmillan, 1943), p. 359.

10. I cannot imagine how I could have been so sanguine; as a matter of fact, this is the very heart of the problem. What I create in my imagination and hence in my art is the concern of myself and my confessor alone, but what I publish becomes in some measure the offering of the superior, the Order, and of the Church itself. It is at the level of public performance that the religious artist, like the prophet, encounters the full drama of the tension between the charismatic and institutional worlds. Christ in Galilee was in a way an in-teresting revivalist, but Christ preaching in Jerusalem was sedition. Dante's version of Hell was unobjectionable until he put a pope there. For there is no phase of social life, not an iota of the collective life, that does not fall under the scrutiny of the institutional gaze. It is a well-known proof-reader's maxim that a misplaced comma can start a riot or break a truce, and the typesetters may never forget the fate of their unfortunate colleague who thoughtlessly placed a question mark instead of an exclamation point after a pronouncement by Hitler!

11. There are two thoughts here. On the one hand, I have been gratified by the degree of sympathy and encouragement shown by some superiors. On the other hand, I have never found a superior who would take the matter to its logical conclusion, because as an institutional man he reacts in terms of conserving the whole. "It is expedient that one man die for the people." Actually, human nature being what it is, practical considerations usually prevail, as well as the hoary, but by no means exhausted thesis, that nothing succeeds like success. There is the story in our Order of the artist-priest who gained sufficient prestige to merit an exhibition. His provincial did not pro-hibit it, but during recreation let it be known that he could not think well of any cleric who so abused his time. At this point someone remarked that the artist had just sold a painting for five hundred dollars. The provincial's attitude changed visibly. "Is that a fact! Well, perhaps there's more to it than I supposed . . . ." Perhaps nothing so poignantly illustrates the perplexities of the well-intentioned man before the charismatic fact!

12. This is a delicate matter. What I meant was not an indictment of Hopkins as either an artist or a religious, but in his failure to fuse the two. The institutional pressure was too much for his tremendous sensitivity. It was not that he did not face it heroically; I believe he did. But he expected too much from his superiors. Religious obedience, to the Dominican at least, is not simply obeying. It is fulfilled in the creative tension between the point of view of the superior and the point of view of the subject. That tension is the

crucifixion. But the charismatic man, the mystic and the artist, like Christ himself, has the obligation to live to the death the essence of his spiritual vocation, and not blindly but intelligently, being, in times of crisis, as wise as serpents and as simple as doves. I am thinking her of the manner in which St. Teresa of Avila founded her reform outside the knowledge of either her prioress or her provincial. Hopkins, if I understand his position correctly, would have waited for his superior to order him to attempt a work he, the superior, obviously did not think was necessary. In the early phases of the religious life, these sentiments are wholesome and salutary, but any seasoned religious knows that he must seize the creative initiative whether it be in scouring pots or writing sermons. In the ideal community the superior is not an autocratic mastermind, but rather an umpire presiding over the creative efforts of the individual members as they engage their projects in the fabric of the assumed collective goal.

13. I meant that St. John of the Cross, in spiritually reconciling himself to his crucifixion, made it a creative rather than a crushing death. It is for this that we honor him as a saint. In the next sentence I hasten to add that I myself make no such claim to detachment. Perhaps I am so hard on poor Hopkins because I am projecting; I fear that if put to the test I would die as he did rather than as did St. John of the Cross. In this regard, Father D'Arcy's words in footnote nine above apply most forcefully to myself as a convert.

14. The tendency of the religious artist is to shy away from the most acute imaginative demand because of the fear of the power of the imagination, and the danger of falling into sin. This is what I meant by the inner censor, the artist's first problem. I call it a pseudo problem because the Thomistic principle is clear: "Now the delectation of the thought itself results form the inclination of the appetite to the thought. But the thought itself is not in itself a mortal sin. Sometimes, indeed, it is only a venial sin, as when a man thinks of such a thing for no purpose; and sometimes it is no sin at all, as when a man has a purpose in thinking of it; for instance, he may wish to preach or dispute about it" (*ST*, II-II, q. 179). Or, I might add, he may, if he is a religious artist, seek to transform it in the universality of the life of man in God, purged of its decadent softness, and epitomized in the extremes of moral consequence through the projected truths of the aesthetic vision.

15. Actually the icon should have been included here. Perhaps I did not think of it because, coming as it does from the hand of an individual artist, and hence resembling easel painting, it does not seem to fit my thesis. But the perdurable convention of icon witnesses to its place in the collective consciousness.

16. This is, of course, conversational hyperbole.

17. I meant that the religious achievement in these spheres, particularly the Catholic religious achievement. Certain writers might be instanced to challenge this view.

18. This statement is highly questionable. I was thinking of the example of the craftsmen-sculptors of the medieval period who were so assimilated into the collective religious attitude, an attitude so authentic that great art emerged under the chisel regardless of the subject matter dictated by the plan. I doubt that the modern, highly self-conscious artist can realize his greatness in that way. Modern art is easel art—individual, non-functional, subjective, introspective, mystical, and charismatic. Of course a Matisse could do an entire church at Vence, but to me this proves my thesis. The creation at Vence is essentially easel painting—a private vision.

19. I meant that a Rouault bears the medieval achievement in his unconscious, by virtue of his anterior position in time, so that his private vision partakes of the earlier collective vision. Unless, of course, one holds that modern subjective art is decadent, in which case the reverse would be true—the heritage of the past is squandered rather than amplified.

20. I meant that the liturgical artists of the collective era transcended the collective ego without recourse to our contemporary objectivized ego-attitudes in the same way the modern artist transcends his personal ego in subjective illumination. It is the transcendence of ego-limitation, the limits set by the institutional world, which characterizes the charismatic man, mystic or artist.

21. Victor White, O.P., *God and The Unconscious* (Chicago, IL: University of Chicago Press, 1952). The chapter on prophecy, "Revelation and the Unconscious," is the section particularly referred to.

22. I was trying to distinguish between the contemplative and active, or rather between the receptive and projective aspects of aesthetic intuition.

23. I meant prophetic utterance as term, or consummation, of prophetic insight.

24. This concluding sentence lacks precision, but actually, in these resolving phrases, my meaning was being carried more by oral qualities, by tonal inference, than by definitive denotation.

The Presence of the Poet

BROTHER ANTONINUS: I must confess I expected something a good deal less structured than this occasion. I don't have too much voice left after last night, and I'm told I didn't have too much then. I'm centering in now on Austin, Texas, and devolving from Norman, Oklahoma, so I'll try not to go "all out," or in any way deplete what energy I have left. You understand that we have to consider these things. So I would just as soon depend on questions from you, if you don't mind.

The presence of the poet. I think that is a good enough starting point. Because the presence of the poet somehow . . . I'm beginning to talk with that Oklahoma drawl myself and I feel self-conscious about it!

About the matter of communication, then. Of what the poet is trying to do. In terms of the *presence* of the poet. For not very many people *read* poetry today. But they do come to *see* a poet, or to *hear* him. And I think this is important. Because this stands behind the point of view I want to take this afternoon. The poet as archetype, we'll say. And what that meaning might be for the collective, for society at large. How it is that people no longer read poetry, and really have a profound distaste for it. But yet they will come to receive—if they may, if it is possible for them—something of the presence of the poet. Why they are more interested in the poet than they are in the poetry.

And I think that's probably true. I think that's true of poetry in a way that it's not true of any other art I know of. I don't think people . . . Almost anyone who goes to a concert goes to hear the music. And almost anyone who goes to an exhibition, though the painter

An informal discourse given before the University of Oklahoma Philosophy Club, October 26, 1962; first appeared in *Windmill* 10 (January 1967). The second part of the discussion, which was not included in the original publication, is presented thanks to the Bancroft Library, University of California, Berkeley.

might be there, goes to see the paintings. I don't know of any other art. The people are more interested in the poet than they are in the poetry. In the *presence* of the poet. And I think that it's explainable only in terms of the *archetype* of the poet. That psychological and spiritual archetype that lies behind the fact of either the poet . . . Of the poetry as written or of the individual poet. In some mysterious way the archetype has kept its validity, its relevance to collective human life. Even though poetry itself has been in serious disrepute as an intellectual form.

QUESTION: Do you mean, perchance, by archetype, the image that seems to be present most vividly in the poet himself, as a person, when he is giving his poetry?

ANTONINUS: Well, I meant it in the Jungian sense of a transpersonal psychological, symbolic reference point in the collective unconscious. . . . What jargon!

Which maintains itself over against all phenomenal effects beyond it. A source of creative energy in the human soul, in the human psyche. A symbolic reference point of creative energy which is not accommodated to the psychic part of man in any other way. The poet maintains a dignity, and a validity, in spite of all he can do himself to damage it. And a large number of poets of the last fifty years have certainly been doing enough to.

Now the philosopher holds an archetype in a similar way. The philosopher is, like the poet, in some disrepute today, due to the tremendous pragmatic context in which the situation of society puts him. Both have in common that they are faintly amusing to the public at large, and are tolerated, in terms of the phenomenal mind, as the "absent minded professor" or the "romantic" poet, or the "beatnik" poet. Any of these images is slightly contemptuous to the pragmatic mind.

And yet when the archetype is permitted, or given a situation in which it can manifest itself, the archetype is operating. People do come to receive, in some way, the presence of the poet. And it is a kind of quasi-religious thing. Because the mystery that lies within the archetype is the mystery of "otherness." The mystery of transcendental valuation. The mystery of the intangibles of life which the pragmatic mind cannot reach but which intrigue it. Even though the pragmatic mind chooses to deny the efficacy of these intangibles.

Nevertheless they lie there, always in some way latent, sometimes activated by a particular situation. And then, in those moments, there is a kind of hushing down. And the poet, or the philosopher, or the religious man, or, it could be, the mystic, emerges.

QUESTION: Would you mind, or would you object to a "core" or—what you call "archetype"—a basic or irreducible way of life?

ANTONINUS: No, an archetype I don't think of as a way of life. An archetype is a symbol that has relevance to a latency, a virtuality. And it can only activate those latencies in a very limited way before it has the opportunity to emerge into a way of life. It maintains a primacy. As you see in the dream; you see it best there. Or in the myth. The archetype in the myth or in the dream emerges in its purity before it has this. We'll say Romanticism would be the way of life flowing from the archetype of the poet, of the romantic poet. But behind that is the psychological efficacy itself. The symbolic first manifestation of the psychological or spiritual latency in the unconscious. And it is *this* which is the source of potency and power behind the image, behind the symbol itself. And then you realize that there's a greater Fact than even the archetype can accommodate. And that it will always be that way. The mind will never be able to assimilate the tremendous *vastness* that lies behind any of the archetypes. Because if it were different from that, there would not be the archetype there.[1]

The symbol is different from the sign. The difference between a symbol and a sign refers to something you know. Like the name of a corporation: you see the trademark on a label and you know what it is referring to. But a symbol is distinct from a sign in that it relates to a mystery. And this mystery to which it relates is the thing that gives it its special operative force in the psyche. So that the "greaterness," the vastness, the mystery, the inchoateness, the profundity, the tremendousness, the *awesomeness* which lies behind and informs the symbol, keeps its creativity alive in the dream-life even when it's denied in the conscious life. You see it in a Pasternak.[2] Or suddenly when the poet speaks, the whisper goes around the room and men are awed by the presence. And when he speaks men know there has been a . . . you see it in all the great symbolic figures of history. Socrates through Christ through . . . whom you will. There's always this profoundness in the symbol.

QUESTION: Would you admit making man . . . I'm sorry, I didn't want to make that a leading question. Is the use of symbolism as you see it in this doctrine you're espousing here, it is too a kind of myth? Nothing derogatory here . . . I want to use the word "myth" in conjunction with it. I believe you used the word "myth."

ANTONINUS: Now the question again is . . .?

QUESTION: Is this doctrine you're espousing, of man as using symbols, a myth? And if so, why? And if not, why not?

ANTONINUS: It is not properly speaking a myth because the mind . . . You rationalize in the proper sense of the word, try to make rational— the mythical dimension. And you do that through a different psychic function than myth itself. What the myth is, is that imaginative projection which occurs when there isn't enough factual data for the mind to make a *reasonable* construct on the basis of its own finding.

In other words, we'll say that a primitive people will see the sun go over until they have enough phenomenological data on hand to make a certain correlation at that level. But not enough to make the total picture. And so they accommodate between what they can know phenomenologically (the sun as it is) and what they must add to it (either falsely or truly, it doesn't make any difference) about the mystery beyond, which they somehow have to explain. They don't have enough data to make a complete explanation of a reasonable kind. So they make an imaginative construct based on some part of it. But that is not the same thing as an archetype. However, it partakes of one insofar as it *relates* to the mystery behind it. Then it satisfies the psyche because it makes an accommodation based on an imaginative projection, an imaginative filling-out of those factors. And it is *true* insofar as it registers the *quality of mystery* behind phenomena. Do you understand what this means, this recognition of the truth of myth by virtue of the archetype, the very non-rationality of it? So the myth is more than any explanation of it. The myth is more than that. To explain the myth, that would be mythology, say as science. Rational deduction from first principles, thus a science—

QUESTION: You have more faith in science than that!

ANTONINUS: I mean science, not in a pragmatic sense, but in the sense of a coherent process of deduction . . .

QUESTION: I understand. I got the Aristotelian sense. More or less. Could you distinguish between the myth as used as an explanation and the myth in the poetic sense?

ANTONINUS: Well, they both serve the same thing. The poem is a myth with the difference that . . . You see, it proceeds from the same *domain* as the myth, from the same domain of the mind as both the myth and the dream. But it's closer to the conscious mind in that it is more structured. That is to say, the myth has to carry everything it does in terms of its pure action, its scenario, its narrative. The poem is one step closer to the conscious mind in that it bodies forth the *quality*, the character and the quality of the myth, through the syllabic texture and the other elements of language itself. In other words, for instance, the myth, we'll say . . . We'll say the myth is that Apollo rides the chariot of the sun each day up and comes down. Well, the poet will take the myth. And then from that commonly-assumed myth of the collective, he will write a poem about it. Or refer to it in a way the myth itself can't reach. That is to say, in the very fabric of language itself. The intangibles which inhere in it (the language) and yet which refer back to the same origin in mystery, will be bodied forth. Or the painter will do it in a different mode. Or other artists will work on the myth in the same way—a bringing forward, closer to the conscious mind.

QUESTION: Isn't it selfconscious? Isn't poetry selfconscious? Would you say that?

ANTONINUS: Selfconscious in the . . .?

QUESTION: Well, the poet they say is conscious. Isn't he conscious that he is mythologizing, where the primitive person might not be?

ANTONINUS: No, not necessarily. The poet believes the myth, the spontaneous utterance of the poet in celebration of the sun. We'll take it in the sophisticated . . . In the late Roman times, yes, that would probably be true. But in earlier times, the poet would not . . . Or in religious times, we'll say. The myth, for instance, today. Take the Christian myth of the origin of the world. Now the religious poet could write a poem about that in an utterly unselfconscious way. He would have the need to bring elements in that myth, in the myth of the origin of the universe, closer to his own emotional needs, without any consciousness of mythologizing. In other words he's stirred by the myth, you see, profoundly stirred by the myth of the creation of the world, and Adam and Eve. And we'll say he accepts its truth. And so in the inchoateness which dawns and burgeons forth within him, he will have that need to focus it in at a closer level to his conscious mind, at the same time not destroy the potency, the imperiousness, the aliveness, of the myth. He doesn't want to destroy that essential element of mystery with the analytical mind. He's not quite the same.[3] And of course he is far different from the mythologist who merely wants to analyze the myth and compare it with other myths and find corresponding features to bring the scientific mind to bear upon it. The poet, the true religious poet, doesn't, of course, want to do that. He wants to bring forward in a closer dimension to himself and his time something of the potency of the archetype itself, and his faith in his belief. So, then, he will write the poem, utterly unselfconscious about the myth of the Creation. His function is to bring it up closer, do you see what I mean? Not so much to make it conscious as to *make it felt.* So really it's not a matter of selfconsciousness or unselfconsciousness. That could be but here it is not the essential property. And it makes a different kind of poem if he does. But really he is not trying to make selfconscious what is unselfconscious.

QUESTION: May I ask just along that point, would you care to make a value judgment here that the unselfconscious poet that you describe here, is he a better poet than the selfconscious, intellectual, abstracting, neatly . . . ?

ANTONINUS: Both types of art are valid because they each do different things. And mankind will constantly use both sides of its mind that way, because both sides of the person, of human nature, have to be met. And so you will have your primitives, your Dionysian artists, always, who go in their courage directly to the infra-rational, the instinctual, the deeps of the memory and the imagination. And out of this exposure of themselves, these Dionysian forces in the human psyche will produce a kind of dissolved state of consciousness, where the ego is not sharply focused, is more exposed and open. And out of this open, intuitive state of being the words will begin to find their center of reference and body themselves forth. And over this gestation the creative mind maintains a kind of civilized jurisprudence and helps it into order and coherence. The quality of that underlying burgeoning thing is being registered—

QUESTION: And what is that?

ANTONINUS: Now your Apollonian type of artist starts from another side of the mind. He sees that there is a deficit, a hiatus, between the myth, we'll say, and the ego-consciousness of the mind. And so he sets himself the great goal of bridging that gap by an adequate symbol. And so he will . . . I'm talking about a Dante here, that kind of a poet. A Dante will sit down, and he will conceive his great work, and he will begin to . . . He knows. He structures it out. He determines the ideal structure that will be useful for this. And once he establishes what that will be, then he gives himself to his great task and exposes himself to his creative depths. But he draws that up and forms it into his intellectual . . . what the structure of his mind has already decreed for him to be necessary.

You see these two polarities or types of art. Almost all criticism of art is built around the function of the Apollonian artist. We have never had an adequate aesthetic of Dionysian art. That's why the Dionysian poet always suffers at the hands of the Apollonian critics of his own time. He brings this material from the unconscious, and to them he violates their principles, and they find this wretched. And they fear this material because they feel that, as the masters of the cultural continuum, they have to protect its purity against these outrageous . . . Henry James, when he first read the *Leaves of Grass*, set down as the opening words of his review: "This will never do!"

And who is to say which is greater? You see, in the end . . . For me, I point to Isaiah, the supreme religious Dionysian poet. And then you have a Dante, who is the supreme Christian Apollonian poet. For me, I prefer an Isaiah to a Dante because I feel he is closer to God—

QUESTION: Which one?

ANTONINUS: I really don't distinguish between them . . . I have not made up my mind as to . . . I think the final phase, the so-called . . . I forget the name applied to the second Dionysian poet who continued the work . . . I mean the second Isaiah.[4]

QUESTION: I question symbolically the possibility of the irresponsibility on the part of the poet with the doctrine of the archetype behind this. He can only fit the archetype you give him.

ANTONINUS: And he's right.

QUESTION: No control. He's not responsible to anybody. He has free license more than anybody, even philosophers!

ANTONINUS: This is his mystery, and why he has such potency before the people. And why he is so dangerous. Why Plato kicked them all out of the Republic. Because they are true to the archetype rather than the formula. And in their truth to the archetype, which they worship and adhere to, they are irresponsible from the point of view of the Apollonians. But not . . .[5]

QUESTION: Would you care to say something about the notion of the persona of the poet? I noticed last night you made an allusion to the mariner in the "Rime of the Ancient Mariner" and I assume that this part of the notion of the poet as a persona. I wonder if you would care to explore this for a moment. And if you could bring in possibly our friend Jeffers as you see him in the light of your own comments.

ANTONINUS: I think that the fascination, the fascination of the poet . . . It seems to me that the more profoundly the poet adheres to the creative unconscious, to the archetype, the more he will emerge as a curse to the complacent mind of the everyday world, because of the nature of the ego structure. Now the ego structure, both of the individual and of the collective mind, is a thing of limit. This is the first thing to grasp about it. Because man is exposed to profound unconscious stimulus from two sides of his nature (both the infra-rational, or instinctual, and the supra-rational, or spiritual, what we have always called the spiritual) the ego is forced to make its correlations within a defined situation of limit, in order to maintain itself in time, in the continuum of time, and it does this by selecting and creating its own myths.

For there are such things, actually, as secular myths, egocentric myths. For instance, a certain ego-set thinks of itself, say, as "scientific," or as "military," each exalting objectivity, and each presuming an exceedingly myth-less ethos. But what gives it away is the fact that it selects, and in selecting, ignores. And the presuppositions by which it makes its selections, the unconscious correlates of its own valuation ("These things I value, these other things don't count") constitute the myth of the scientific and military communities at large. And so its own myth, then. Confronting a mysterious cosmos and forced to myth-ologize in order to maintain its cognitive associations, each selects and discards consonant with the assumptions based on its type of operation.

And so you have in any culture a system, an interlocking and inter-referential system of valuation based on correspondences which form, as they become tightly knit, a limit, an unconscious limit, within which values are acknowledged or denied. And so, then, in order to protect itself (the conventional mind of any society, or any discipline) from either the disruptive energies of instincts form below, or the exposure of the utterly awesome, supra-rational forces from above— the collective mind resists, with a tremendous reflex based on fear, any threat, from any quarter, to that self-containing mythological and self-perpetuating continuum of its own valuation.

Now then, the poet on the one side, and the philosopher, the madman, the mystic, the saint, the prostitute[6]—all who come from the unconscious self bearing their witness and their potency, which they have acquired and bear forward from that unconscious self—enter the terrain of the conventional awareness and valuation of their time, and stand in a singular position in relation to it, because they possess, actually, both sets of value.[7]

That is to say, they carry forward the potency. Because the convention, sooner or later, becomes a sterile thing, no matter what it is. And the reason for this is that forms are material, sensible. It doesn't take the mind very long to exhaust the latencies it perceives in the material forms of any system of valuation which it inhabits, unless the archetype behind them, the mystery, is acknowledged. Otherwise it exhausts the latency of the material forms and the aridity sets in. This, in turn, sets up an unconscious thirst for those very intangibles which it had rejected as valueless, outside its own system of valuation.[8]

At the same time it is fearful, because having excluded those things, it has abandoned any mode of accommodation of them into its own system. It doesn't know how to make the bridge. At this point the archetype throws forth another poet, the man designated to make the bridge. And when the man who makes the bridge emerges, in his own person, he carries the stamp of both the fascination and the stigma, the curse and the blessing, of the deliverer and the accuser.

And as for the prophet . . . This is why the prophet . . . Behind all these archetypes: the philosopher, the artist, what-not, which ever you have: insofar as he does come from the outside, as Outsider he both teaches and accuses, both delivers and indicts. The archetype behind all these is, of course, the Prophet archetype. The one who comes from beyond, bearing that trace of the divine in both its awesomeness and its fear, its deliverance and its terror.

QUESTION: You use the word archetype in the singular?

ANTONINUS: There are many archetypes.

QUESTION: Just right now. From what you said right now I have the impression that you used it in the singular. And this was behind my former question which you answered in this way, that for you, the term "way of life" was an actualization, a visible embodiment of an underlying vision. Perhaps you might use that word instead of archetype. Do you agree to that?

ANTONINUS: No, we must think more concretely than "vision" to understand the archetype. The archetype is an actual, concretized symbolic referent, a direct psychic manifestation, which carries its force and power because it is not merely a concept but a concretized, factual, obvious, energetic, mysterious, potent, operative . . . I'm bringing as much emphasis to it as I can in order to reach the emphatic specification behind the image. To avoid the essentially static connotations that words like vision, image, symbol, and so forth, carry with them.

QUESTION: How do you know this?

ANTONINUS: Well, actually the analytical psychologists have compiled a mass of evidence demonstrating the existence of the archetypes. The problem is more a superfluity than a deficit of evidence. For you can have a dominant one, a one-to-one, singular manifestation, or you might have combinations of various interfusive ones, as I said before.

QUESTION: The interfusive is that one-to-one division which, when equated, would be one?

ANTONINUS: No.[9] Actually, the archetype is based upon the recurrence of a specified image from the collective unconscious of man. The archetype of the prophet occurs in all races and at all times. It emerges in the dream life of the individual. It emerges in literature as an unconscious manifestation, as something not deliberately specified by the writer.[10] Its presence is denoted by its power rather than its configuration. This is really the criteria of its objectivity, the fact that you can change the configuration, but the power, the effect, persists. Thus, speaking practically, we say that Hitler was responsible for the rise of the Third Reich. But that is only half true. It was Hitler plus the *archetype*. Without the archetype a Hitler cannot constellate the collective behind him. His power lies not in himself, but in the archetype. You see, that's the great mistake we make. We think that when we've got rid of Hitler, we've got rid of the difficulty. But the next man is right up there, just over the horizon of time. And all he needs to do is to avoid the label of the one who preceded him, and in so doing side-step the hostility occasioned against his predecessor, and proceed to concretize the unconscious fascination within his own presence.

"And I say unto ye that he who listens to my voice, he who is within the sound of my voice, cannot escape the destiny which, because I possess the archetype, and in that possession I command the Truth latent in the movement, binds us together. And if any one thinks he can leave this room untouched, he leaves in delusion. Because it is not *I* who am speaking to you, but the Mystery that lies beyond me, and which I possess within myself. Because I have no fear of my self. I have subsumed its reality, and I hold what it is, if not to command, for I despise command . . . I would never be a Hitler. But I stand in the dignity of the archetype of the prophet, and that transforms—"

QUESTION: Those whom you reject, you have objected . . . Now, couldn't it be that, say, a Lenin would be possessed by a myth of pragmatism? Could it be that this pragmatism you have rejected . . . you have contrasted the unknown and unexperienced, which you are talking about, against the merely worldly or technical or pragmatic? (I realize your use of the word "pragmatic," and I would agree with your use of the word "pragmatic" completely). But I wonder whether a man like Lenin or Karl Marx would not be just as much possessed by their pragmatic myths?

ANTONINUS: That's true. But their potency is not in their pragmatism. Their potency lies in the unconscious power which, because they are in some way close to it, they have the capacity to concretize the collective energies within their person, and to convert these back into action.

QUESTION: That's right. Wouldn't you then have a conflict between these archetypes? Not only a plurality, but a conflict?

ANTONINUS: When the archetypes come into conflict, and I think they do in all great men, I think that what destroys a Hitler is the fact that the archetypes which he had touched were those for which he did not possess the final point of synthesization. Because he lacked the transcendental dimension wherein alone they can be resolved into a thing greater than his own ego. And because he, in his egocentricity, thirsted to use the archetype *for* his egocentricity, appropriating the power to himself, instead of yielding himself to its uttermost depth, and delivering his nation, as he had the power to do. He had the power to deliver his nation instead of to destroy it. But the archetype, as it possesses a man, inflates him incredibly. And because of his inflation, his ego, because of his . . .

QUESTION: Your point, then, is that you really need and must have something supra-rational, if you will, transcendental, from above, to maintain the person in his wholeness, in his integrity, during any time in which he is contacting, if you will, or utilizing, or embodying the archetype.

ANTONINUS: Precisely. And whether or not it destroys him, or whatever it does to him, is in large measure determined by two factors. One, his humility, and two, the truth of his metaphysic. The truth, really, of his notion of what reality is. If he has an utterly false notion of reality, no matter how humble he is, he is going to be destroyed because he is not . . . Look. Here are two charges coming his way. His function is to stand between them, and receive them, to transform and to manifest. But if it's coming from a totally . . . now, what's a good example of that? There should be plenty of them. Let's take . . . yes. The Hitler is the man who chose to activate the archetypes that emerge from the instincts . . .

QUESTION: Blood. Soil.

ANTONINUS: Yes. But he had an imperfect metaphysic. He could only make the transcendental reference in terms of his national state. He could only conceive of . . . His notion of the transcendental was limited to his own collective. And therefore when he tried, through the imperfection of his metaphysic, when he tried to activate the archetype from below, and to solve the problems which confronted him, he could only be destroyed, and so destroy his nation. Because he could not *be* that thing which concretized the relation between the Absolute and the Contingent.

QUESTION: Are you saying that the archetype itself, or the archetypes, are not themselves good or evil, but the relation of the archetype to its embodiment, fulfillment, manifestation—the individual under the control of his ego or the supra-rational may make a difference.

ANTONINUS: If I understand you properly, yes.

QUESTION: How do you account for the fact that so many poets in history have come to bad ends?

ANTONINUS: Because like so many dictators they secure the relationship to the archetype, expose themselves to it in order to secure its power, then seek to specify it in terms of their own egocentricity, and are destroyed by the very power they possess, are consumed by it and destroyed by it. Among primitives the *shaman* has a social support in his people, and as long as they believe, he is sustained. Even with a Hitler, as long as his people believed, he held his psychological unity. But when they began to wake up, to withdraw belief . . .

Yet there's another factor. It is something that, in a sense, destroys every prophet. I mean, in the end, if he lives out his archetype, every prophet is . . . The ego is always inadequate to the burden that comes from the archetype, the insuperable force. This is why, in the end, he is crushed. Christ's cry in Gethsemane, "Let this chalice pass from me!" And this is why, in this greatest of archetypes, the prophet lays down his life for his friends. Because he did not seek to secure, for purposes of egocentricity, his own preservation. But delivered himself, and through his death rather than through his life, perfected his final transformation. But you can't fake it. It is said, in fact, that Goebbels actually convinced Hitler that he should appropriate that archetype by committing suicide in secret, being consumed by fire (the primal symbol) to emerge again, phoenix-like, in spirit, somewhere in history.

QUESTION: What about those poets that modern criticism has tended to exonerate, Rimbaud, Baudelaire, Crane, who all came to bad ends, yet seemed to have both metaphysic and humility. Dylan Thomas?

ANTONINUS: Well, Dylan Thomas.

QUESTION: Oh, let's except old Dylan. Except Rimbaud.

ANTONINUS: Actually we exonerate them precisely because they were destroyed by their charismatic potential, and we make virtual culture-heroes of them, for their self-destruction confirms in our unconscious minds their possession of the archetype. But, let's except Rimbaud, and get down to, let's say . . .

QUESTION: I'd like to hear what's wrong with Dylan Thomas. That'd be a good number.

ANTONINUS: Well, it's the same thing: an imperfect metaphysic which does not permit sufficient ego-relation, so that when deliverance emerges from the instinctual forces below it, the ego cannot serve as an adequate prism between these two energies. Because the ego, by virtue of its cultural presuppositions, is forced to deflect, rather than specify. It responds in disastrous ways, because the context can't support what's given; the doubt is killing. Whereas, you take an Isaiah, we'll say, where the metaphysic is adequate to the historical situation, and yet the full reach into the instinctual is . . .[11]

You see, almost all artists fail in two ways. The artist . . . we'll just use him as an example of this particular archetypal situation. In a highly cultivated society, the artist becomes ego-centric, and he learns the techniques, the appropriation of proper materials, his words, to make what his tradition has found to be the most adequate form. So, knowing these things, studying them and learning them, he stands in a position, then, where he can at last approach the unconscious, engage the creative force.

Well, if he's a Dionysian, generally his form is too slack—no structure, and nothing happens. Blah, blah, blah. But if he's an Apollonian, generally speaking he relies too much on his structure. And he does not reach deep enough into the instinctual level to fully tap the archetype from below. Do you see what I mean? Because he is concerned most with containment, here. And he thinks that if he . . . For you see, the function of reason is right here in the middle, where it can specify the conception and the form, and determine the field of this particular operation. This is reason. Then the infra-rational down here, the creative depths, emerges. Finally, the supra-rational up here, where the universal intuitional implications are manifest . . .

But if there isn't enough Apollonian tension in the center, here, in the cruciality of conceptual form, you won't get the compression. And if there isn't a deep enough reach down here into the Dionysian infra-rational, the power-source, you are not going to get the propulsion, the ascent into the upper register, the bloom, the supra-rational proliferation, which is, properly, the aesthetic synthesis of the creative intuition.

And that's why so many of your religious poets, who are actually most interested in reaching a transcendental elevation, don't get there. Because they are afraid of the infra-rational. They won't approach those libidinous dark forces. So that they start from here, the center, with a traditional form, but they never get any aesthetic height, because the passion, the energy is lacking. That's where the energy comes from, down here. It's down in man's inchoateness, his matter, the material side of man, his energies, his instinctual forces, up from the roots of his being. This is where his great volition comes from, and it's in terms of this . . .

Now you see the problem before your artist is that he has to go two ways: He has to be both exposed, himself, to the dark forces within him, and maintain himself in those areas of the mind which . . . Now we're going back again to our idea of the society with its limitary . . . And his ego stands in direct relation to that, you see, so that he has the same fears. But because he hungers for the universal relevance, seeing the stagnation of his time and its insufficiency, longing for a more universal perspective, feeling arid also because the conventions of his time have closed out the archetypal forces. Around most . . . A perfect example of this is a highly rational situation in France where both instinctual lines and metaphysical lines had been reduced to a conformism, through a bourgeois society, with a stagnation within its transcendental values.[12] He reaches into the violence and the passion within him. And he looks toward the deliverance in the supra-rational realm which lies beyond that rational core.

QUESTION: Well, why is he destroyed then?

ANTONINUS: It's the problem of faith. You might say only in faith can a man expose himself to these things and not be destroyed by them. And what that is. . .[13]

QUESTION: You speak of metaphysic, especially in conjunction with humility. Are you speaking of an intellectual derivative of some sort, perhaps just a sense of presence with the universe, or what?

ANTONINUS: Of a metaphysic. No, I mean a system of thought.

QUESTION: You actually mean a system of thought?

ANTONINUS: A metaphysic I attempt to define as a system of thought, a system of thought of the nature and structure of reality, and therefore out of the metaphysic rather than out of the conduct . . .[14] "Reality being thus, I conduct myself thus and so."

QUESTION: What I mean is, do you refer to a system of thought as something intellectually derived?

ANTONINUS: Yes, something intellectually derived. There is in this metaphysic a system of thought in which the whole person is not engaged. All of the mind isn't engaged. But the intellectual capacity has to be in operation from the rational level. Otherwise, there is no real tension in the form.[15]

QUESTION: Let's go back to your example of Hitler, whom you contend did not have an adequate metaphysic. I want to take you to this point here again. Not an adequate metaphysic. I translated that a little bit. I got the impression in viewing that history of Hitler, that what we are saying is that his vision, his world image, if you will, world vision, did not coincide with what you or I would probably call reality, meaning that the world wasn't structured the way he would like to believe it was, what with Valhalla and everything thrown in, as I recall. And so your contention, then, is that he imposed upon the world an invalid metaphysic, and invalid world view that was bound to fail—

QUESTION: I have no structure![16] He didn't guess the materialism of that ! He just didn't have enough rockets at the time!

ANTONINUS: Well, even if he had succeeded in the battle, the forces of men's nature would not have permitted the continuity of—

QUESTION: Hypothetical!

ANTONINUS: It is hypothetical, yes.[17] But to me . . . All right, we don't have to take it any farther than that. Let's say he didn't have enough rockets. He obviously didn't. But suppose he *had* invented the Bomb—

QUESTION: There's one point. This is just a point of information. Science defines mystery as a mark of ignorance, something we don't know, something we have to push behind. What do you think, what is your basic justification for this constant feeling that mystery is a special disclosure of meaning, or proof of the supra-rational dimension, and so forth? Does this anticipate what you've said?

ANTONINUS: Yes.

QUESTION: How do you go about satisfying that, from your point of view? What's the most basic point in your justification of this feedback?

ANTONINUS: Psychological.

QUESTION: Do you mean scientific?

ANTONINUS: Yes, empirically so. I believe that the empiricism can be demonstrated in terms . . . I think, as a poet . . .

To me, the mystery is not an hypothesis, or I'd never be a poet.[18] It is an empirical fact which I discern within myself. And on the basis of my empirical situation I deduce from this that the "X Factor," the mystery, is not merely ignorance, that is to say, a deficiency of knowledge, but of itself possesses substance . . . Because I intuit beyond the empiricism a latency, a virtuality—I will say no more than that—a virtuality which is operative, and in its operative manifestation . . .[19]

QUESTION: Could I take a crack at this? I want to see if we're talking about the same thing. I'm concerned with this question, too. Would this, from the poet's point of view . . . You are dealing with the problem also of creativity, are you not? You're dealing with a formulation in symbols of something, and this act is a creative act. It is partly, presumable, ego-conscious structure, Apollonian if you like. But you also insist that if it has anything behind it at all beyond that, it has this latency coming into fruition, bearing its own fruit through you if you can stand it. And you feel this. You experience this. You can't stop it. You can't say on one particular day, "Today at 5:30 I shall create a poem." It comes to you, in some sense. It's not a planned program. This is the kind of experience you're talking about, in part when you say that this is a matter of empirical evidence, a very intimate and vital experience.

ANTONINUS: Yes. Yes. But I want to say something about that just for a moment. And that is this: that the reason why a poet creates, then, is because he intuits the latencies, the complex of archetypal factors within himself, which, in contact with their corresponding exterior realities, activate. So that as he encounters this person today, that person tomorrow, a father today or a mother tomorrow or a bride the next day, a child the day following, behind each one of whom subsists an archetype, until, in the complex of contingent but impinging forces from within the psyche, stimulated by the encounter from the outside, he has the need to make coherent in a way that both captures, that both evokes the latency, and at the same time objectifies and specifies the concrete exterior situation. This is why reality itself, the phenomenal world, cannot, for the poet, ever be enough. Because these things are coming forward out of their inchoateness, but lack a mythological dimension to give them coherence and structure. And so in the moment of creativity he exposes himself to that complex. And suddenly the father image, the mother image, the bride and the child, begin to find a proportionality within the dimension of his own intellect, and his own ego. And he subsumes these in the creative act, bodies it all forth in the texture of his art, which in this case is language. And he delivers himself both of the necessity of this intolerable state of inbetweenness, and at the same time gives back to the collective some witness to itself of its own unconscious dimension. And a poem is born.

QUESTION: You've used the word awesome or awesomeness several times, first in relationship to ephemera, and then you said that people are in awe of the archetype. I don't think that there are people in this world who are in awe of anything! Now, are you trying to show that there is something to be in awe of?

ANTONINUS: Yes. But I won't presume to dictate to the collective about it. That would be preaching, in a way that I don't do. To me the awe, going back to where we came in on the thing, is in the archetype, in the *presence* of the poet. Because he does possess his archetype, if he is a true poet, out of awe . . . The structure of our prevalent attitude is such that *has* depotentiated the mystery of all things, and in this depotentiation the prevalent self-satisfaction, or lack of transcendental inquiry, or the compelling preoccupation with tangibles which a technology demands, does make what we call an aweless or demythologized, or detheologized social complex, so that, as you say, people are not in awe of anything. *Until the poet appears.* Until the prophet emerges. Until Hitler arrives. Or . . . who else? You name him. He is in yourself. Out of our own unconscious will emerge the hidden force which concretizes for you the mystery and the awe. Then you will say: "I know what you mean!"

Notes

1. The meaning is that it takes the undifferentiated energy or power behind the archetype to produce the particular constellated image or symbol by which it reveals itself.

2. The reference is to the way that the figure of Pasternak, by constellating before the world the archetype of poet, held in check the hostility of a powerful organized State when he stood forth against its presuppositions.

3. That is, not quite the same as the secular poet using a religious myth for purposes of secular culture: the difference between Homer and Ovid.

4. "The Book of Isaiah," writes Northrop Frye in *Anatomy of Criticism,* "can be analyzed into a mass of separate oracles with three major foci, so to speak, one mainly pre-exilic, one exilic and one post-exilic. The 'higher critics' of the Bible are not literary critics and we have to make the suggestion ourselves that the Book of Isaiah is in fact the unity not of authorship but of theme, and that theme in epitome the theme of the Bible as a whole, as the parable of Israel lost, captive, and redeemed."

5. The meaning is that the poet must be true to his motivation if he is to fulfill his archetypal efficacy in the social whole, even if the ideas by which he engages the archetype happen to be wrong. This is not Art for Art's sake. Rather the evil of error is taken up into the aesthetic dimension, which is not action but contemplation. Thus the difference between Wagner, wherein erroneous ideas activate a powerful archetype in the collective psyche, but where the destructive consequences are subsumed in the aesthetic dimension, and a Hitler, where the same ideas are projected upon the world disastrously, is the difference between contemplation and action. Art permits man to purge his illusions without jeopardy to his social life, as we see in *Romeo and Juliet.* But its first function is to transmute primal energy into comprehensive truth, and to do that the poet has to directly engage the energy subsistent in the archetype.

6. The prostitute finds herself in this company because she was once sacred, a temple priestess, and still bears, in man's unconscious psychic life, something of her divine origins. Something of the creative divinity of sex still inheres in her, by virtue of her archetype.

7. Formed originally by their culture, they naturally possess the values of that culture. But having experienced the transforming power of the archetype in the unconscious, they possess, for good or for evil, its values over and above the other.

8. The meaning is that the creative power emanating from the archetype must be given to the culture through material forms (the poem itself, the

painting itself, etc.). But the function of reason is to strip things of their materiality, abstracting forth their underlying principles. When it has accomplished this, it thirsts for new material. Thus new work is always needed, new poems, etc. "Of the making of many books," says Ecclesiastes, "there will be no end."

9. Actually, the answer to this question would be "yes," but I didn't grasp its import. Many archetypes are combinations of others. The archetype of Priest, at this late date, subsumes those of Celebrant, Sacrificer, Preacher, Cleric and Confessor. Of course men have always spoken of certain clearly recognized *types*. What Jung did was expose the unconscious power, fascination, fear, dread, behind certain dominant types, and then, on the basis of this, postulate the *archetype* behind the type. But their numinous character reposes in their symbolic rather than their conceptual aspects.

10. For instance, in *King Lear* the character of the Fool fulfills the prophet archetype, insofar as he both indicts the King while effecting his deliverance form his course of disaster.

11. The full reach into the instinctual was not avoided out of nicety. Isaiah could be as earthy as Dylan Thomas. But Dylan Thomas, like Hart Crane, inherited the culture of doubt, in which the Mystery is rejected, instead of a culture of faith, in which the mystery is received. The tremendous tension between profound infra-rational and profound supra-rational responses was frustrated, in both men, by an established doubt at the central, the rational level. The archetype could find no ultimate transforming prism in the reason, and hence destroyed them both. But not before they had written magnificent verse——done, that is, what they were "sent" to do.

12. The meaning is that these conditions prevalent in nineteenth-century France produced the extreme poets of revolt, Baudelaire, Rimbaud, etc.

13. The modern artist without faith is destroyed because the doubt-ridden ego cannot accommodate for long the essentially religious energies the archetype pours into it. On the other hand the prophet *with* faith is destroyed because he is a rebuke to the complacency of his time. It should be understood, however, that all are not going to live out the archetype completely. An important element of the archetype of the prophet is that he be stoned. Yet all prophets are not stoned. An important element in the archetype of the Poet, at least the Romantic poet, is that he die young, as did Keats, Shelley, Rimbaud, Crane, Thomas, etc. Yet Whitman did not even begin young, and certainly died aged. He fought through to another archetype, that of the Sage, as did Frost. But survival finished Whitman as a poet, even as it saved his life. Goethe is the supreme example of the poet who began young, lived young, died young at the age of eighty-four, and remains young despite posterity's efforts to transform him into a sage.

14. That is, metaphysics must precede conduct.

15. "Intellectually derived" in the sense that the total personality is abstracted from in order to pursue a rationally consistent, conceptually "pure" process. This conceptualization is necessary, even in art, to provide adequate structure, otherwise there is not enough formal tension to precipitate aesthetic realization.

16. Apparently the speaker is appealing to the witness of his own continuing existence without benefit of metaphysics.

17. Hypothetical or not, historians seem agreed that Hitler lost his war more through the contradictions in his own nature than through deficiency of material.

18. That is, the poet deals with the *concretizing imagination* rather than the speculative intellect of the philosopher. Until he has *felt* something he cannot validate it in the poem. This *being felt*, a different thing than mere revery, is his certitude of objectivity. Therefore, as a demonstrable psychic manifestation, it has the credibility of empirical fact.

19. The appeal is to introspection as a universally practiced and reliable process of establishing certitude. The Mystery is verified by correlation with the experiences of poets and mystics throughout history. It is questionable whether from the point of view of science, mystery is equatable with ignorance alone. From the point of view of the poet, the Mystery, though he cannot know what it is, is not nothing, because its presence is felt as a substantive. It is not illusionary because its reception integrates form rather than disintegrates it. Because as a processive accommodation in aesthetic form it perfects, it cannot be Nothing.

A Conversation with
Brother Antoninus

QUESTION: We talked last night about the separation of Apollonian and Dionysian poets and perhaps we should start there. Do you think that contrast underlies the Academic vs. Beat poetry?

BROTHER ANTONINUS: What has confused the contrast is the attempt to create a middle ground, for instance by William Carlos Williams. I think Williams is an Apollonian, that is, not a Dionysian like Whitman or Ginsberg, who move right out of the unconsciousness.[1] He uses all his powers of consciousness to realize his impressions, and this bearing down of the conscious on the poem becomes extremely mental—not rational, but deliberate registration of experience rather than vague reception. A guy like Jeffers is much more unconscious in his effects, especially meditative effects. It's that element in the so-called Beat side of things that centers around W. C. Williams and Charles Olson, which I can't think of as being Dionysian.[2]

QUESTION: Do they crack the ego?[3]

ANTONINUS: Occasionally Williams does, in a poem like On the Road to the Contagious Hospital, but generally, no. You see, most of them are eschewing rhetoric too deliberately.[4] Rhetoric for me is the device by which the consequentiality of the emotional situation and the mood is in some way registered. Williams is antirhetorical because of his metaphysical premise that no reality exists except in things. So you get a

Conducted February, 1962 at Lowell House, Harvard University, with Albert Gelpi, Sidney Goldfarb and Robert Dawson. Originally appeared in The Harvard Advocate (Spring 1963).

phenomenological poetry in which the object is registered as much as possible. To me that involves certain preconceptions of the ego-structure and it isn't the sort of thing that opens up in poetry, except occasionally, as in the poem I mentioned, where Williams does become rhetorical.

QUESTION: How about *The Gulls?*

ANTONINUS: In some poems like that and *The Yachts*, almost despite the poet the language takes on consequentiality in its abstractness, which is almost a violation of his principles. In *Paterson* he's rhetorical in his release, but that is not what his followers follow.[5] Creeley and Jonathan Williams use satire and conscious devices.

QUESTION: Does Apollonian mean academic?

ANTONINUS: No, though academic poetry is Apollonian usually. I think academic poetry is marked by the use of literary convention. Wilbur is an example, and I suppose most people would say Lowell is, but I don't think so myself, although I can see his academic sources. I think he has a great unconscious. All the greats are men who have great unconsciouses—tremendous feelings of consequentiality. Opposed consequences within themselves have to be resolved in aesthetic form.[6]

QUESTION: Do you think the rhetoric of the Beat Generation will ever result in a great poet?

ANTONINUS: I don't think there was any rhetoric in the Beat Generation except in Ginsberg.[7]

QUESTION: Is it the unconscious that forces the rhetoric? Can't you take rhetoric and consciously fill it up?

ANTONINUS: So that it becomes academic? That's what academic is. Berryman did it in *Mistress Bradstreet*—there's another case of a man with not as great an unconscious as Lowell, but in that poem he succeeds on the rhetorical level because the issues of it meant so much to him that they provided a bearing-off point.[8] Actually we talk this way you know, but the possibilities of language have become so complex, you can develop schools around many things, like Berryman, who isn't going the same way as Lowell at all. You see the possibilities of a school and yet I don't think it would ever develop. You can talk in generalities, but when you dare become specific[9]—like myself, am I Apollonian or Dionysian? I say Dionysian, but not anywheres near as Dionysian as Ginsberg.

QUESTION: Do you think one influence will predominate? What way is poetry going now?

ANTONINUS: I asked Lowell that and he said that it's in an in-between state, between the Beats and Academics, that everyone is fighting shy of the extremes and trying to come forth with a statement which embodies both the vigor of the Beat and the structure of the Academic. Which is just what you'd want to do; but it's not something probably that can be worked out, since that is already an academic position.[10] Anything really good has to arise from something in the self. The Beat generation's function was the opposite—to break things open, and it did that[11] and everybody was glad, though they spend most of their time putting the Beats down as hopeless. It seems to me the only solution to this problem is to see it in terms of the creative personalities. Until they emerge no one can know what to expect. Until the leader emerges nothing happens; when he comes, the politics will go the way he goes.[12] If you can establish the primacy of personality over idioms and schools, then you can make sense of it. Otherwise, just about the time you think you have your school going, along will come a real original creator and you have an apocalypse of poets.[13]

QUESTION: Then the Beats gave new birth to American poetry by the fact that they did lend personality, even if not a sustaining one. I think of the Beat generation not in terms of forms, but in terms of Ginsberg, Gregory Corso, etc.

ANTONINUS: Yes, the trouble with the poetry of the earlier fifties was that after Lowell, academic or not, there was no one of his stature to vitalize it.[14] Suddenly somebody comes along like Ginsberg and with his poem *Howl* captures the imagination. That thing sold over 50,000 copies in no time. It was read everywhere. In bars people were looking over shoulders to read it. It had a fascination about it and when the label—Beat Generation—was applied to it, it went. There had to be a creative personality, and Ginsberg (and Kerouac) supplied it. How great they were remains to be seen. The academic people who followed Lowell, like Wilbur, Merrill, Merwin, and Sexton, lacked the creative energy that made him unique. They lacked the capacity to get enough energy into their material to crack the reader's ego. They wrote non-academic poems in an academic way.[15] So, you don't like to quarrel with poems as good as some of theirs—as authentic, I mean, as moving to the point of consequence—you don't like to quarrel, but of them I find my reservations the same as in Lowell's later poems.[16] *Life Studies* is a book I don't like very much. His utilization of the conversational didn't operate for me. I think he switched to the conversational in the later book because he had the problem of losing belief. When you don't have belief, you have to make do with what attitude you have, but not having belief, the psyche can't generate sufficient energy to move others, to crack the ego. It's only in belief—I don't mean the formal sense—I mean this in the sense of an unconscious which affirms the authenticity of reality against its dubious aspects—which assert that authenticity and which denies the dubiety to register the consequence of its own needs—well, Baudelaire could make poems out of disbeliefs[17] that were shudderingly profound because his unconscious was locked on desperation. But modern unbelief, even anguished unbelief in *Life Studies*, fails somehow. Maybe it's the period in history, I feel something has happened to Lowell's poetry (and this despite that fact that people like Anne Sexton and Elizabeth Bishop think *Lifes Studies* is an advance over *Lord Weary's Castle*, which I would think is the received opinion)—this is a great thing to me[18]—it's not true.

QUESTION: The accusation against the whole current generation of poets is that they run down somehow, that their early poems are better then their late. Do you think this pattern is fair?

ANTONINUS: I think success has a way of leasing off the psychic energy into extraneous elements. You write out of your unknown state, out of your need for recognition, your need to produce, to discover yourself and make the impact upon your time. This is man's masculine ego. When success comes too early in life to an artist, it raises problems that are almost insurmountable for him in order to maintain the primacy of his original commitment. It's like the religious life. You can make tremendous acts of asceticism, of discipline, courage, charity, when you first enter the religious life. Then after you become adapted, you find you don't have the capacity. You realize that you were operating on only one level. With poetry your initial creative insight carries you on with a great burst of energy and makes a breakthrough. Now to discover how to transfer over into another system, another psychic frame of reference is extremely difficult, and only a guy like Yeats, somebody like that who can go through about three generations in his own self, can do it.

QUESTION: Does that mean building new cosmologies to be able to write new poems?

ANTONINUS: That really isn't the problem. The problem, which has to do with the subconscious, is of the content in man of belief. The capacity of the poet must be invigorated by the capacity of belief in himself. This is not just egocentricity. Every poetaster in Greenwich Village believes he's great, but the idea is to prove it. Belief in talent isn't what he needs, rather a different kind of self-belief, the self-belief of a saint. An artist has to be a kind of saint in that he has to have an unconscious assumption of the primacy of his place. It's as if he inhabits his place, having found it himself. Then he has something that cannot be taken from him. Not even by success. I think Lowell would have maintained that if he hadn't gone through the crisis of losing the faith by which he achieved his prime work. When he'd lost that faith, it put a different bend in his career than you would normally expect. Yeats never suffered the loss of faith, in terms of content of it, when he lost his religion. If he hadn't been a religious poet there might not have been any problem in regard to his art.[19] When you are a Christian poet, or a Communist poet, and lose your faith, the loss of commitment reduces you to a different level of activity.

QUESTION: Isn't that Pragmatism? Do you mean the will to believe?

ANTONINUS: Not in the sense of the ego willing it. The main thing is to acquire the craft. Then the unconscious genius can transform the formal knowledge and the acquired craft into something that's both personal and collective. The accusation against the Dionysians is that they become so personal that they lose the impersonal framework which sustains a literary production. But I think the Dionysian really has to have a deeper control of rhetoric than the Apollonian. Deeper, because those unconscious qualities are to be manifested in terms of consequentiality. What rhetoric does is establish the moral consequence and primacy of the materials, and by moral primacy I mean something else than conventional morality, something more like survival value.[20]

QUESTION: That seems to imply something like "thesis, antithesis, synthesis."

ANTONINUS: Hart Crane.[21] There was a man who has to speak, out of his belief, and that necessity creates the rhetorical, consequential structure. He was one of those men whose unconscious need and whose conscious commitment and craft burn and fuse together. Craft and unconscious seem simultaneous. There are the marvelous pieces like *The Dance*—where the rhetoric is perfectly believable; it's believed; the commitment of belief is there.

To me that unconscious power, or rather power rising from the unconscious, is recorded in what I call rhetoric. It's possible to be rhetorical in an academic way, but it won't register anything. That was the Georgian fault which Pound and Williams rebelled against. They discarded rhetoric because it could be faked up. Yet when Pound himself or Williams breaks through into consequence, when his implicit knowledge and belief in the consequentiality of the thing he's doing shows through in terms of opposed tensions within it, as in *The Road to the Contagious Hospital* but not in the red wheelbarrow piece where he's merely drawing down the object, then all of a sudden rhetoric begins to operate. Even the guy who's antirhetorical cannot dispense with rhetoric when he becomes committed in the unconscious, not just the conscious art of delineation.[22] Like a Goya, whose drawing is perfect, who has controlled skill, suddenly in *The Disasters of War* his unconscious dynamism will emerge in consequence, fill up the rhetoric of art, transform the forms. The art becomes great and is identifiable in the conventions and tradition of art, because that's what holds it all together. Minor art can go along between, but suddenly, boom, the big ones appear, with maybe a handful of poems in their whole lifetime. They are the bearing-off points. Their rhetoric is so original, profound, and true that it doesn't seem like rhetoric or craft but some real thing achieved. The punch is in the rhetoric. That's the way Shakespeare did it. That's the way Whitman, Crane, all the great ones, operate. Eliot, when he becomes great, does it. Afterwards, there are poets who will come along and fill in and make a pattern with an anthology poem or two, and you enjoy it because it's extremely well done. For instance, in Anne Sexton or James Merrill you find a consciously assimilated rhetoric in the Georgian sense, but better done because they're astute enough to avoid sentimentality. You don't like to quarrel with poems that good, but you never believe in their consequentiality. They are too much dedicated to creating an aesthetic object.[23] The Beats revolted against the poem as an object in order to reassert that the vatic commitment in the poet's unconscious is the thing and not the aesthetic object. The vatic commitment must break through the object we call the poem. An icon has to lose its nature of instrumentality in the reality of the thing it is registering. It becomes transformed by something greater than instrumentality in the reality of the thing it is registering. It becomes transformed by something greater than instrumentality, and that, when it happens, is what I call rhetoric.[24]

QUESTION: You mentioned war. Do you think the unavoidable commitment that a war produces explains that short burst of good poems in the postwar forties?

ANTONINUS: Yes, there was Randall Jarrell and Karl Shapiro. Jarrell is still writing good things, though he emphasizes the Mephistophelian in himself. Even Wallace Stevens wrote his by far best poems in that period and after. But those poets of the war who wrote merely out of ego-need to participate were no good at all.[25]

QUESTION: And what do you mean by a vatic poet?

ANTONINUS: Basically, one kind of poet or artist creates a world of his own making, while another stands witness to a world beyond the world of his making. The first is the visionary and the second is the vatic or prophetic poet.[26] It's not a value judgment; I would say that Leonardo Da Vinci was the visionary and Michelangelo was the vatic. It's a matter of archetypes. Visionary and vatic are archetypes of the poet's nature. In literature, James Joyce falls into the visionary category because he's content to create a world of supreme fiction, whereas D. H. Lawrence is vatic. Lowell, because of his loss of faith, stopped being the vatic poet he was in *Quaker Graveyard* and became a visionary one. But I doubt that a prophetic poet can do that and survive.[27] I don't believe Lowell can, despite his craft. If he is archetypally a prophetic poet, all the visionary alleluias in the world won't substitute convincingly.

This standing witness to reality doesn't necessarily imply a religious one. Sometimes it's moral, like the better poems of Wilfred Owen; after the war the registration of moral consequence that was breaking through the indignation became vatic.[28] To my individual habit of mind, there's no comparison between the prophetic and the visionary archetypes, because it seems obvious that the man as maker cannot fulfill himself. Reality always lies outside to be broken through to. What good is it to me to create vision? A mirror to look at myself in? What does it come to in the end any more than that? I don't know. I suppose it's all right. But oh to break the mirror, you see, in one blow.

Yet you remain frustrated, you come back to the visionary in the end because you realize that you're doomed as a prophetic. You're doomed to the anguish of not being able to cancel yourself out in your role of standing witness.[29]

QUESTION: If you're an academic poet you have a better chance of staying sane?

ANTONINUS: But have you in the end? I understand what you mean facetiously, but when you start fooling with dynamite, you'd better make what you're doing dynamite. The man who can do tricks finally blows himself up—but it's greater than that, more to do with psychology. In this vocation, given the nature of the material you work with—a word from the visionary point of view is the self-contained object, or from the prophetic, is a filament that relates the receiving object to a charisma—you're going to expunge yourself, burn yourself out by making that filament receive contact. The liabilities of the visionary artist are like those of a priest who disinclines to engage himself. To heck with those mystics, says the young priest, I'll dispense the sacraments, I'll be a functionary in the community, and I'll get along. So he thinks he will. But if the medium he's dealing with is real, the danger is obvious. There is no asbestos glove to protect you against the reality of words if you don't recognize it. The Apollonian can't use his art as a method to protect himself.

Whereas your Dionysian is overkind—by yielding himself to what he does, he maintains the salvation of kind.[30] He liberates his spiritual dimension and it is comfortable to the reality which he speaks. He is received by it. The person who falsifies that relationship because he doesn't know better can never recognize what he's dealing with. This is neurosis. It's the neurosis of the organization man, who sees the material he's working with only as units when they're loaded with unity, as objects when they're loaded with reality, and it's the reality that drives him into the neurotic condition. The organization man and all the other neurotic symptoms of the times result from the fact that reality has been theologically depotentiated. The attempt to depotentiate the material world, to manipulate it as you will, can only end in disaster to the person who tries it, because the truth is simply the opposite. There's enough reality in this book of matches to blow me apart. Yet I can't avoid facing it just to keep my sanity. I will either be consumed by what I give myself to, or be broken down by the world I refuse to give myself to.

If on the archetype you're a salesman, that is, an intermediary between the manufacturer and the consumer, one who knows what the people need and what has been made, this man is protected in his vocation by his belief that this is what he does. He is a kind of teacher.

To me the thing that destroys a man or makes him vulnerable to neurotic diseases is that intellectual work has its liabilities of inner frustration and of the whole sensibilities, when it is involved in doing things on one level for another level. The organization man, who does things not for himself, is in danger that the inner refusal of the body to be any longer exploited thus will set up a counteractivity and he will die of cancer or heart failure. The negation of his whole way of life reverberates back through his sensibilities, and collapse comes because reality is denied.

If you can teach with life and commitment, go ahead, because this is life-giving and health-giving; you move, you radiate, you walk through your skin, you become an epiphany. You are in the prophetic dimension.

Find the archetype of what you are, and then if you are a poet, you'd better just not compromise with what you can't be. When the poet compromises and gives the better part of his time to what he isn't, then he becomes the academic. He loses even what he had.

QUESTION: Then you don't agree with Robert Pack's introduction in *New Poets of England and America?*

ANTONINUS: His logic is so beautiful and careful, but I have misgivings that I can't really tie up. If the poet goes into the university, as he recommends, then he ought to make sure the two vocations aren't hostile in himself. Some can do both, but if he is merely serving Mammon, if he isn't committed to teaching, then he's practicing self-deceit, which is hostile to his real commitment.[31] Life will come along and drive him to a lower level. Here's a man, say, who gets married, has children, and he has to take a teaching job to support them. All right, that's a different thing, that isn't what we're talking about. Life often forces us to do things we are committed against, but we are purged because it's not our choice. We're not trying to fool anyone. But even that is dangerous. The great men are like Blake who live in the hands of God, who have courage not to do what they have to do, if it violates their archetype.

I don't know how you find these things out. The mistake I made in my own life in regard to being an artist, the first great mistake, was when I married I sacrificed the inner viability of my marriage to my career. In other words I accepted my art, in the religious sense, but at the same time I entered into a relationship with a woman which was based primarily on my need to stabilize my passional nature. Unless I had the stability, I could not have peace I felt, but I didn't want to sacrifice either way. I wanted to maintain the primacy of my career and at the same time secure through the woman the equanimity of passional adjustment. The mistake I made was that I denied the primacy of her person. By reducing her to an object and sacrificing that object, even to a school of thought,[32] I denied the reality of the situation. So when the war came and I was drafted, caput, she just found another man. There was no primacy in our relationship, and that's why in my second marriage I'd learned my lesson. And I replaced the primacy of our relationship, not on the career, but on the person. And the career went right along better than ever, because I had freed it from an over-intensity that was false at this other level. By asserting the primacy where it belonged, the art began to achieve liberty. Now then, this marriage terminated because it was founded on a misconception. When I became a Catholic, since we'd both been married before, we gave it up, and I entered the religious life. Of course I was faced with the same problem of primacy again, but I'd learned my lesson,[33] from which I made a better art and a more continuing one. I secured the inner freedom to relate to life as life moved upon me.

The primacy of personal relationship is what generates the creative energy and liberates the charisma in the depths of one's unconscious. Out of this the art prospers, but by objectifying his art or reducing it to an object, he reduces himself to that object.[34] He is the egocentric who has great mastery of his material, but where it should expand it remains closed. When one yields to life and is an artist, his art takes on the abundance and somnolent beauty of life, and the truth beyond the tangential phenomenological object.

Well, a man of fifty can always tell a youth that, but I think if someone had told me in the first years of my marriage, I would have insisted it was what I was doing, that I was really putting the intimacy on the personal. What I should have been able to see was that the primacy wasn't even on my person.[35] And until I made concessions to the personal thing, I was living a lie. I had a vasectomy and no children, and in that kind of thing I was cutting myself off at the roots. Life-denying, no matter how much I said I was life-celebrating. Denying my biological immortality and my capacity to have sons, trying like

Rilke to make my poems my sons. And they became crippled children because I had crippled myself. But we've talked this way about as long as we can.

QUESTION: Well, since this is an interview, perhaps we should talk a little about critics. If you want to go on, that is?

ANTONINUS: Ask me a leading question.

QUESTION: Like the questions Dylan Thomas spoke of? "I carry Kierkegaard in my pocket. Who do you carry?" All right, I'll try. Do you think the critic affects the poet?

ANTONINUS: Supposedly the critic represents judgment. But I think he complicates the task of the poet by bringing in collective[36] reactions not within himself, which he gets from convention and tradition. The poet himself is the first and purest critic of his work. He also knows and writes against traditional backgrounds. But he has a knowledge of himself within himself, and he produces in a state of tension between these two attitudes. When a poem goes into the world it has two destinies. It provokes a reaction from professional critics and it provokes a reaction from the people who read it, if they read it. Novelists needn't bother so much about the critic because the people support them, but the poet is so far from the people in our time that he doesn't get the normal assurance. So he has to think of the critic. They're eyeball to eyeball. The magazines are the critic's chief tool in his attempt to manage poetry, since book publishers respect mostly poets introduced through the magazines. One of the main objectives of the Beats was to crack this system by going straight to the presses. *Howl* sold[37] 50,000 copies by direct appeal to the people. This situation is unfortunate for the poets, but its unfortunate for the critics also. I don't think the poets will ever bring the critics around however. The creative mentality and the critical mentality operate on different sets of reactions. The trouble will always be there, but the tension is necessary. The poet makes do with his times, but he shouldn't waste too much energy trying to solve a problem which is based on archetypal division.[38] He does what he does, and shouldn't worry if he is always conscious of an outside[39] point-of-view which he has and which brings a lot of pain.

The same problem confronts those who are trying to pretend there's no difference between negro and white, as if the differences weren't archetypally operating. We've put up an abstract concept, justice, and true, we have to work in that frame, but it can't be solved. It's the same with poets and critics. The difference will not be solved as long as there are negroes and whites. Ideally, these archetypes give life its tension, and there's nothing more tragic than to see colored people abandon their archetype just for white mannerisms or whites becoming deliberate negrophiles to the extent of certain Beatniks.

These archetypes are hard to overcome sometimes. As a West Coast poet, I carry a lot of regional bitterness against the East, because I feel the power of criticism lies in the East, while the power of creativity seems to be out West. I feel it's a more open situation; there's so much just around San Francisco now. But I'm realist enough to know that if you're going to make it, you have to come East.[40]

QUESTION: Let's tie two subjects together here. Why do you think Robinson Jeffers, who's the first person that comes to mind as a West Coast poet, wrote some of his worst poems during the war?

ANTONINUS: Because he denied it too much, that is, the reality of it. Still he produced some short poems out of his denial of war that will gain strength as the world worsens. *Such Counsels You Gave to Me*, for instance.[41]

A poem like *The Stonecutters*[42] works through a meditative, philosophical tone, which from an academic point of view may not be satisfactory, but nevertheless it comes out of a part of the psyche that's very permanent:

> Stonecutters fighting time with marble, you foredefeated
> Challengers of oblivion
> Eat cynical earnings, knowing rock splits, records fall down,
> The square-limbed Roman letters
> Scale in the thaws, wear in the rain. The poet as well
> Builds his monument mockingly;
> For man will be blotted out, the blithe earth die, the brave sun
> Die blind and blacken to the heart:
> Yet stones have stood for a thousand years, and pained thoughts
>   found
> The honey of peace in old poems.

In some ways it's a man thinking out loud in a profound and serious way, which is a great deal different than writing about a red wheelbarrow. Many of Jeffers's poems I could never be satisfied with if I had written them. As a poet I have to make a denser statement. But then his poems bear off and satisfy some important part of my nature, and I'm content that he did them. You know, though, there is not another poet I've ever read whose work I would put my name to, except my own. Even poems I recognize as masterpieces, I would never publish. I would have to tighten them or change them, even make them less than they are perhaps, but I couldn't let them stand.

However, for the present, the language can support a whole shoal of academic poets without much loss, but as I said before, we just have to keep our eyes peeled for the next break, the next masterpiece. And it will come from personality, not from any trend. The charismatic man with his creative energy will jolt everything forward, and then another shoal of academics will come, and the institution will support them so they can give themselves to their craft and not be involved in betrayal.

QUESTION: Do you think when the poet appears who can go directly to the masses that he will be committed to involvement by his archetype? That is, involvement in society perhaps, rather than writing articles on verse forms for the *Hudson Review*. I mean, will the people recognize what he's thinking about?

ANTONINUS: I don't know if that's possible still in poetry. Maybe in the novel, but people don't read poetry. The only way to reach the people now is through the spoken word. They will come to hear, as you see. They will come because they want the poet, they know they need him; they can't stand what he writes, but they want HIM. You see it in the case of Frost at the inaugural. It's not even the entertainer, but the poet's presence that they want. After successful reading, sometimes people come up to touch me, nothing more, just to receive the presence of the poet. And it's not the guy, it's not Brother Antoninus— it's the archetype. That's why when a great poet is in the archetype, free in it, he possesses,[44] and he can mount the rostrum.

QUESTION: You think there's a need in the people for a poetic personality?

ANTONINUS: Of course there is. I feel it myself. But there's no formality yet by which they can be reached. The poet properly belongs on television where he can reach his own audience. We've been dominated by the literary audience so that the sense of the present[45] has been lost, and that's why the people aren't reading this garbage any more.

QUESTION: Do you think television is a possible medium?

ANTONINUS: I don't think people would turn it off. They would have to be tricked into it; like slip the guy into Ed Sullivan's show. If he's real, he'll take ahold.[46]

QUESTION: Even better, the late shows. Get them while they're nodding.

ANTONINUS: A regular weekly show wouldn't work because it would be dominated by the culture vultures. It would be another *Wide Wide World* feeling. Anyway, the poets who could do weekly shows are far between. Ginsberg is a great showman, or Ferlinghetti, who isn't too good in terms of specific gravity.[47] Yet they are marvelous performers with a broad appeal.

QUESTION: So you think that has merits?

ANTONINUS: Yes. There is a dimension there which you perceive. You laugh or you are mesmerized, and days later you realize you've been put through an experience.[48]

QUESTION: I suppose Dylan Thomas is the perfect example of how a poet's voice and personality can make his popularity, even when he is difficult. Everyone heard him on the BBC.

ANTONINUS: The thing about Thomas is that he's British in the sense that he sounds Shakespearean. I think the average American would stand very little of Dylan Thomas, though seeing him on TV would help. The American is much more charismatic. Ginsberg is more acceptable with his "I saw the best minds of my generation." In America it's the moral tradition, not the Shakespearean, not the Dylan Thomas literary revision, that has to be followed. Thomas is very good, and British and so on, but it isn't the vatic voice.[49]

Notes

1. The terms Apollonian and Dionysian refer to attitudes, only secondarily to form. The Apollonian utilizes the mind's power to shape, to objectify; the Dionysian the mind's power of spontaneous registration. The difference is one of degree. All poets, all artists, compared with, say, scientists and philosophers, are Dionysian, yet among themselves the distinction is pronounced. The term of the Apollonian is specification, that of the Dionysian is ecstacy. Yet like any dialectic it is only initially valuable; carried too far the distinctions blur, and it becomes ludicrous.

2. "Modern American poetry begins with the determination to find the image, the thing encountered, the thing seen each day whose meaning has become the meaning and the color of our lives. Verse, which had become a rhetoric of exaggeration, of inflation, was to the Modernist a skill of accuracy, of precision, a test of truth." Thus George Oppen in *Kulcher 10*. Although commonly placed on the left in company with the Beats, it is this concern for accuracy, precision, that makes the wing represented by Pound, Williams, Zukovsky, Oppen, Levertov, etc. (in short, the Modernists) not Dionysian at all. But neither, of course, is it Academic. Certain others, say, Olson or Duncan, while Modernist, stemming from Pound, are not precisionists in Oppen's sense of the note above, but cultivate a freer imagination. Actually the work of Duncan as a whole is quite Dionysian, though he is in no sense a Beat. Uncritical journalism, however, labels all poets represented in the Grove Press *New American Poetry* as Beats, whereas in reality it was simply that the Academic entrenchment in the Fifties impelled Modernists and Beats alike to unite against it. Williams (an Apollonian) sponsored Ginsberg (a Dionysian). It is this situation that I am seeking to clarify.

3. "Crack the ego." This was my own term, introduced before the tape was started. By this I designate that moment of aesthetic illumination when the poem, whether Apollonian or Dionysian, succeeds in its function—creates an expansion of consciousness. Academic poetry seeks this through recourse to unconscious collective values latent in the Tradition. Modernist poetry seeks it through concentration, reduction to a few concrete images. (As Oppen says, "It is the arbitrary fact, and not any quality of wisdom literature, which creates

the impact of the poets. The 'shock of recognition' when it is anything, is that.") Dionysian poetry seeks it through mysticism, "cosmic consciousness," dithyrambic exhortation, hortatory urgency, etc. Academic poetry tends toward morality and rationality; Modernist poetry tends toward the pure aesthetic object; and Dionysian poetry tends toward religious ecstacy. Thus it is the Modernist movement that is anti–rhetorical. Both Academics and Dionysians readily use rhetoric, but for different purposes. It is actually the rhetorical element in Beat verse that makes the Modernists so uneasy in their forced alliance.

4. The emphasis on the specific, or absolute formal specification, tends to preclude the presence of those transcendental intangibles which both the Traditionalists and the Dionysians appropriate through rhetoric.

5. Williams's transcendental side is rarely acknowledged by Modernist apologists, who concede only his "objective" element. But when he cannot contain himself, he appropriates the transcendental:

> It is a sea of faces about them in agony, in despair
>
> until the horror of the race dawns staggering the mind,
> the whole sea becomes an entanglement of watery bodies,
> lost to the world bearing what they cannot hold. Broken,
> beaten, desolate, reaching from the dead to be taken up
> they cry out, failing, failing! their cries rising
> in waves still as the skillful yachts pass over.
>
> "The Yachts"

But in his Collected Poems as a whole his Modernist aesthetic precludes this, and we get mostly objectification.

6. I trust these hopelessly uncritical utterances will find greater force in the restatements of them to follow later in the interview.

7. This is tantamount to saying Ginsberg is the poet of most consequence in the Beat Generation, and that he is a great Dionysian in the Whitman sense.

8. I meant that Berryman, as a traditionalist consciously constructing his rhetorical base, touched in this subject meanings so consequential to himself that his skillful elaboration becomes transformed into true rhetoric, in the sense I am trying to establish it in this interview:

> Bone of moaning: sung Where he has gone
> a thousand summers by truth–hallowed souls;
> be still. Agh, he is gone!
> Where? I know. Beyond the shoal.
> Still–all a Christian daughter grinds her teeth

a little. this our land has ghosted with
our dead: I am at home.
Finish, Lord, in me this work thou hast begun.

9. At this point the impossibility of sustaining the Apollonian–Dionysian equation in a free-running interview became hopeless, and I tried to break off. The introduction of myself seems precipitate, but was an attempt to nail the fragmenting context down with a concrete instance. As a poet I seek a synthesis between Beat and Traditionalist positions. I have little affinity with the Modernists.

10. I meant that to attempt to opt for even the Beat position, conscious-wise, is to surrender to the Academic polarity. Thus opponents often charge that the Beats created a new academy of their own.

11. That is, the authentic Beat instinct was originally unpremeditated and charismatic—to crack the hold classroom poetics had got on American poetry. It delivered the Academics from the dilemma of their own impasse by providing them a fresh *oppositorum* to fill the vacuum left by the collapse of Modernist verse in the moral extremity created by the War. With the Beat breakthrough, the new Modernists, such as Olson, Creeley, Levertov and Duncan, swept into prominence.

12. This shift from dialectic to the primacy of the creative personality, the individual genius, who transcends the categories, was occasioned by my exhaustion of the dialectic above; but in this discussion it was inevitable. The creative personality represents the term, the synthesis of the thesis–antithesis dialectic which the interviewer raises later.

13. "Apocalypse of poets." If the transcriber took this term down correctly, I have no idea what I was thinking of. Perhaps I had in mind the way in England the Apocalyptic school tried to mount an *oppositorum* to the Auden-Spender hegemony in the late thirties, only to be completely obscured by the emergence of Dylan Thomas.

14. In the thirties the proletarians and the surrealists captured the anti-traditionalists movement, but the issues raised by the War discredited both. In this collapse Neo-Modernists like Duncan could not be heard, and the emergence of Lowell was the answer to the Academy's prayer: a creative personality of the first magnitude. Thus the image of Lowell dominated, until Ginsberg could constellate sufficient creative energy to establish an *oppositorum* in the late fifties.

15. This is nonsense. They wrote academic poetry in an academic way. I was thinking of work like Merwin's "Leviathan," an archetypal subject handled in an academic way.

16. I meant that Lowell's new confessional verse was moving out of the security of the tradition, but doing so in a too conscious way.

17. An error in transcription. It should be singular, "disbelief." "Shudderingly profound" refers to poems, not beliefs.

18. "This is a great thing to me." I meant, this displacement of value in the estimation of Lowell is of great concern to me, because of its implications for the problem of belief in poetry.

19. That is, Lowell. The essence of my thought is that it was Lowell's conversion to Catholicism that constituted the spiritual awakening and precipitated his tremendous gifts. Certainly it gave him the point of view and the metaphysical position to mount the awesome frontal attack we find in Catholicism would tend to impugn his creative self-belief, due to the identity of the two in his work. Yeats moved out of his Protestantism before he experienced the real discovery of the intellectual and metaphysical principles that sourced his greatest work. Therefore he did not have the same problem. Poets whose intrinsic belief is identified with their objective, formal belief (the Catholic and the Communist) have a crucial problem when they can no longer sustain the commitment that precipitated their genius.

20. Here I am at last approaching something of what I have been trying to establish throughout the interview, the relation between consequentiality and rhetoric. Because the Apollonian through conscious craft can *construct* a rhetoric, he commonly misses the very consequentiality he sought to achieve. Thus Oppen's indictment above: "the rhetoric of exaggeration, of inflation." But the Dionysian has only his intuition, his almost preconscious organization of speech, to tap the origins of consequentiality which he intuits from his mood. By consequentiality I mean the implication, intuited but not yet established, in the crisis of choice, with the potent admixture of conviction and dubiety it entails. Because the Modernists validate the "arbitrary fact," they disdain rhetoric, considering it a deceit. In their pragmatism, no consequence hinges upon the fact, so there is a minimum of consequential choice.

21. Normally I would answer "Jeffers" to this question, but I could point to Yeats, or Rilke as well. Each of these men sourced their verse primarily in a mystical intuition of the cosmos, which for me places them above the traditionalists like Eliot, Pound, Tate, Ransom, Winters, Auden, Spender, Frost, although Frost comes closer. Jeffers' aloofness form the aesthetic culture, the thing that makes him so impossible for most critics, is to me the greatest sign of his supremacy. In the end this is what makes him greater than Yeats, greater than Rilke. It is true that his cosmology is limited by nineteenth-century conceptions of science, but his freedom is that cosmology (and it is the great imaginative creation of the period just closing) is a tremendous

thing to experience. With every decade that goes by, he will emerge as its supreme poet. But for the purposes of this interview, I was right in citing Crane as the answer to the question. I could have said the same for Dylan Thomas.

22. The intuition of consequentiality evokes the need to convince; rhetoric is the vehicle of conviction. Thus when Williams becomes really concerned he rises into rhetoric despite his principle: it is a movement of the soul.

23. Actually, I was thinking of Merwin's "Leviathan" here, and I meant him rather than Merrill.

24. At last I got to the point, what I was trying to put my finger on all along.

25. This question took me by surprise, and I didn't center in on it at the level of the questioner's intent. I do like the early Shapiro, but Jarrell doesn't interest me as a poet. The whole problem of the relation of the War to my generation is infinitely complex.

26. I had just been reading Roy Harvey Pearce's Introduction to his facsimile edition of the 1860 text of *Leaves of Grass* and so had direct recourse to his distinction between the visionary and prophetic types. "Visionary poetry projects a world which the poet would teach us to learn to acknowledge as our own; it comes to have the uncanniness of the terribly familiar. Prophetic poetry projects a world which the poet would teach us is alien to our own yet central to our seeing it as it really is, a world built upon truths we have hoped in vain to forget. As the characteristic manner of visionary poems makes us feel, we say of the visionary world that we could have made it, at least in dream-work. We say of the prophetic world that we could not possibly have made it; for, as the characteristic manner of prophetic poems drives us to assent, it was there already."

27. I profoundly regret this statement for its personal tactlessness. "Survive" here means literary achievement: the poet's capacity to forge a continuing body of work.

28. I meant after he went to war. The experience of the war crystallized his profound moral sense, and in the uncheckable moral indignation his work became prophetic, thus he serves as an instance of the transformation of a visionary artist into a vatic one. Recognition of this led me to contradict my earlier statement (that the two types were equal in value) by opting for the prophetic in the next sentence.

29. I'm really saying that art can't be the ultimate vehicle of transcendence. In the end the poet has to pass beyond poetry.

30. I have no idea what this means. I don't recognize it at all.

31. I have seen young poets waver and choose teaching because academic position resolves the anxiety of their social alienation, thinking they can still be poets in the summer months, whereas that very anxiety should have been the substance of their poems.

32. "School of thought." I mean an attitude, a mere point of view, a habit of mind.

33. I meant the experience of the marriage taught me how to place the primacy on the religious life rather than on my career. Not that I have perfected this. The pursuit of career still triggers me into many unfortunate reactions, but I do not believe in Hopkins's solution of willed forbearance from career. If, "on the archetype," you are a careerist, as I am, then that has to be perfected through the religious life, not denied.

34. This is my complaint against the Modernist aesthetic, no less than the Academic one.

35. "My" should have been italicized. I meant that modern pragmatic, materialist and mechanistic concepts, as picked up in our secular education, had closed to me the true freedom of the person. We tend to think of man as a bundle of drives seeking object goals: sex, fame, success, security.

36. The word should have been "collective." I mean the critic's integrity as unconsciously representing the voice of tradition blinds him to originality when it is before his eyes. Often he sees it plainly, but can't declare it because he fears his colleagues won't understand. Thus critics tend to band into coteries, celebrating a few safe poets (good poets but agreed upon and hence safe) and ignore others they secretly admire because the risk is too great professionally.

37. I meant "*over* 50,000 copies."

38. I meant that blasts like Shapiro's *In Defense of Ignorance*, while understandable enough, are doomed to ineffectuality, because moral protest cannot obviate archetypal realities.

39. This should read "outsider point of view"; the anxieties that come from being a maverick.

40. In regards to one's career, to establish one's place among his contemporaries. But it threatens one's writing, if one is a Westerner.

41. The First World War was extremely traumatic for Jeffers, and the Second aroused an excess of feeling that in *The Double Axe* was virtually hysterical. But some of the short poems in the volume I mentioned are profoundly resigned and reflective.

42. There seems to be either a break in thought or a hiatus in the transcription at this point. Or perhaps my mind made a silent bridge around the idea of Jeffers' meditative strength, directed by my desire to elevate this above the Modernists.

43. That is, entertainer as minstrel or troubador.

44. This should read, "he possesses it."

45. This should read, "the sense of the presence has been lost." I meant that since the invention of printing poetry has shifted from an oral to a bookish art, with a bookish audience, so that the presence of the poet, as an archetype, has been diminished. Academic poets tend to look and act like scholars. The Beats sought to reconstitute the archetypal image around the vatic idea of the bard.

46. This seems a very specious recourse to the traditionalist mentalist. But actually poets like Ginsberg and Ferlinghetti have great stage presence, and could have made the bridge over from highbrow audiences to the mass media as easily as Mort Sahl. Ginsberg would have been terrific on Sullivan's or Parr's show in the Beat days, but they were afraid of him.

47. I meant that in the bookish, traditionalist scale of values, where the emphasis is on verbal texture and conceptual density, Ferlinghetti's street poems do not appear too well. But the way he reads them on the platform is another thing. When he read his "Chinese Dragon" at a writers conference at the University of Lima in Peru, he brought down the house. So did Ginsberg.

48. I am tiring badly here, and the creative force has gone out of the interview. What I meant was the personal presence of the oral poets persists long after the experience. I was thinking of a reading by Duncan in San Francisco when he read over two hours, and we were simply smashed, his voice and inflection were somehow changeless, and the whole audience was mesmerized, out of it. But later, a few days further on, you realized you had been put through a supreme aesthetic experience. He is a remarkable, Dionysian visionary artist. On the other hand it is Ginsberg's prophetic intensity that pulverizes his audience.

49. I was really tired here, and should not have attempted to reply. Actually, Dylan of course was a great presence on the stage and would have been so on television. The germ of what I wanted to clarify was to distinguish between the theatrical, Shakespearean tradition of the British, of which Thomas was an exemplar, and which is essentially visionary, and the flat, more intense, more "committed" prophetic stance of Ginsberg which is closer to the American ethos.

An Interview with David Kherdian

DAVID KHERDIAN: As a poet do you find that in the twentieth century the Church can still serve as muse? Hasn't the Church become too masculine and defensive for this to be possible any longer?

BROTHER ANTONINUS: No, it's still possible. More so, in fact, than, say, a hundred years ago. There's been considerable recovery, largely unconscious, of the feminine spirit in Catholicism, as Jung pointed out regarding the recent Marian dogmas. I think in the Latin countries there was never any substantial loss. Certainly at the end of the Middle Ages the Church was everywhere the Great Mother—Holy Mother Church. It was with the uprush of erotic energies at the Renaissance that this feminine element began to transmute into another dimension and transform the entire culture. That great moment of radiance and ambience that was the Renaissance. The true feminization of culture in terms of poetry and art emerged then, together with all the social graces.

All that produced a wave of reaction, however, because of other, once powerful residual elements in the religion itself. Ascetic norms were being jettisoned in high places. The great wave of the Renaissance was followed by the great wave of the Reformation. There began the puritan attack to extirpate those feminine delicacies from the Great Mother and force all back on more ascetic norms, make her more "natural" in the Old Testament sense, by making her more simple. Simplicity and permanence, and to hell with art.

The revival of Old Testament patriarchal norms coincided with the rise of national states, the cult of kingship, the codification of Roman

Conducted by David Kherdian in 1967. Originally published in *Six Poets of the San Francisco Renaissance* (Fresno, CA: Giligia Press, 1967).

law, all severely masculine sensibility in the Baroque, but that was doomed by the triumph of rationalism, industrialism and, in the nineteenth century, scientism. As for Catholicism, the commercial victory of Anglo Saxon and Teutonic Protestanism did put the Church on the defensive, and legalism and moralism carried the day. It was a bad time for the artist.

Being a bad time for the artists, they left the Church in droves. As a class, intellectuals generally did. With the capitulation of the intellectuals the new proletariat lost its natural ally, and it too fell away. The Church was left in the hands of the bourgeois. In the keeping of the middle-class, urban Catholicism inevitably became a conventionalized moralistic religion. Because the middle class doesn't have enough intellect or enough vitality—it has neither the mind nor the instinct to sustain the true religious spirit. It can only conventionalize material existence, and it clings to the priesthood as father image, as security principle, the anxiety fixation of a rootless mercantile people. It is no life for the artist. They left in droves.

Now, however, with the breakdown of traditional middle class values and the recovery of authentic religious ones due to the universal crisis brought about by the double onslaught of two world wars, the breaking down, you might say, of both secularized middle class assumptions and proletarianized lower class ones (not to mention rationalized intellectual ones) shaken by two great wars hurled against their closed systems, and which will hurl again until those systems have utterly succumbed, we are forced, for better or for worse, toward a new, surely more open, way of life, and in that just-glimpsed openness a new freedom promises.

Now, the return, at one level or another, by sensitive men to religious values, means that the more feminine side of Christianity, repressed since the Reformation, but retained in its sacramental deeps, is emerging. I do not refer to the Big Mother image projected almost superstitiously by so many elements of the lower classes, and by a certain sentimentalizing portion of the middle class itself. Rather the artist senses the recovery of his Muse in the Church by virtue of something else, the emergence up from her depths of the feminine instinct as Sophia, the Divine Wisdom. This spirit comes to us from the Old Testament. We find it in the Book of Wisdom which the Protestant

Bible excluded. But in the Vulgate the Book of Wisdom manifests the Spirit under its feminine aspect. It was so in ancient Jewish thought and it is so in the deeps of the Catholic intuition. Listen:

> Wherefore I wished, and understanding was given me,
> and I called upon God, and the spirit of wisdom came
> upon me.
>
> And I preferred her before kingdoms and thrones, and
> esteemed riches nothing in comparison of her.
>
> Neither did I compare unto her any precious stone:
> for all gold in comparison of her, is as a little
> sand, and silver in respect to her shall be counted
> as clay.
>
> I loved her above health and beauty, and chose to have
> her instead of light: for her light cannot be put out.
>
> Now all good things came to me together with her,
> and innumerable riches through her hands.
>
> And I rejoiced in all these: for this wisdom went
> before me, and I knew not that she was the mother
> of them all.
>
> Which I have learned without guile, and communicate
> without envy, and her riches I hide not.

See what I mean? This is the Muse, pure and simple. And she is splendid, the Bride of Christ. I have myself written verses to her, which can't match those above, but again listen. Not the whole poem but some stanzas out of the middle. I have tried to get something of the passion, the instinct, which make up the wisdom of life, the terror and the awe of the Night of Nights.

> Savage and awesome as the birth of suns
> She treads a tumult on the stippling shore.
> Keeling the fleets of kings about her knees
> And drowning the sailors that her daughters bore.
>
> She is the Mother of Life, mistress of depth,
> Before her feet the tiger coughs and dies.
> And the bony elephant gives up the boast
> Of those vast passions that once filmed his eyes.

She is the Mother of Life, of Death the pride;
Nothing in nature broke that Maidenhead.
Man's glory entered life between her knees,
Yet does she keep inviolable the Bed.

Dung and all death are hers to keep and fend;
The thirst of mules, the semen of the stag,
Beat of the flesh and the flesh's diffidence,
The sperm-swift cusped in the dreaming Bride.

When arrows beak the ridges of the bone
Hers is the hand; and when the widow weeps
Hers the invincible will that took the man,
Shovelling the dead up for her windrow heaps.

She is the Mother of Life, the Queen of Death,
Her only Lover lives beyond the skies,
Coming to cover under the lightning flash—
The impregnation of the prophet's cry.

Upon a night of geysers by a sea
When the lost tribes stirred in their urgent dust,
And rain walked pelting through death's random slain
Stirring the whirling rapture of their lust

She was accosted on a lonely hill
By what no man may guess, but in her womb
She bore the impact of the sacred Seed;
Her instinct broke the lordship of the Tomb.

Fire and passion, energy and source,
The blood's distemper and the mystic cry—
She met the wild Lover face to face
And drank the hunger of the naked sky.

And so on. As Muse she holds it all, all life, it's all there. When the poet speaks, when he finds his voice, it's Sophia, the wisdom, who is speaking through him.

KHERDIAN: If the Church is recovering her power as muse for the poet, what of the crafts? You reached, I believe, the apex of your career as a printer with the printing of the *Novum Psalterium PII XII,* which is regarded by many to be the finest book printed by an individual in this century. Did you feel that you had gone as far as you could, or did something happen in the printing of that book that made it impossible for you to print again?

ANTONINUS: Something failed. Certainly the Church as muse inspired that book, and certainly there was a breakdown, a snapping of inspiration. I don't know. Maybe if we talk about it we can find out why.

I began to get into printing after I'd reached a certain peak in the writing of poetry. You generally struggle through life to activate certain potentialities within yourself. You begin to score early. You score by activating those potentialities and finding your way into life, working your way into the collectivity in terms of what you can do. I began as a poet. When things opened up for me they came forth in a clear flow, pure sensibility. Then ideas developed, and I had to labor in a craftsmanly way in order to explicate them, and the whole problem of formal exposition arose.

The first book of poems I did was, as I say, relatively easy, clear flowing, just right out of the unconscious. But with the beginning of *San Joaquin* I really had to start to labor, to perfect a craftsmanship in order to get those ideas across. This became more and more a developing thing as the war came on. I was impelled to struggle with that problem in my verse. And I was struggling through my life, writing it out as I was struggling, until the war ripped me out of the San Joaquin Valley, that great womb in which I'd been gestating, and I was thrown on the Oregon coast among ideationally motivated men, and other sides of my personality were forced to develop. Then came the failure of my marriage, and the great truncation and release brought a breakthrough in the writing of "Chronicle of Division." Now, surprisingly, after that great pain had been worked through, had settled, it was as if craftsmanship itself had matured. I felt I had finally achieved a point from which I could engage ideas without struggling with craft. The craft became unconscious, at my fingertips, and it was at this point that I began to veer over toward another medium, the medium of printing.

I suppose it was inevitable that I should take up printing, since my father had been a printer. I knew something of the atmospherics of printing from working around the shop as a boy, and it was natural that I should gravitate toward that mode of expression next. Initially, I am inhibited by technique. It's the sensation side; that side of the psyche which has to do with concrete things—what Jung calls Sensation—this has always been my great limitation. I have always been impaired on that side (as well as on the side of more speculative processes like philosophy, mathematics, even arithmetic) so that I can only—I proceed only through techniques that have been fairly established in me by necessity, by the practice, experience, and requirements of life. And so it was natural that at Waldport, when the group turned to printing. and I found others there to help me, that I should veer into printing and work out that potentiality within myself as a problem, as a life problem. I'm looking back on it now, but of course I didn't know these things at that time. You just go where you have to go, where life takes you.

As we worked on the press, and I gradually developed skill, I began to think in terms of the absolute typographical achievement, which, I had heard, had come only from the handpress. As I have related elsewhere, when I went to San Francisco on furlough I bought one and after the war I set that handpress up. I set about in a very determined way to master the craft finally and produce a book that was a consummate work of art. My idea was to write my poems, and then concretize them in a perfect format. To write a perfect poem, a perfect book of poems, and concretize it in a perfect format established on absolutely authentic materials. It was basically out of such motives that I launched into private printing.

Now you ask about the term of this process, the printing of the *Psalter*. That's partly compounded with my problem in the monastic life. By the time I'd done my second book on the handpress, *Triptych for the Living*, I was once again, from the craftsmanly point of view, approaching facility, just as I had painstakingly approached it in poetry. You struggle and struggle until you get what you want, but after a while the craft becomes natural to you and you don't have to struggle so much. You're not simply fighting to perfect a craft, but to reach a point where the craft becomes implicit, where the craft becomes unconscious. Until the craft enters into you, until the craft is memorialized in your very person, your very presence, you are not a master. When it achieves that point then you have the freedom of the craft and your genius, what you are, can manifest itself directly without equivocation.

I am known as a perfectionist in printing, and, I think it fair to say, an anti-perfectionist in poetry. I disclaim the distinction. It speaks more of the typographical and literary situation than it does of me. Actually there are printers so perfectionist that I have no interest in rivaling them. I was born under the sign of Virgo, but in the pursuit of perfection I know there is a point beyond which you cannot go, or "perfectionism" sets in. The norms of perfection begin to work against themselves. In either art I seek to approach that point, to achieve that point, but never to trespass beyond it. To go beyond it is worse, believe me, than to fail to reach it. What is still yet-to-be retains some of the power of the inchoate, the potential, whereas what is over-done is more than finished, it is finished off, "finalized"—the thing that has happened to so much modern poetry. Perfectionism is total violation, the violation of the tomb, whereas imperfection, as for instance in the gash, actually liberates the charisma. But there is no reason for either. Perfection, in the true Greek sense, avoids either excess. She offers herself in her nakedness and is there to be had. Possess her.

The trick, of course, is to know when she arrives, to recognize her when she shows up. And that is not a trick at all, you only have to know what she is. One can't rely on judgment, I mean in the sense of *estimation*. The craft has to be memorialized in the flesh, and the flesh has to be memorialized in the spirit, the life principle. Then you are free. Your work becomes what you are, and you have peace in it. Your flaws and imperfections become operative in the substance of what you do. You are delivered. She, perfection, delivers you.

Now, as concerns printing. When I finished *Triptych for the Living*, this process had not been achieved, although it was approaching. And when I swung forward into the *Psalter* it was in the hope of realization, of perfecting something. The problem of why I abandoned it is complex. Upon entering religious life I plunged into what I can only call my "monastic phase." Conversion had come in 1949 and within two years I found myself a monk in an Order. I was ambitious, spiritually ambitious. I wanted to produce a great archetypal work which would concretize something, complete something. I had always maintained that the end product of the craft of printing is the production of a masterpiece, and that, of course, requires a great text. So it was that when I perceived the opportunity of taking on the new Latin translation of the Psalms, the Great Work archetype simply invaded, as the Jungians say, simply possessed me, and I threw myself into it.

Now this isn't a bad thing, actually, this possession by the archetype. Because every great work, any kind of real work, is accomplished in some loss of self, some yielding of the self to the object, to the work you're doing. You have to lose yourself to the work in order to outdo yourself, in order to do that which is greater than your own estimation decrees. This giving of the self to the work, to the subject, is crucial. To give yourself to the *subject*, in the writing of the poem, is of the essence. To give yourself to the subject, to lose yourself in the subject. Then if the craft has been memorialized in your very being you can realize that subject in your loss of self to it. And it is the same with printing.

So I gave myself to this effort. I lost myself, I lost myself in the great project. I swung into it and I began to print this book, which I was determined to make a perfect book. Actually, I was trying to do too much, too many things. Although it's true that I was approaching unconscious knowledge of the printer's craft I was not approaching assimilation of the monastic life. I was no more than a novice and I had no integration. If I myself were a Superior I would never let beginners undertake "masterpieces" in their novitiate, no matter how accomplished they might be. In fact I would be pretty darn sure they wouldn't launch into something stupendous until I saw signs that they had fairly matured in this new way of life. It's too much to bring off. More than once I've seen young painters come in and some Superior will give them a whole wall to paint. The kid is all fired up and the Superior is reluctant to discourage him. After all it's only a wall. If it doesn't pan out simply paint it over, and nothing lost. Actually a great deal is lost. Because once you start painting a wall a whole series of resonances are set up which utterly complicate a youth's capacity to work, you know what I mean? A wall, even in a monastery, is a public thing. The problem of community comes back on you. It's not as if you are experimenting in your studio. Art becomes a collective act and all the ambiguity of your problem with your group, which in the novitiate period is severe, begins to bear down in a fantastic way.

Now all this was happening when I began printing the *Psalter*. Furthermore it became known up and down the coast that I was doing this work. First I had to appeal for money to finance my paper, and after I got started people who had seen sheets of it began to praise it. In short a whole series of pressures began to develop demanding I make good. Which, actually, is not a bad thing—part of the normal incentive of the craft. But at the same time my relation to the Order, the monastic life, was not formed enough for me to sustain this kind of pressure. I say that now. After fifteen years I have reached a point from which I could start a work like that with at least some assurance of completing it, some assurance that the monastic problem would not be riding me at the same time I was confronting the technical ones, which were monumental.

But I didn't do that. Instead I began to print, and the first year was spent perfecting the technique necessary to print folio, at the same time refining make-ready to get absolute perfection from the impression. This meant a concomitant refining of my method of damping paper, and the subsequent handling necessary to keep it damp, to keep it proper over four runnings through the press, you see. Printing quarto, four pages up, you work and turn, two times through the press, one for the black, one for the red, and that's the end of it. The original damping keeps. Printing folio, two pages up, you can't work and turn. The sheet goes through the press four times. How was I going to keep paper damp through four runs? Four slow runs on a slow handpress? And especially since I had reduced the original moisture content in order to gain crispness from the impression. Then too I was devising a new method of rolling out the ink, in order to improve on the quartos—greater evenness and uniformity, matching side for side in utter perfection going through the press. These problems had to be fought out, but I could meet delays and crises, and much chagrin, much hopelessness.

Well, so I entered the Order in 1951; I began the book that fall. I struggled till the fall of 1952 before I began to really print with consecutiveness. Through the winter of '53 and all that year I labored, but other setbacks occurred. When I started, a certain amount of manpower was available for the general monastic maintenance work, but a lot of those vocations left, and some of the jobs were reassigned to me. My time was cut down till I was really carrying a double load, getting maybe only four, five hours a day on the handpress, if that; not enough to make a complete run, and the problems were beginning to really bear down on me. Still I did get launched on it and was finally printing, and the sheets were coming out somewhere near what I wanted. I felt I had stumbled onto a magnificent format. I felt the relationship of the ink to type and type to paper was just about ideal, a terrific incentive. But it was going on too long. I had set myself a five-year period, two of which were already gone, and the problem of the monastic life was getting harder and harder to cope with. By the beginning of 1954, at a real impasse with myself, I blew up.

Now when you blow up, in order to save face, you blow from the lower position to the higher one. You don't just quit. If your psyche is acute (and whose isn't?) it finds ways of relieving itself of one project by going to a greater one because it can't face the failure. So at this point I began to dream up the idea of becoming a priest. Not that it was entirely an unconscious ploy. I can look back on it now and see genuine charismatic elements at work there. Certainly the platform side of myself had to develop, I mean the poetry reading, lecturing, public speaking—all that had to come. And at the time I saw it as being fulfilled in the preacher, for there seemed no other outlet for it in the Order. But at the same time I cannot deny that there was this tremendous impasse working against me with the book, and so I abandoned it. I just threw it up. As is well known, the sheets were taken by Mrs. Doheney, the wealthy Los Angeles collector, bound separately, and now reside as individual copies in certain libraries. They are, as you say, famous, but they are fragments.

So I went on to the priesthood. Or rather I entered the clerical novitiate and washed out in six months. And I arrived back at St. Albert's in just a frightful state of mind—a worse one than I faced with the *Psalter*. That taught me something, believe me. You know, I had nothing. I had neither the book, nor the priesthood, nor, really, the vocation, for had I not renounced the lay brother state? I entered upon one of the worst periods in my life, which carried through till the summer of 1956, when the inner break occurred and I went down into the unconscious to find the solution to the problems that were destroying me. The Great Work archetype, which in me approaches obsession, just about finished me off. The image of the Printer and that of the Priest were both wiped out, and just in time. I began then to throw myself into the analysis of the unconscious, and went back to my poetry.

I went through a period of four or five years there, maybe more, maybe five or six years of self-analysis. As I say my poetry, which had gone dry in the clerical novitiate, was coming again. Nothing has ever wiped out the Poet in me! And it was at this period that the San Francisco Renaissance broke and I began to be called out on the platform to read my verse. Suddenly I found myself doing what I'd gone to the priesthood for—facing a living audience. I'd gone toward the priesthood in order to be a preacher, to develop the oracular dimension, the potentiality, of the voice. First, remember I spoke of developing the writing, as a potentiality. Then came the development of the printing, the concretization of writing in print. Now I had to take the poem to the oral dimension. You see these steps? Each one moving toward a state of perfection in itself. So now it would be so with the voice, but I am ahead of myself. We left me midstage in printing, hung up back there around that unfinished masterwork, which I had flung off but could not escape. Why? Because I did not complete what I had begun. Of what worth is a magnificent fragment? All fragments are failures.

Now at last we are in a position to answer your question. In the interval after I got back to St. Albert's, before I began to go out on the platform, I tried to print. I tried two or three projects then, but none of them came off. It was as if something in me, some nerve, had broken on the *Psalter*. I had strained myself up to a decisive, perhaps fatal, psychic pitch. Perhaps the Church as muse, because she is so powerful, overstimulated that Great Work archetype—sucked me too far out of myself, the source of my own responses. Perhaps if the text had been my own poems, something more intimate of myself, so that the work seeking completion continued the process of relating the inner and outer man, I could have finished it. As it is, I'm like a horse that's been run too hard. He has been driven beyond a point within himself, and after that can't race. Oh, he can run well enough, but he can't race, he can't *win*. So me. I can print. I've worked as a production printer for the Order, even printed *Crooked Lines* on the machine press. But to commit myself once again to a masterwork—which for me is what printing means—with the total unconscious dedication that went into the *Psalter*—I can't do it. Something chills me about it. As if, as I say, some nerve had been strained there, and, well . . . I guess that's all I can say about it.

KHERDIAN: If the Church as muse can precipitate an overextension of self, does that not endanger the basic religious vocation? For instance, does not your ambition as a poet conflict with monastic humility? Or is this a misunderstanding on my part of the notion of humility in the Church?

ANTONINUS: There is a convention of humility, caused by the grades or the levels of the spiritual life. In the early formative phase values are conventionalized in order that they may be participated in by the incoming members, and this conventionalization of a given virtue is necessary to the whole collective enterprise. In a large corporate move-ment of vast scope and long tradition like monasticism, with generation after generation of men coming into it, the conventionalization of the particular virtues becomes reflexive, almost automatic. In the early phases the novice lives the conventionalization. He cannot do otherwise because he has no direct experience of what he undertakes. So you conventionalize the life, and you live it by appropriating the image that the convention sets up of the ideal, in this case humility. The function is to break a certain fixation of the ego—a certain ego-iden-tification with the world. For in secular life the worldly continuum with its own goals, its secular ambitions, has done the same thing. You have the image of the successful man, and then you enter the monastery and transfer to the image of the supernaturally humble monk. He becomes your model.

Well, after a while you exhaust this conventional stage. It is the same in the world. Remember in Mark Twain's *Life on the Mississippi*, that marvelous description of the cub pilot? The novice in all these skills which have a pronounced social bearing moves forward by this artificial but necessary process. So it is with monasticism.

For in time there comes a certain crisis in the spiritual life. After the novice has become a proficient he passes through a certain dark night phase. This means that the conventionalized attitudes are no longer serviceable, and there begins an almost systematic, processive breaking down of these factors. They have now become inhibiting factors, because the end and term of the spiritual life is, really, freedom, and image-living is not freedom. What is the free man? Who but the one who has the capacity to respond to the movement and stimulus of grace, of life as it comes to him? In the beginning, as we saw, this spontaneity is inhibited by the necessity of established norms over against the unslaked ego, which has never accomplished anything. Loaded with ambition it has never participated in finality. But once it begins to possess what it desires, then it advances from proficient to expert. In the world such a one becomes an old pro. He can take ambition or lay it aside. That is to say, he does not let it impair his work. No matter what honor comes to him, no matter what fame comes to him, he performs his work. You see what I mean? He becomes the old pro.

Well, in the spiritual life it is the same. You might say the saint is, spiritually, the old pro. The young ones come in around him with all their ideals of humility, all their ideals of self-effacement, self-renouncement, self-denial; they go through their terrific efforts to achieve self-immolation. The saint, we'll say, or at least the veteran monk, if we don't want to speak of the saints. But every real monk is a saint, though few are canonized; and if he's a veteran, really up on what he's doing, he takes on a kind of sanctity. And, actually, every kind of superior dedication does that. Rexroth says somewhere of Mardersteig, the hand printer, that the craft had endowed him with a kind of sanctity, because he had entered into the freedom of his craft. It's that freedom that we intuit and know to be the saintly element. The man who truly possesses his craft is saintly because he possesses freedom in it. And sanctity is freedom. The capacity to move where the need is—to respond to actual need, rather than an *a priori* formulated need. And believe me this predetermined, formulated need is a terrible thing to break, a very hard thing to break in the spiritual life.

Now, to your question. When I began to move toward that break, it was part of the same problem I was speaking of before, as a printer, in the monastic life, when I had to cease living the image because the image broke down. So now, in regard to Fame. I couldn't sustain the life any longer at the image level, yet I hadn't fought through the unconscious resources, the opening of the inner psyche, of the Self, as Jung would say. Before I could break back into that I had to go through the Dark Night period, and at this point fame began to come to me again. I say "again" because at the moment of conversion I had worked up to Guggenheim rank as a poet, and I renounced the possibilities it offered to enter the monastery. Now, suddenly, I began to be called out into the world. The San Francisco Renaissance issue of the *Evergreen Review* travelled around the world. I was featured in *Life* and *Time* magazines. Suddenly Fame, the desire for fame or the need for fame, repressed during those long monastic years, flared up. I laid aside the presswork and took up the pen, and I laid aside the pen to mount the platform, to confront the world. I had to move out into the area of my passion, my obsession. I had to assimilate it by working through it. Of course I could have thrown up the wall again. I could have said, "No! No! Not that! I renounced all that! (laughter) Never will I again submit to the temptations and the blandishments of the world!" Well, you see, it just won't do. That's just not freedom. And since it isn't freedom, the only way you can get through to it is to eat the toad, or, better, go into the belly of the whale. You have to be like Jonah, devoured by your obsession. There comes a time when you are delivered willynilly into the bowels of your obsession, devoured by it, and you have to come out the other end of it—defecated or puked up, one of the two, but you've got to go through the system of the monster. For the monk, this monster has two mouths: Fame and Women. So I stand here, reeking of whale-vomit, but digested. I have gone through the gut.

KHERDIAN: You spoke of the Church as Sophia, or Holy Wisdom, and related her power to serve as muse to that. This takes on a kind of cosmological significance, doesn't it, which was given point a moment ago by your reference to yourself as a Virgoan, or perfectionist? What is your relationship to astrology?

ANTONINUS: That's difficult. It's still considered so intellectually disreputable that most thinking people refuse to take it seriously, which means the usual assumptions underlying discourse go by the board.

I've come to it late. It's the most vast and complex of all the studies I've undertaken, except theology, and in some ways is the mediation between them. But I'm not very good at it. Too much arithmetic. If you can't do simple sums, how can you possibly calculate transits?

I'm very glad I got through self-analysis and experienced the archetypes of the unconscious before I came to it. I doubt very much if I could have grasped the singular force of astrology unless I had done that. It's more real to approach astrology from the archetypal point of view, though anyone who is adept in astrology is certainly ready for an introduction to the unconscious. But generally the type of mind that can't grasp the concept of the archetypes, or refuses to, can't grasp the concept of astrology.

For me, astrology provides the objectivization of what is potential within me. I don't know quite how else to state that. I got into depth psychology out of personal need. Speculation for speculation's sake interests me, but I'm no good at it, no philosopher, that is. I have to fight through the battles of my life as they come up; only then do I turn and engage techniques that can help me through those battles. So with astrology. After I'd gone through the whole depth psychology bit and returned to engagement in the active life, I was ready for more objectivization. A year or so ago a friend named Terry Nichols showed me my chart, my horoscope. Suddenly many things that I'd tried to resolve in terms of depth psychology—the depth probe—became apparent to me, simply scaled out right there on the chart.

For instance, all my life I have cried out in pain when alone, or even when with someone, if I'm preoccupied. When my thoughts wander from the external situation, and the attention span drops back on inner processes, then I'll hit some kind of snag, and in this momentary hangup, this tension in myself, I'll cry out. Well, I don't like this. It is very disconcerting, not only to myself, who have never got used to it, but to others, especially others. So when I got into depth psychology I figured that it must be part of my early conditioning, and it was my hope that in dream analysis and the scrutiny of events of the prerational life, I could come up with some answers, some traumatic experience that I could lay bare and dispel, but no luck. Then when I was shown the chart and saw Saturn posited in the Ninth House, the House of Religion, and was told something of what that meant,

I realized where the whole Dark Night of the Soul syndrome was originating, where the interior anguish was localized. I realized, for instance, that no matter what liability in my relation to my father I might pursue in order to pinpoint that particular symptom, the chart showed me that it was originating in a deeper area. Eventually I came to see that if there was a problem with the father it too was localized in the chart in the same way. The chart posits determinants that both my involuntary cry of anguish and the father-trauma turn upon together. See what I mean? The cry, the trauma, Saturn in the Ninth, these things, if not actually one and the same, are at least beads strung on the same thread. As mutually responsive symbols I suffer them out with the whole drama of reality.

Astrologically speaking, reality clicks on the principle of synchronicity. At least, that's what Jung feels. I wasn't aware of Jung's interest in astrology when I got into it. I was studying it simply because I saw something there, something relevant. But later I learned of that principle, synchronicity, and it was something my studies in mysticism enabled me to grasp quite clearly. The great simultaneity of all being from beginning to end of the temporal process and the deceptive character of time. The mystic sees the whole of reality in the unifying instant of total perception, the moment of birth and the moment of death telescoped together, the shape of the entire life posited in the single act of being. What astrology does is structure out that total act of being as it occurs for you. Your chart becomes a *mandala* upon which you meditate, widening your consciousness until all your potentialities come alive under your gaze. Call it a paradox and a mystery. But it works.

Actually, the development of modern physics has thrown the whole prospect for astrology into a more palpable light. Under the old Newtonian system a planet was nothing but a hunk of dead matter wheeling lifelessly through space, essentially inert. Modern perspectives see it as an intensively active thing, not so much an object, though of course it is that, but all objects are simply localizations of energy complexes: the conversion of energy into mass. The existence of that tremendous presence out there must mean that the invisible rays or transits that compose the cosmos intersect in such a way that their potencies are activated into mass, and that this mass, being objectivized, can transmute from material to symbolic efficacy. Symbolic efficacy is the transmutation of materiality into value. For the energies to register in a meaningful way they must be translated in terms of symbolic force.

A couple of weeks ago I wrote the first poem I've written all year. I'd seen the film *Dr. Zhivago* the night before in San Francisco—not a good film, either, unfortunately. But the way Zhivago lost Lara, the loss of her, turning the corner out of his life—that haunted me. Too much of myself in it not to be moved by it. And the next day I sat down and this poem began to come, the closing of a love. And naturally I took it as something to do with the movie, because that had been on my mind. What could be more obvious?

Well, a week later I happened to look at the Ephemeris for the month and noticed that the planet Venus moved onto the 29th degree of Capricorn the day I wrote the poem. The Sabian symbol is feminine: a gypsy woman reading tea leaves, "the mind has its ultimate focus in eternal and universal coordinates, and ever tends to fit the exigencies of practical living into some pattern of possible consummations." Now Uranus is the planet of inspiration, and is in my Fifth House, the House of Creativity. Anything that touches that degree is going to stimulate the Uranian response. Not only so, but a few days before that, Venus had entered the Virgoan Fifth House, once again the House of Creativity, the House of Love, of Pleasure. The fact that Venus was not only in the house, but went straight across Capricorn 29—well, this poem emerged. Let me read it for you.

> Cold gropes the dawn. Time wavers on the interdicted face.
>   A sovereignty of distance shapes and fashions
>   The contours of those long abandoned passions.
> Charred fragments of desire flake upward from that place.
>
> Outside, the visionary rainfalls veil the day.
>   The mystic semblance of an ancient sorrow
>   Trembles the nighttime of our vast tomorrow.
> Reluctant as the light they fade and glide away.
>
> Her face reenters time. God of all tangled deeps
>   Revokes the sureties of old reliance.
>   Darker than the stonefalls of defiance.
> She murmurs in her dream, and stirs herself, and sleeps.

Well, what does it mean, astrologically speaking? To me it means that the poem and the planet and the residual potentiality inhering in the degree from the presence of Uranus there at birth achieved, in some metaphysical dimension, approximation. What I said earlier about symbolic force, the efficacy of symbolic force. Anyone who knows the archetypes knows that symbols have force, awesome force. The archetypes of my unconscious were touched at that moment, and the deep, most profound roots of my experience were stirred. Venus, the love, Uranus, the inspiration or quickening, these two archetypes momentarily converged, like a musical chord. Some finality was placed on an old pain, something was healed. I was delivered. The sensitivity of Saturn is in there too, because in my chart the three of them make the Grand Trine. That sensitivity of loss, Saturn, touching the spirit of Love in the creative throes of inspiration. No sense in overstressing it, however. None of this is necessary to an understanding of the poem— that can go on at an entirely different dimension. But as an artist I have learned something of what sets them in play.

For when I look back over the chart and see a thing like that, it confirms the mystery, rather then dispels it, in my own mind. I am at one with the wholeness of things. I don't feel like a mechanical agent, as if something out there triggered something in here. I feel more as if the cycle of the cosmos had moved around in a certain way, and out of that movement I, too, was moved. I responded, the poem was my response. And the poem is increased in its dimension in my mind, for having emerged out of such a context, than if I were to localize it back at simply the more personalistic level—that I had happened to write because I happened to see a film the night before. Well, I did. The personalistic element is here also; but the larger dimension, the greater form to me is the fact that the sum of things was centering upon that particular point in time. Nothing is lost, but a great deal is gained. For a very short interval, Venus swims into my Fifth House, crosses Capricorn 29, and is gone. Like Lara! Just turns the corner and enters another dimension, something I can't see yet, may never possess. It's very meaningful. And many old pains, many old scars, are transmuted into accent marks that glow with a life they never had before. What was once my pain becomes not only bearable, I had already gained that. Now it became beautiful. What more can one ask?

From *The San Francisco Poets*

WILLIAM EVERSON: Leaving the Order was more of an upheaval than a decision. That's one reason I'm still at sea. I just plunged out. I should have waited for the expiration of my temporary vows next October when I would either make final profession or leave legitimately.

The reasons I didn't are really personal ones and would take too long to lay bare. I've been too close to them to analyze them. I . . . . Susanna . . . when the father of her child, you know, that off-again, on-again thing . . . when that wouldn't resolve, when they really couldn't find their way to make a life together, it kept throwing me back into the picture as a—as a what? Not an alternative, certainly. I was in her life before him. I think, really, that her bid for a marriage with him was an attempt to find an alternative to me. And when it didn't work out—even with the arrival of their baby, no marriage was forthcoming—I began to sense that my number was up. So I went to Europe last summer, really an attempt to get away, to change the focus so as to allow every opportunity for their thing to prevail. Then I came back and it hadn't and it didn't and it wasn't. In November I went on my regular eastern tour. By the end of that month I realized that what I was returning to was something permanent, that I could no longer delude myself that this was a transitional involvement. That did it. I moved then to make the break with the Order. At my final reading at Davis in December I closed by pulling off my habit and leaving the stage. The price I must pay, of course, is that I am out of the sacraments.

JACK SHOEMAKER: That must have played some part in influencing your decision. You knew before, didn't you, that you would be out of the sacraments? Will you attempt to get some dispensation?

Excerpted from an interview conducted with David Meltzer and Jack Shoemaker in 1970. First appeard in *The San Francisco Poets* (New York: Ballantine Books, 1971).

EVERSON: Yes. It seems we may be able to marry in the Church. At least, that's my hope.

DAVID MELTZER: You really haven't left the faith as much as the Order?

EVERSON: That's right. I'm still a Catholic.

MELTZER: How long were you interned at Waldport?

EVERSON: Three-and-one-half years.

MELTZER: When you left Waldport, where did you go?

EVERSON: Right back here to San Francisco, because of Rexroth. You see, when the war was over and they began to demobilize, they could have closed the entire system of C.O. camps right off. But because of their notions of equity and the political instinct to prevent the complaints of returning GIs that we got first crack at the jobs, the government made us wait until they could demobilize those thirteen million fighting men. We found ourselves waiting interminably. V.J. day was in August of 1945 and I was not released until late in July 1946, and I wasn't the last by any means. And the only reason we were kept that long was so that we would not be released ahead of the men who were inducted at the same time as we were.

MELTZER: When did you first come in contact with Rexroth?

EVERSON: Let's say about 1944. I got a letter from him when I was in camp. Somebody had sent him one of my C.O. pamphlets, *The Waldport Poems* or *War Elegies*, I don't remember which. On my next furlough (we got furloughs on the same basis as the soldiers) I came down to San Francisco to meet him, and his presence here was the real reason I returned after the war. Not only was he the acknowledged leader of the new literary ferment, but as soon as I read his new poems, *The Phoenix and the Tortoise*, I took him to be the best poet of his generation.

I've never really doubted that. It was a tough generation to be born into, because following the brilliant coterie of writers born in the nineties—the Hart Crane generation—those born in the first decade of this century couldn't sustain that kind of esprit de corps, and the baton went to England: the Auden-Spender generation. But of the Americans, Rexroth remains the best. Better than Eberhart, who has won all the awards. Better than Kunitz, the supertechnician. Better even than Roethke, who is of course the ranking poet of that generation.

Both Roethke and Rexroth were born in the Midwest, but whereas Rexroth came West, Roethke went East. It was fatal for him. He could have been—ought to have been—the Theodore Dreiser of American poetry, but he opted instead for prestige and technical proficiency. The prestige he got but the proficiency remained very limited, actually. He constantly celebrated rapture but could never let go. He mastered certain forms and these are impressive, but his open-form experiments of the later years were not. In contradistinction, the open form of Rexroth is brilliant and vivid, his sense of the earth is immediate and pungent. Gary Snyder, for instance, the best earth-man now writing, stands squarely on Rexroth's shoulders. Rexroth is more uneven than Roethke, granted, but that's because he risks more, attempts more. Though in the modernist tradition actually his classical sense is far more haunting and evocative than Roethke's doctrinaire aesthetic classicism. His masterpiece is the title poem of *The Phoenix and the Tortoise*, in my view the best poem of World War II. Unless Lowell's *Quaker Graveyard* is really that. I've long wanted to do a piece on Kenneth, but his erudition is overwhelming. I'm not capable of coming to terms with it. Anyway, it was his presence here in San Francisco that drew me when the camps finally closed.

Of course, there was the fact that my wife was here. But we were so estranged by that time, it was hopeless. Sometimes she came up to Waldport but we were never able to straighten it out. She fell in love with a young friend of mine even before she left the Valley for San Francisco. That affair went on all through my time in camp and it was this that I couldn't abide. "Chronicle of Division" in *The Residual Years* spells it out. So by war's end there really wasn't much hope of salvaging the marriage. When I look back on it I think we could have resumed our life together, but I was sensitive and proud, and very very hurt. I'm certain now that she was ready to take up the relationship again but I was just too proud, just too hurt.

SHOEMAKER: Did you go back to cannery work?

EVERSON: No, I came down here and joined a group on a farm outside of Sebastopol. We were going to make a life on the land together—the commune idea that's so fetching now with the hippies. Rexroth was going to join us. I actually moved my handpress there and installed it in an old apple dryer, but I met Mary Fabilli, and as soon as I met her I fell in love with her. I left the farm and followed her back to Berkeley. The poems in the third section of *The Residual Years* are all the product of this change. In Berkeley I got a job as the janitor at the University of California and then moved the press back and began to print my poems.

MELTZER: Were you a Catholic at that time?

EVERSON: Lord, no. I was anti-Catholic. It was Mary who converted me. She was fallen away herself but had already begun the painful process of struggling back. You might say I was her last fling!

MELTZER: Did she actively try to convert you?

EVERSON: God, yes! Mary dominated the relationship to the end. She's a powerful personality, and I was confused, lost within myself and really looking for an anchorage. It was her strong hand, no doubt about it, that drew me into the Church.

On the other hand, in my own defense, I'm not saying that a masterful woman simply got me by the nose and pulled me into this monolithic religion. I was really looking for what the Church is, though I didn't know it. I didn't know I needed the sacramental life. She brought me that, and I've never regretted it.

MELTZER: The ritual, the structure . . .

EVERSON: Yes. If you are a religious man without a religion you're in trouble. Mary gave me that religion, the vocabulary, the conceptual background. And also the faith, the belief. It was really the great turning point in my life.

MELTZER: Do you think that initially it was a philosophical conversion and later an emotional one?

EVERSON: No. The other way around. It's possible that I sensed a whole new field of engagement remaining untried even as I met her. Certainly my pantheism had reached its term. In the breakup of my first marriage I would cry out to God and there just wasn't any answer coming back. Pantheism is really a great concept, but there's not much help from it when your life needs help most. It just isn't personal enough to meet the absolute demand of the spirit.

SHOEMAKER: In conversion, you generally think of the mind leading, or the heart . . .

EVERSON: Well, this was a conversion of the heart, but with the mind running like crazy to catch up. I went into the Order to enable the mind to catch up with where the heart was.

MELTZER: Then you and Mary split?

EVERSON: Not just to enter the Order, I would never have done that. But before I could be baptized we had to separate because of the validity of my first marriage. And of course her first marriage was valid too. She married Grif Borjesen in the Church even though she was no longer a committed Catholic. In order to satisfy her parents. Which is foolish. But that's the way born Catholics do.

SHOEMAKER: So you couldn't get special permission to . . .?

EVERSON: The norms then were so tight, so legalistic. To get an annulment you had to produce legal evidence of coercion or of nonbelief. Apparently the Church is more willing to take your word for it now.

SHOEMAKER: You were both struggling Catholics and yet they wouldn't allow you the sacrament?

EVERSON: Not as long as we stayed together. We tried to get permission to live "as brother and sister" as it's called, cohabitation without sexual intercourse. But they said we were too young. And we were. They were right!

MELTZER: After all this trouble, what did you and Mary decide?

EVERSON: It wasn't a matter of having to agree to enter an order or anything like that. We just had to separate to receive the sacraments. Once we were not living together she was free to reenter the sacraments and I was free to get baptized, which I did. I stayed on in Mary's house because my press was there. She was most generous about that, renting another room for herself and letting me stay on alone there. And as luck or grace would have it my Guggenheim came through at that moment. Boy, that was a beautiful year, in spite of the pain of another separation. I worked that Guggenheim year! I was printing and binding and writing like crazy, just like crazy! 1949. Twenty years ago! Oh, man!

So I didn't travel on my Guggenheim, which actually I should have done, from the point of view of tactics. New Directions had published *The Residual Years* the year before, and if I'd used my Guggenheim to go East and stump the campuses, that book would have sold. But I hung right in there and wrote. I wrote so much some of it is still unpublished.

I bound *A Privacy of Speech* that summer, and in the fall was getting ready to print *In The Fictive Wish*, but my need for a more structured religious life was beginning to assert itself, and instead I began to search for an order.

I couldn't find one to meet my needs. The Domincans were there but I never approached them. They didn't seem reclusive enough for me. I talked to the Benedictines and the Franciscans. I didn't go to the Trappists because Merton was there, and his *Seven Storey Mountain* had made that route a bit too faddish at that time. Besides, their

entrance requirements were strict, and with the impediment of a marriage in my background I stood little chance of acceptance. So I talked
to the Benedictines and the Franciscans, but neither would satisfy me
as to my own creative needs. I would ask, "What about my literary
career? What about my capacity as a poet, my talents as a poet?" Each
one told me that I would have to put that matter aside on entering.
If in the decision of my superiors those talents were useful, well and
good, but I could claim no mandate. Well, I could understand but
couldn't accept it for myself. I knew the necessity to write was too
deeply founded in me to renounce.

When my Guggenheim year came to a close in the spring of 1951,
I applied for an extension, which was denied. I didn't want to go back
to my job. Instead, I ended up in a Catholic Worker House of Hos-
pitality down on Skid Row in Oakland helping indigent men. But the
real event there was meeting an ex-trappist monk who taught me how
to pray. He watched me work for a week or so and finally approached
me and said, "You aren't praying enough." "Why," I protested, "I pray
three rosaries a day!" He said, "Three rosaries a day. That's nothing.
That's chicken feed!" So he said, "You follow me. You pray ten rosaries
a day for ten days and I'll guarantee you results!"

So I began to pray those ten rosaries a day. I did. I really began to
bear down on those beads. Ten rosaries a day is a lot of prayer. But by
golly, before those ten days were up we were praying fifteen and twenty
rosaries a day. That's around eight solid hours of prayer. I took it on
because I had read of the *Jesus Prayer* of the Russian pilgrims, repeating
the holy name hour after hour as they walked. I mean we would walk
around Skid Row jumbling those beads like a couple of idiots. I'd say
"Hail Mary full of grace . . ." and he'd be right behind me with "Holy
Mary Mother of God!" The winos thought we had gone out of our
heads.

Well, on the tenth day we went to Mass that morning and I was
almost sick with fatigue. But right out of the tabernacle came a bolt
from the blue. I'm telling you it was my first great mystical experience,
and the primary one. It hit me right in the heart like a sledgehammer.
I went down like a poleaxed ox. I dropped in my pew and the tears
poured down my face. It was so great, so beautiful. From that point

on I knew. Up to then I had been searching, but from that point on I knew. And I still do. After twenty years nothing can erase the awful reality, the terrible truth of that experience.

Well, to get on with the story. On the strength of this experience the parish priest sent me to a Dominican. "This stuff," he said, "is too strong for me!" He never cottoned to all those rosaries in the first place.

The Dominican listened carefully and asked me a few questions. They were the right questions. When I answered as best I could, he nodded his head and said, "Yes, that's real. That's true." After a few months' work with him I began to read Dominican books. From them and from what I sensed in that Dominican priest, it began to dawn on me that maybe the Domincans were where I belonged. But there still remained the problem of the literary career, and the poetic faculty.

He was dubious about my being a Dominican. I seemed too far out to fit into the local community at least. But he sent me to another priest, a theologian. When I asked him the telltale question about the talents he never batted an eye. "Of course you will develop your faculties," he said. "St. Thomas insists that the talents are God-given. I once had a superior who claimed that if the order accepted a man with a fine tenor voice it was obligated to develop it, even if it had to build him a soundproof room!" I stared at him in disbelief and exclaimed, "Let me in!"

MELTZER: What were the aspects of D. H. Lawrence's work that attracted you?

EVERSON: The affinity to nature, and the celebration of sex as the central archetype of the natural. The first great impact in my creative life was Jeffers, the celebration of nature as divine, the divine made concrete, a kind of agonization of divinity in the concreteness of natural forms, what I would rather recognize as incarnation. Then in 1937 someone, some friend, smuggled into the country a copy of *Lady Chatterley's Lover*. Lawrence delivered sexuality from the torment of Jeffers and sang of it in its joy. With this book I adopted him as my number two formative master. Both the Jeffers and Lawrence interests led me to Lawrence Clark Powell, and through Powell I encountered Henry Miller. All this before the war.

Powell told Miller about me, and he came up the Valley from Los Angeles with Gilbert Neiman and stayed at our house overnight. Edwa and I had read all his books before we met him. They were quite unknown in this country except by hearsay. Powell had lent us his copies, until a Trotskyite seaman in Fresno named Carl Palmer smuggled in pirated editions from Hong Kong. As a revolutionary Carl repudiated my pacifist stand, but the poor devil was torpedoed in the Caribbean by a German U-boat and never seen again. I remember how impressed he was with the purity of Chinese whores. When they ganged up on you in port you could scatter them just by saying "Suckee! Suckee!" But the first pirated edition of *Black Spring* that Miller ever saw was a copy Carl got for me.

MELTZER: Was Miller's work influential?

EVERSON: Not in any stylistical way. What Miller taught me was . . . how shall I put it? Not just the desirability, but the *necessity* for going-for-broke. And not just in the aesthetic sense.

With both Jeffers and Lawrence there was always the primacy of the aesthetic. Traditional literary values were used to orient the mind into violational areas, sexual explicitness subsumed in the aesthetic intuition. Miller taught me the truth of going-for-broke even without the blessing of the aesthetic. Just the raw force of language humping you through, that preaesthetic draft into the unconscious, the sexual surcharge lifted out of the pornographic, not by aesthetics as other writers had done, but by the naked energy invested in language itself. That alone. I never attempted it for myself, but at last I began to realize what was possible. With those three masters behind me I was set up for the work I had to do.

MELTZER: I remember I came to San Francisco to seek my poetic identity and found a lot of people just sitting around. Not the archetype, but the stereotype media created in multitudes. What did emerge at that time was the rise of poetry into more of a public art . . . the poet as spokesman, the poet as conscience, as well as the poet as entertainer.

EVERSON: That's why I always identified with the Beat Generation—the point you're making just now. I'd never let any kind of negative aura around the Beat image deter me from the primacy of that fact. It put poetry back on the platform. We had been trying for a whole decade to get something like the Beat Generation going. We tried it back in the late forties with Rexroth, and were successful enough to get attacked in *Harper's* as "The New Cult of Sex and Anarchy." But the nation as a whole wasn't ready for it, what with the postwar preoccupation and the cold-war freeze. It took Korea and the second Eisenhower administration to make the country ready. It took the man in the gray flannel suit as the national image and the crew cut as the prevailing college mode. The tranquilizing fifties. I remember that *Life* magazine titled its big feature on the Beats *The Only Rebellion Around*, almost begging for dissent. Now they've got their belly full of it.

As I say, out here in San Francisco we were ready for it long before the rest of the country, but we couldn't have pulled it off alone. It took something outside ourselves, something from the East Coast to make a true *conjuntio oppositorium*, a conjunction of the opposites. As it turned out Allen Ginsberg and Jack Kerouac provided the ingredients. They came to San Francisco and found themselves, and it was *their* finding that sparked *us*. Without them, it would never have happened.

MELTZER: What made you emerge from seven years of a rather closely regimented monastic life?

EVERSON: I was called out, really. The Beat Generation broke with the second issue of the *Evergreen Review*, the feature that announced the San Francisco Renaissance. Our poems were there, but more importantly our photographs were there. Harry Redl's portfolio of portraits was added to that issue almost as an afterthought, but in my opinion it made the issue. It's astonishing how a photographer's point of view can give to a group a collective identity it doesn't actually possess. I'd never even met Ginsberg or Kerouac, but under Redl's somber lens we all looked like brothers. Soon requests for readings began to come in. My superiors would evaluate each one on its own merits, then give me the permission to take it. And actually it wasn't the readings that got me in trouble, it was the interviews.

SHOEMAKER: How was that?

EVERSON: Well, the image of a Roman Catholic religious poet as an exponent of the Beat generation was sensational enough to attract the press. It was this image more than anything I actually said that set the hierarchy's teeth on edge. After the *Time* feature on me in 1959, the archbishop lowered the boom. I'll never forget *him*. John J. Mitty, Archbishop of San Francisco. His clergy didn't call him "Cactus Jack" for nothing.

MELTZER: You mean he silenced you?

EVERSON: He tried to. He silenced me locally and tried to silence me nationally. My superiors had to go along with his wishes as far as his own diocese was concerned, and they began to be more choosy about where I could read. They made me stop giving interviews to the press. And they denied me the use of the religious habit on platform. Lord, I suffered during this period. I thought they should stand up and fight him, but they said they couldn't possibly win on an issue like that. I submitted. Within a couple of years he was dead and the ban was lifted. I saw his death as divine retribution. But I had a beautiful Mexican friend named Rose who saw it otherwise. Unshakably loyal to both the charismatic and institutional aspects of the Church, she declared: "This lifting of the ban proves that his grace is already in heaven and moving to correct the natural mistakes of his episcopate!" Meantime we had a new provincial also. The ban was lifted and I was back on platform, interviews, religious habit, and all.

MELTZER: It must have been unusual to leave that closed life and find yourself on the platform with people you hadn't seen for seven years.

EVERSON: In the beginning all I could do was just get up there and lose myself in the voice, let the voice itself carry me through. That's what you heard in Fugazi Hall.

SHOEMAKER: How did this influence your poetry? Did it happen to occur at the time when you needed something?

EVERSON: Well, the poetry had dried up, all right, but that was in the novitiate studying for the priesthood. *The Crooked Lines of God* was finished there in 1954 and I didn't write again until 1957. It was the crystallized monastic ego that dried the poetry out of me. Heap big monk. I had no way through until the summer of 1956 when I underwent a real psychic break, a real invasion of the unconscious. This took me into depth psychology. Out of this inner break, almost as a lifesaving thing, the poetry began to flow.

SHOEMAKER: What do you mean by depth psychology?

EVERSON: Jung. I began to study Jung. I took up the analysis of dreams. The years between 1956 and 1960 were spent primarily on dream analysis. At the same time I was writing *The Hazards of Holiness*. But the main force of my thought was in depth psychology, in dream analysis. Jung was the master who showed me the way through that.

MELTZER: It seems your creative cycles are always led by a master, a guide.

EVERSON: That's right. When I need knowledge the masters always appear to guide me. But in terms of instinctual impasse the guide is usually a woman.

MELTZER: How about some of the younger poets here in 1959? Did you get to know any of them well?

EVERSON: No, I wish I had. But my image of a monk was such that when we occasionally met we were never really free with each other. The fault was mine. As you say, to come out from so many years of monasticism wasn't easy. My first meeting with Allen Ginsberg was not a happy one. In those days he used to come up to anyone having a religious orientation and open with, "Have you had any mystical experiences?" I shouldn't have let it turn me off, but I couldn't be so free about such matters.

I'll always remember a story about Allen seeking across India for the absolute guru. Finally he found this ragged holy man, half gone with visionary rapture, sitting by a path in the lotus position. Allen rushed up to him and in broken Hindi stammered: "O Master! I have come all the way across the ocean to find you! Tell me, have you experienced the *Paranirvana*, the nirvana beyond nothingness?" The old adept opened his eyes and focused them blankly on Allen for a long moment. Then he replied in perfect English: "None of your fucking business!"

That's really unfair. Allen Ginsberg is one of the crystallizing forces of this time. His poem *Howl* remains what Rexroth first called it: "The confession of faith of a new generation." Few people yet grasp how so much of what is happening now goes back to the writing of a poem in the Drake Hotel cafeteria on Powell Street in San Francisco.

MELTZER: During all these disruptions you were spending a great deal of time on the reading circuit. How did you regard that experience?

EVERSON: I regard it always as a witness. On the college campuses the emphasis is on communication, what you know. I can communicate, but the witness is greater. It's something like this: what you can communicate maintains the point of contact, but it isn't the essence of your total effect, which is witness. By witness I mean a personal confrontation, a personal encounter, a psychic crisis deliberately precipitated to produce a change in attitude, a new center of gravity, a displacement of consciousness from cognition to faith. I don't mean faith in the Catholic sense. I never proselytize. I mean faith in the sense of commitment to life and to living. To live by faith, rather than by the mental thing that our education inculcates. To enter via the ideational world, yes, but to move through it. To be able to field the questions as they come to you and at the same time to throw back into the questioner a different principle of life. We are familiar with this from the example of the Zen masters, but my point of orientation is not Zen.

The Beat Generation began it back in 1959. And it took, you know, it really took. It took more than any of us thought possible. Certainly the image took. The credit is usually given the Beatles, but the Beatles can't be compared with the Beats. They were the middlemen between the Beats and the rising generation, because the Beats alone could never make that image all that popular. Nevertheless it began in a different place, another point in the psychic hemisphere. Not Liverpool but San Francisco.[1]

SHOEMAKER: Is the platform also a testing ground?

EVERSON: Not really. I never considered it that way. The testing ground was back in the monastic cell, where the interiority of vision was fought out and preserved. The testing ground was in the writing of the poem, not its utterance on platform. Once you are on platform you have to be absolute master or you're lost. The long periods of withdrawal build, they build fantastically. They fill you up, and you move out into the world. And at the point of contact, the crucial issue, you respond. It's not that you have it programmed like a good debater, all the answers, etc. It isn't that at all. It's just that when the point of issue actually occurs you are there to meet it. And you do meet it. Because you know what you are. There isn't any other principle, really, than that.

For me, this will go on. It's not something that will end with my change of life. True, I learned it in the monastery. I learned what it is, the meaning of it, and its tremendous value. From the monastery I brought out to the world an image consonant with its essence: the religious habit, the robes. But now that the robes are gone, the same thing will go forward, and in going forward a new image will emerge. I don't know what it will be. I won't know until the first encounter.

The monastic life gives you terrific capacity for reflection. There is awesome power in it. Separation from the world really constitutes a kind of power. I'm sure that the Orders are by no means finished. It's just that so few in the Orders ever discover how to utilize the power they possess. The shift in Western culture from a religious orientation to a secular orientation has left them in a kind of backwash, and they haven't been able to free themselves because their parochial constituency prefer them as fixated security symbols in a transient world rather than moving and living dynamic charismatic entities. As a brother, I really feel that I perfected the accommodation of that religious power to the point of issue in the world of today. Perhaps that's why I left. As someone has said, "What you've perfected, you've condemned."

As I look back on it . . . and I hope I'm not bragging, only just musing about something that is no more . . . it seems my approach was an almost perfect equation between the monastic life (the principle of reflection) and the point of application that youth was asking for on the campus. If it wasn't absolutely perfect, it was because it took so long to perfect it—ten, twelve years. As you yourself saw me there in the beginning, in Fugazi Hall in 1958, it was so utterly stark. There was no point of mediation except the primal voice of the poet. But after awhile I began to orient myself.

I'm just wondering what's going to happen now. This great break that I've made, I can't justify it. Not in terms of my Catholic beliefs. But I feel God has something in store for me that I could not accomplish in the context of the Order. What it is I don't know. It remains to be discovered.

MELTZER: You were inside the monastic life for sixteen years?

EVERSON: Eighteen, almost nineteen years. Even though I was out of the monastery a good deal on reading tours, nevertheless the monk was always there. What's going to happen to the monk?

I find there are two different worlds, the domestic world and the monastic world, with the prophetic role bearing the same relation to each. The domestic world is much taken up with trivia, and the Church ranks the monastic life higher because its detachment from trivia renders it so accessible to spiritual infusion. But it seems to me that once the domestic life, the life of trivia, is constituted as a permeable reflective form, then the prophetic role, the poet's role, may draw on it with the same accessibility as it does on the monastic life. What I'm saying is that, monasticism or domesticity, the prophetic function must go on.

Yet it's difficult, for I don't know the world, really. I don't know

how much money you need to live, to get by on. I don't know anything
about that. And I don't know where to throw my energies in terms
of it. Before the Order I was able to constitute the domestic life as a
permeable reflective form, but I had no children. Very likely that was
the reason I feared children, why I became a monk. But now I have a
boy to raise to manhood. So the life of a parent, the life of responsibility
in trivia, confronts me.

EVERSON: I distinguish between the poem written and the poem read.
The poem read is the confrontation with the world, but the poem
written is the confrontation with the self, the unknown part of the
self, which is hidden. This is carried on at an entirely different level
than the blazing confrontation which the world exacts. We begin as
introverts, the reason why so many poets are poor readers. For the art
of the platform is an art of extroversion. You master the problem by
throwing a more challenging confrontation back to the world than it
is prepared for. This enables you to survive even as you insist on your
own terms. For this reason I will sometimes outrageously exploit my
poems when I read. Whereas when I write, it is as private a thing as
my love life. There is all the privacy of the bedroom about it. Procreation and insemination. Except that the dialogue is with the self, the
unknown self. In the act of creation we find the pagan in ourselves,
the primitive. We find *him*, or *her*, or *it*—whatever it is that has not
yet yielded to formality.

And it taunts us, and rebukes us, mocking us with the limitations
of formality, suffering itself to be accepted only under the most specifically appropriate terms. And so the poem emerges, the ritual in
which the dialogue with the mysterious self is consummated.

These truths are weapons. I have this knowledge, this secret knowledge. And it is the knowledge that enables me to confront the world,
convert my introversion into a true extroversion. What I have achieved
is irreducible. No one can take it from me. Nothing that happens out
there can nullify it.

And the heart of encounter, as I said, is witness. Witness is the passion that propels me, as monk or citizen. A man is seldom honored for that. The world wants to be entertained. You have honored me when you spoke of the primacy of the voice at that Fugazi Hall reading, but a poet can take an audience to the depths and have it spit in his face. That is what being a prophet means. No performer alive can hold such power over a people, for the poet is the archetype of the performer. But that power brings pain. Any psychiatrist, any counselor or confessor, will tell you the same thing. A psychiatrist will wait weeks for the moment he can truthfully tell what he has truthfully discerned. The patient leaves his office exalted with a kind of received wisdom. But the next day he is back glaring and muttering accusations. "Human kind," as Eliot has said, "cannot bear very much reality." The same thing goes for your audience. You can shake them to the bone, move them with a religious revelation they never before experienced. But the responses the next day are mixed, and the reviews, if you are lucky enough to get any, say "excessive" or "emotional." Or they speak of the performance as "uneven." Uneven! Good God! I seek perfection, in my life and in my craft, but I will jeopardize it if need be, and sometimes sacrifice it deliberately, in order to touch, to move, to change attitudes, confront lives. This is the meaning of witness.

"Ah yes," the critic replies, "but it is not art!" I deny the distinction. In his *Essays on the Philosophy of Art*, Collingwood spells it out: "The artist must prophesy not in the sense that he foretells things to come, but in the sense that he tells his audience, at the risk of their displeasure, the secrets of their own hearts."

I have emphasized the prophetic role of the poet because of the relevance of the prophet's moral confrontation as it derives from our Old Testament heritage. But now that I'm out of the Order and experiencing the recovery of nature (not so much probing it as letting it invade me), I feel that those young San Francisco poets who localize the matter in the image of the shaman are closer to the truth for our time. The more you study the function of the shaman as archetypal creator and poet—as seen, for instance, in those fantastic bison preserved for us in the Altamira caves: figures replete with that unbelievable delicacy of abstraction that could only have come from sources of the utmost psychic cruciality (even if, unfortunately, the performance was "uneven"!). A function brought right up to our own times in the tribes out here on the coast, for whom the shaman served as tribal psychic stabilizer, as well as master of ecstasy in the dance and the peyote cult. So I am becoming more aware of the deepening relevance of the shaman for our time, and the poet's archaic connection with him. In fact, come to think of it, the first time I ever read the term was in Duncan's poem "Toward the Shaman," printed in the *Experimental Review* before the war.

And the more I reflect on what actually happens on platform, the more I am convinced it is shamanistic rather than prophetic—the trancelike rhythms, the unspeakable silences, the incredible psychic polarization in the audience—these are all ingredients of the shamanistic syndrome. Of course, this function has now been largely taken over by the rock band. The infusion of oriental tonalities into rock in the sixties is the clearest indication of its appropriation of the shamanistic role. We Beats were a manifestly poetry-oriented generation, whereas the voice of the succeeding one is indubitably rock, so that poetry is relatively unemphasized right now. I think this is to be expected. But this does not mean that the place of poetry has been altered. Pure tonality augments, but does not supplant, the primacy of concept, for it is founded on the priority of inception: "in the beginning was the Word . . . ." I believe that in the field of expression, music emerged and developed as an augmentation and extension of the Word's latent nuances which poetry's limited tonalities of necessity could not articulate. Sometimes the Word must retire in order to let these latencies find their activation. But it can never be a matter of primacy. I have experienced too much on platform to fear that any music can usurp the poet's place in the field of man's awareness. For his verse clinches the point of cognition, the bone-cold nucleus in the vast connotative flux. What poetry concedes to music in the area of the implicit is more than recovered in the area of the explicit, where music never can challenge it.

Anyway, it's this consideration, this complex of considerations, that makes me feel the transposition from the religious habit to, say, buckskin, if that's the way I am meant to go, has an unconscious validation that authenticates it as something more than affectation. The deep work now confronting man is to touch the roots of his symbolic motivation. It was shaman's work once and it is the poet's work now, and it will be met.

Thinking of this struggle, I remember that I listened to you both read on the same program at Santa Barbara a little less than a year ago. David, I could see, had had more experience on platform, and had through pain been liberated into a direct feeling—rapport, a true discursive, with the audience. Whereas you, Jack, had not had so much exposure. The audience had not yet clarified you and purified you through the suffering of your prophetic witness as poet, or I should say your shamanistic witness. For the shaman this purification was done in solitude, immersal in the wilderness. The wilderness was then man's problem, and deliverance comes only from being swallowed up by your problem, like Jonah in the whale's belly. But it is increasingly evident that such solitude is no longer feasible, for the wilderness of the race itself, the vast, anonymous, terrifying, and inscrutable population that everywhere surrounds us, and which for the poet is symbolized by his audience. For him, paradoxically, the solitude and the suffering are undergone on platform.

I know this contradicts what I said earlier in answer to your question of whether or not platform constitutes a testing. I was struck cold by the realization that the platform is too late for testing. It is the arena. And yet so was the wilderness for the shaman. The platform for the poet, like the wilderness for the shaman, is not a place of testing. It is a place of survival. For me, my testing was my solitude, and my solitude was my cell, and that solitude formed me. And yet that is nothing compared to the terrible solitude, the isolation one undergoes on platform. I think it is crucial to see the audience as the active force, the dangerous unconscious force. Then the audience is the bull and the poet the matador. Until you have been gored a few times, your vocation has not been confirmed. We wait always for the baptism of blood. In her book *Waiting for God* Simone Weil quotes with approval the saying of French craftsmen, that until an apprentice has been hurt by his tools, "the craft has not yet entered into his body."

MELTZER: Your view, then, that in his platform role the poet accommodates to a persona, or mask, which in your case the religious habit

confirmed and which, as you say, the transposition might well extend—
this is a different thing, as you have indicated, than the creation of
the poem itself.

EVERSON: Actually, I believe that in every response, the psychic element
we designate as the persona is in play, that it is not only an indispensable
factor in the creative process but in the psychic process itself. It complicates, but in some strange way it precipitates cognition. Among the
implicit criteria of sanctity in our time, the one that presupposes a
totally unstructured awareness, pure spontaneity responding without
inhibition or equivocation or any suggestion of predetermination. Thus
I have heard Allen Ginsberg called "our only modern saint" because of
his apparent liberation from our collective taboos. But this assumption
is one of our myths; insofar as it is entertained as an ethos or value it
is itself memorialized as a constitutive persona. Let's say that the persona
is the ineluctable concomitant of concept, which is attitude. Persona
is the prism through which subjective attitude is conferred on objective
reality. It is only objectionable when it is not really one's own. The
poet might as well accept its presence as something given, something
ineradicably present in the creation of his poem.

It's harder to speak of what happens in the writing than what happens
on platform, because in the writing everything is introjected. The
creation of a poem is like a love word uttered; you are not aware that
you have spoiled it until it is too late. If when you speak to your
beloved you are unsure, it is implicitly revealed in the signature of the
inflection. Then you find trueness in yourself, maybe out of your
experience, certainly out of your suffering, always, if you do, the grace
of God, and the uttered word comes true, not a quiver of uncertainty
. . . and you and your beloved understand each other. So it is also
with the writing of the poem, only the achievement is permanent.

This makes it terrible. From one point of view it is horribly like
photographing your beloved in the moment of giving herself to you.
Who would do that? Yet as a poet you do it. Except we deal with
more intangible forms.

For there is this inscrutable character of the language, its capacity
to both withhold and manifest at the same time. This is so strange.

Everything that happens in a poem happens in terms of language. You cannot exceed the language. You can never say more than it says. The collective nature of the language is the boundary you can never cross. Your personal language, yes, you can rattle off. The baby babbles. But the collective nature of language remains intransigent. You finally begin to realize that the other self—the *he* or *she* or the *it* whom you address—is your collective self. This mysterious one is really all men. We talk about it as the most deeply personal self, and so it seems. But who does it turn out to be? It turns out to be the race! This is the explanation of craftsmanship, and why it works, why it is necessary. It liberates the impersonal through efficiency. But if it is merely effectual it's like the lover who is merely skilled. Who ever heard of an efficient lover?

This is why it's easy to write the first poem. A minimal craftsmanship is endowed in your tongue. The problem is how do you keep doing it. Again, it's like in love. It's easy to make love the first time. The act is so much its own motivation that it blows your mind. But making love the five hundredth time? My first true poem was written with tears pouring down my face. Then the tears turned to sweat.

MELTZER: You say you have begun writing a new sequence. Do you have a sense of the work's direction?

EVERSON: Actually, I write out of the crises of my life. For Virgo, this is the permanent condition, since it is the sign of crisis. We see this in Lawrence, a true Virgo, the condition of the sensibility in permanent crisis with itself, from which his art could not deliver him, and which burned him up. But my sensibility is not all exacerbated, and my religion came in my life at a time when the crisis became absolute, and gave me comfort. Nevertheless, the contour of crisis constitutes the contour of formality in what I do. The only sense of direction is the sense of crisis engaged.

However, I simply wasn't prepared for this terminal break with the Order. As I say, leaving was more of an upheaval than a decision. Now that I have truly begun again, I rejoice. Because I see how right it is. I don't mean in the moral sense. I only mean I am delivered from having to elaborate what no longer required elaboration.

For in beginning again, right or wrong, you are restored to fundamentals. Nature, love, the touch of woman, Susanna. And something never before in my life, or in my poetry: the child. Little Jude makes it all new.

Note

1. The answer should read "Not Liverpool but Monterey." Chroniclers of popular music point to the Monterey Jazz Festival of 1967 as the breakthrough event of Acid Rock's sweep beyond conventional rock 'n roll. It had entered the scene in the wake of the Beat generation, a primarily literary movement, was taken up and amplified by the catalystic energies of Acid Rock in the sixties to emerge in the seventies and eighties as the obsessive apocalyptic strain in the mainstream of popular culture.

The Poet as Prophet

QUESTION: What is your conception of the poet's prophetic function?

WILLIAM EVERSON: Prophet, of course, is a highly loaded word, and that's the source of its power. In popular parlance it means a predictive capacity, but we don't speak of it here in that sense, although without doubt that certainly is a part of it. Undeniably prescience or insight into the future is intrinsic to the prophetic function, some would say its deepest dimension. Yet mere prediction is not what we're interested in when we speak of the poet as prophet. Nor is the supernatural dimension that is ineradicable from its association with Old Testament literature. The historic shift from that kind of religious prophecy to other visionary forms, such as the aesthetic intuition, is what we are seeking today.

QUESTION: Then what does the poet-prophet do if his primary concern is not prediction or futurity.

EVERSON: Encounter. The prophet not merely predicts but confronts. By the moral force of encounter he exposes the people to the miasma of their own inertia. The shock of encounter is intended to correct. To change the attitude is the primary force of prophecy, rather than prediction. To dispel the preoccupation with merely transient things. To break the drift of temporal process. To bring an awareness of transcendent value which is always the gauge by which the temporal is measured. The force of the prophet from time immemorial has been to register that dimension, and the inheritor of that function in modern life is the artist. Let us take this quotation from R. G. Collingwood as our text:

A Seminar conducted by Albert Gelpi for the Lilly Foundation, 10 August, 1976 at Stanford University. First appeared in *Sequoia* (Fall 1977).

The artist must prophesy not in the sense that he foretells things to come, but in the sense that he tells his audience, at the risk of their displeasure, the secrets of their own hearts. His business as an artist is to speak out, to make a clean breast. But what he has to utter is not, as the individualistic theory of art would have us think, his own secrets. As spokesman of his community, the secrets he must utter are theirs. The reason why they need him is that no community altogether knows its own heart; and by failing in this knowledge a community deceives itself on the one subject concerning which ignorance means death. For the evils which come from that ignorance the poet as prophet suggests no remedy, because he has already given one. The remedy is the poem itself. Art is the community's medicine for the worst disease of the mind, the corruption of consciousness.

For me that is a good entry into the archetype but it does not exhaust it.

QUESTION: Yesterday a student suggested that a good analogue for a poet-prophet is shaman rather than priest.

EVERSON: Well, the shaman partakes of that same archetype but is a markedly different version of it. There's not the element of confrontation that we associate with the moral dimension of the prophet. The shaman is much more involved in the actual drift. He depends upon the tribal ethos and a mutuality of identity in an almost symbiotic relationship with the people. Aboriginal societies are sometimes spoken of as being "termite-like," meaning a condition of pronounced "participation-mystique" among the people. Without the shaman, the society cannot exist because it has no polarity, no connection with the transcendent world. The shaman is the charismatic personality who maintains polarity by virtue of his penetration to the other world. As with the prophet, this is distinguished from the ritual functions of the priesthood. The shaman is prophetic in that he serves witness to another state of reality, but he is more of a living link to this reality than precipitating confrontation with it. Thus he cannot shamanize unless the tribe performs with him. He goes out into the wilderness, yes, to gain his prophetic identity in solitude where his charismatic destiny is revealed to him. But he returns and shamanizes by involving himself, in the most possessive sense, with the entire community. It's not as though he can do it alone.

At a higher state of social evolution the prophetic archetype emerges in a different way. The tribal cohesion is past. There is instead formalized law and the possibility of life degenerating into legalism. Everywhere the conceptually abstract imposes its definitions. There are more stratified social categories, and the possibility of their degeneration into insularity: the pharisee and the bigot. This is the moment when the prophet emerges out of the desert to confront.

But on the primary level of the shaman it's a much more centripetal thing. Usually it's a descent, whereas the Biblical prophet ascended in order to bring God's power down to the people. You might say the prophet operates on the upper register of the horizontal plane of quotidian reality whereas the shaman operates in its underbelly. The totem of the shaman is usually some sort of diving bird, or a burrowing or hibernating animal, symbolizing the going down into the unconscious, where the tribe is troubled. In fact, among the American Indians it is this animistic element in their shamanism which sets it apart from the Asiatic variety, and I believe the American poet retains something of this unconscious predisposition, this identification with the animal as ancestor, as *imago*. Well, look at it (pointing to his bearclaw necklace). I wear the totem animal. The shaman and the poet both trace this link down to atavistic forces, the deeps of instinctual response, in an effort to resist an excessive cerebral consciousness. The basic mode is rhythmic. The drum and the rattle constitute the shaman's essential implementation, undercutting the horizontal plane, the entry into the visionary netherworld. But there's a direct link between the shaman, the prophet and the artist, established along the primacy of the Word. In the focus of all charismatic acts it is the utterance, the voice, that holds the clue to the inflection of creative release.

QUESTION: Then you see yourself more as shaman than prophet?

EVERSON: Well, traditionally I have seen myself as prophet, especially having gone through a certain span of experience in a religious Order. I aspired to the prophetic in terms of the Hebraic tradition evoking divine inspiration. But this post-monastic phase I find myself in, I see as more shamanistic in the sense of involvement back and down to the cthonic forces of motivation, the cthonic as the element of the source of life, in reaction against an apotheosis of consciousness in our technological age. You might say that my leaving the Order marked a shift in identity from the poet as prophet to the poet as shaman. But always the poet, first and foremost.

The validation of wilderness and its forces of primordial response in the psyche today is an attempt to tie back to the springs of biological motivation along the animistic bridge. From one point of view, this is simply a natural archetypal break resulting from any over-extension of consciousness, an attempt to balance out. In other words, the farther you go in one direction, the sharper becomes the reaction back to its opposite. You're going to find a charismatic figure of some kind redounding against the dominant trend, striking the balance back the other way. And today the poet as shaman is precisely in that position. Gary Snyder is the best example of it, but all the poets of the counter culture bear the same impress.

QUESTION: The distinction that you are making between prophet and shaman, and your talking of the moral dimension of the prophet . . . Does that mean that prophetic poetry always has a kind of political dimension? Political engagement as it has in Ginsberg?

EVERSON: I would fight shy of that because we generally think of politics merely in terms of particular issues or programmatic factors. But in the wider sense of politics, the shaman-prophet addresses not just his private self but the whole people, the "body politic," as audience, they who hear. I think the word "audience" is good here, especially in the prophetic context, rather than "constituency," the political term, because it bears the connotation of a dramatic context. Always the political equation resists the aesthetic, erases the aesthetic dimension. But the whole function of the poet as shaman is to maintain the aesthetic, not in the Modernist view, the hypothesized aesthetic object, but to maintain relevance to the archetypal world, the transcendental world, which is nonpolitical, and sacral. It's the identity between the aesthetic and the transcendental world that is the key to the poet's prophetic function today. Coomaraswamy in *The Transformation of Nature in Art* develops this correlation from the Oriental point of view, and St. Thomas Aquinas spoke of the aesthetic as a kind of "participated beatitude" inherent in form due to its source in the Creator. Thus in modern times the evolution in sensibility from a sacral to a secular consciousness compels the artist to assume the prophetic role, because it is in the secular context that the aesthetic dimension becomes the link to the transcendental. Do I make myself clear?

QUESTION: It sounds as though you're saying that there almost can't be political poetry.

EVERSON: No, there can be. One of the strongest elements in American poetry is the populist movement, more recently called the protest movement. This is highly political in motivation. It is the presence of the moral factor in the political situation that is the opportunity there for prophetic poetry. But the break-in-plane between the phenomenal and the transcendental worlds presents a serious problem for all poetry of social protest. The politician distrusts the artist and vice versa. Moments of crisis bring them together, but afterwards each tends to go his own way. Remember Collingwood's statement that *the remedy is the poem itself*. What politician would buy that? But whatever the political poem does it certainly doesn't simply invoke or celebrate the political solution. Art is not the handmaid of politics. It is its own remedy! And its healing is sacral.

QUESTION: The finished poem becomes a sacred artifact to which the reader comes for revelation. Is there something sacred in the form itself once the language is fixed?

EVERSON: The history of art as epiphany is an indication of that. With the decline of religious and mythical attitudes, and the emergence of objective form as a primary principle of value, the aesthetic object has come to carry the archetype of icon: a self-constituting numinous object. Such "hierophanies," or manifestations of the divine, were seen first in nature, then became, through man's own artifactual creativity, his ongoing attempt to strip away the extraneous and liberate the quintessential meaning, the numen invested in form. It is thus that the aesthetic object emerges as the vehicle of the sacral. Of course that too can degenerate. Decadence is simply the art of contrived surfaces. We may admire such performances, but we soon tire of them and eventually dismiss them since the meaning, the sacred content, has gone from them.

The great challenge of consciousness for the prophetic poet is to forego the intellectual lust for aesthetic perfection before he crosses the line into perfectionism, which is the triumph of ego over instinct. To avoid that I myself depend on the penetration to the archetype inherent in every subject, which is inexhaustible. It is the core of symbolic value that gives the subject its vitality, its numinous potential, and through its embodiment yields to form its sacral detachment. The prophetic poet's first and only intent is to find the way through to that archetype. Once fully invested there the problem of perfectionism is largely solved, for, as I just said, it is inexhaustible. You recognize its arrival by the basal pulsation, the vibration of implication and consequence emanating from it. And it cannot be faked.

QUESTION: You spoke of Gary Snyder as an example of the poet-shaman, and of course he has many followers and imitators, recently dubbed the "Bear-Shit on the Trail" school of poetry. What advice would you give to the young poet of today who aspires to the mantle of shaman-prophet? Is there anything he can do to avoid imitation and achieve authenticity in his own right?

EVERSON: If poetry is truly your vocation the mantle will come with it. The penetration into the archetypal world is properly done through a calling, for only thus are its findings channelled back to life. That is what vocation means. *Vocare*: to be called beyond the known. Thus vocation constitutes the link between our normative world and the collective unconscious, the inchoate potentiality out of which the race evolves.

We enter collective consciousness in childhood through the meanings ascribed to things by our parents. At first that is all there is, all we know. But in adolescence the Other begins to make itself felt as an ominous presence, the mystery that lies beyond the borders of our awareness. By adulthood it has become the problem, for it constitutes the future, and vocation is our orientation-point, our entry into futurity. It is to this that we are called.

But the call is answered only through surrender and this is done only in faith-submission to your own vulnerability, which is terrifying. Only in surrender can you suffer invasion by the archetype invested in your vocation, your link to the mystery of futurity. For instance, the vast world of medicine is made up of many professions, but the archetype of the Healer stands behind them all. It is this symbolic core, this nucleus of psychic energy, powerful, austere, mysterious, challenging, that must be surrendered to or its power remains simply "out there," not a part of one, not invested in the finger tips, the touch, where it must be realized in order to be effective.

So too with the poet. There are many literary professions, but the archetype of the Poet stands behind them all, informing them each with its root-core of symbolic energy, and it is just as powerful, just as mysterious, just as challenging and terrifying as the Healer, for both are constellations of the same Spirit. It is this challenge that constitutes the calling, and it is this to which one must surrender or there is no genius, nor divine inspiration, no creative wonder. You may enter a writing class and learn how to write a poem, but that is not a calling, though it may precipitate one. But the essential thing is *surrender*.

Now surrender is made through the medium. For the surgeon that is the scalpel: he gets at the mystery through the blade. But for the poet it is the language: the mystery calls through the power of words. Though the poetry indeed lies in the subject, it is only got at through words. Thus it is the authority of speech that seizes him and sweeps him beyond himself, beyond his known world, into the abyss of the future, the mystery. Like all rites of initiation this is a terrifying thing, for it can induce insanity, and generally it is done only with the help of a guide. The guide is not the instructor. The guide is the Master-Poet whose aesthetic strategy makes, for you, the single most efficacious path into the mystery, the jungle of words. Immersing yourself in the atmospherics generated by his passage through time, you, the novice, acquire by osmosis the techniques of the sacred by which he, your Master-Shaman, entered and sustained himself in the archetypal world. This is more than imitation, it is approximation.

For this approximation is done not primarily through acquired technique but through an invasion of spirit, the Master's habit of mind, his mood, his attitude, his profound point of view, his ethos. But though you may feel sometimes that you have been invaded by your Master's spirit, never fear, it is his own mastery over language that is being reenacted within you. Nor is it wholly passive. It is extremely intense, almost obsessively so, and a prodigious writing effort is being expended. It is only that the intentness is not directed to a method but to a presence, a spiritual substance, and the mood of your Master sustains you, shelters you. You get the feel of his mantle, acquire his habitus, the disposition of his soul, which like a cocoon is enfolding you, until you have become thoroughly acclimatized within it, the womb of his words. For me this period lasted five years.

But you cannot remain there forever. Sooner or later the process of osmosis wears thin and you have to move forward or remain fixated forever in the Master's shadow, a mummy, a lifeless replica. In this exigence reality brings forward new experiences, situations your Master never had to face, and you are compelled to rely on unprecedented solutions in order to survive. This is the moment at which calling is confirmed and profession dawns. It is not as if your work up to this point has been without value, for you have been true to the archetype and the archetype is substantive. The early Beethoven is not without value simply because he sounds like the late Mozart: his own subsistent stature is evident in everything he does. I consider my work of that period derivative, but after forty years it is still in print and still being anthologized. Yet the break-in-plane that vocation requires is not complete without an ordeal of extreme reach, what we call full-stretch, a crisis of consciousness in which only an original contribution suffices. Until it is undergone profession cannot really take. You may get the diploma but that won't help you when the real devils arrive.

This is the point at which you must jump through your Master's shadow, out of the zone of his protective coloration, and establish your own signature in a work of unmistakable originality. Nothing less will do. It is the point at which the language ceases to be your keeper and becomes your servant, your genie. From this point on you begin to be a true practitioner of the craft. Sustained in continuous performance you can become in time a prophet, a prophet in the sense that you are now a fit instrument for the transcendental energies that are groping their way forward, endeavoring to enter human history through someone, hopefully you. When you have become annealed in the prophetic fire, have mastered the techniques of survival in the prophetic mode, then the larger and more awesome enterprise begins to cry out to you, the wilderness within calls you deeper down.

Suddenly life grabs you and you move back and in like a crab, scuttling in protest, from the prophetic to the shamanistic. *Pull down thy vanity*! Retracing the historic evolution of charismatic consciousness from artist to prophet to shaman you descend, deeper and deeper into the underblows of the race, its obscure sources of motivation, seeking to purify the murky and turbid waters of the unconscious with the electrifying kinesis of the creative act, groping for the vibration, the utterance and the Word that will crack the sleepwalker's trance of the world above you—one stroke to touch the most elemental nerve in the plasmic night out of which all life evolves, and a new age of consciousness can begin.

On the Poetic Line

WILLIAM EVERSON: Free verse (for want of a better term) is the dominant form of poetry in English today. It may be said to have originated with Christopher Marlowe's introduction of enjambment, the so-called run-on line, into Elizabethan verse drama. It is the breakthrough moment of linear energy into the ancient matrix of metrical verse. Generally, poetry is cyclical, built on the principle of recurrence, while prose is linear, that is, specifying a cause and effect relationship. Metrical lines in particular are cyclical, while free verse lines incorporate the linearity of prose, to form a hybrid potentially superior to either parent root. Consequently, the syllable is the basis of the metrical line whereas the phrase is the basis of the free verse line, because it forms the link between the syllable and the sentence. Now, the strong fusion of these cyclical and linear properties produces a torque that neither metrical verse nor straight prose has to contend with. This is revealed by the jagged configuration of its shape on the page, and is endemic to the breed, a kind of Achilles heel, or the flaw of Original Sin in human nature, etched in the jagged glyph of its typographical profile. And like the pearl in the oyster, this is the paradox of the flaw that perfects. Moreover, in considering this visual eccentricity we must not forget that no matter how irregular the typographical variation, all lines in a poet's work are aurally alike. Of course we don't mean literally identical, but rather share a kind of constituent equivalence. When the mind ponders it the aural emerges as a vast undifferentiated resource, out of which lines and phrases and sentences may be fashioned, consisting of a fundamental auditory substance, like music, with its own subsistent properties. We speak of the aural here rather than the oral because initially the writing of a poem is a hearing rather than a

An interview with James Stalker conducted at Michigan State University in East Lansing in the autumn of 1981. Previously unpublished.

saying, and the poet a man more spoken to than speaking, which, incidentally, validates his prophetic stance, the answering of a call. The oral is speech in focus but the aural prefigures it and is more pervasive. It is chiefly evoked through the diction, and it is a certain consistency of diction that determines a poet's "ear," his unique style, and subsumes the pervasive aural equivalence sustaining the eccentric shape, its purely visual aspect. When it at last informs his speech, it becomes synonymous with a poet's identity, his authentic voice, and in the mystical tradition until he achieves it, he has no name, no signature, no presence. Resuming the interview, let us bear in mind that the dynamic of free or open form poetry in our time lies in the creative tension between sight and sound, the aural dimension prefiguring and sustaining both the oral urgency of the voice and the eccentric dazzle of the visual lines, to touch at last the source of its power, the torque, the subtle but incorrigible cleavage between cyclic and linear patterns in the body of the poem.

JAMES STALKER: When I've asked students to break a poem printed as prose into lines, I could not explain why, as a group, they agreed with the poet's original choice on how many lines a poem should have. I also couldn't explain the wide variety between individuals. You're suggesting that some of them may be giving the aural line and some may be choosing the printed line, and since there are two systems working together, that would explain this range of variety that comes out.

EVERSON: You see it in a poem like E.E. Cummings's: the fragmentation of the printed line to syllabic, vertically stacked structures—words broken down to their naked syllabic essence—but the aural line goes right on, unmistakably a Cummings poem regardless of the typography. And we ask of it what we do of any other poem: Is it whole? How does its meaning move through its texture? Is it firm, that is to say achieved? What is it trying to tell us?

My point is this: the recognition of the phrase as the norm of the aural line is basic to writing or reading contemporary verse. Poets will vary it typographically, from Whitman at one extreme to Cummings at the other. Where the truth of the matter lies, in any given case, is

the poet's special gift of phrasing, to achieve the organization of tonalities within aesthetic wholes. Let's pick a poem at random. Here's
one by Diane Wakoski: "Water under the Bridge."

> If I watched the Atlantic
> when I crossed it
> as if the waves formed their white crests
> in my mouth
> and the whole body of water were a saline solution
> piped through my body
> intravenously
>
> I could have seen
> reflected in each drop your
> face

That's a sentence. But the lines are staggered typographically to confront the reader with an almost umbrageous disregard for the conventions of normal discourse. But the aural line is something else again,
"If I watched the Atlantic when I crossed it # as if the waves formed
their white crests in my mouth # and the whole body of water were
a saline solution piped through my body intravenously # I could have
seen reflected in each drop # your face." Certainly this could have
printed as prose, but the reason it's not is because the prose format
tilts toward the idea, whereas the poetic format tilts toward feeling.

Now in the Jungian theory of Psychological Types, you get thinking
and feeling opposite each other in the schema. But the secret of it is
that whereas thinking deals with ideas, of course, feeling deals with
value. Thus poetry emphasizes value over content. Mostly, the ideas
in poetry are stock. There's very little direct thought in poetry, but
rather a range of feeling, a tremendous range of valuation, if you please,
by virtue of the feeling-quotient inherent in the subject. To me this
was a mind blower because I had never thought of feeling as value at
all. We tend to associate value with concepts, and we think of the
concept as substantive and feeling as accidental, mere affect. But if you
think of feeling as *value*, suddenly you're in the realm where the poet
is really engaged, shaping the modification of value around the core
of traditional ideas—what the race lives by.

STALKER: Can you speculate on how the line causes that focus on feeling
and value rather than on ideas?

EVERSON: The line does it through the quality of energy issuing from the numen in the subject, that vibrates through the syllables, the tone and the accent, those two things, tonality and rhythm. There's a densening, an intensification of these two elements. The three elements of rhythm itself are the syllabic, the verbal, and the phraseological. The important thing that free verse did was to replace the metrical line with the phrase, in the manner of prose, yielding the true play of value in its extension and recession. The phraseological line emerges through the sentence, the major unit. The minor unit is the syllable, in between are the word and the phrase, the collective component. The sentence relates to the idea; it controls the flow of ideation. The syllable has almost no ideational properties at all. The word has more, of course, but it is severely restricted, can work only in combinations, which throws the balance to the phrase, the unit that ties the syllable to the sentence.

STALKER: That's a neat idea. I like that.

EVERSON: And that's why it becomes the line. Just selecting at random again, let's take the opening lines of Diane's "Angry at the Weather."

> You shake your fingers and the raindrops fall;
> a confused dream about leaving your wife and child with
> bloody leaves dropping off the elm tree,
> and the weather here gets gloomier,
> the sky insulated with rough clouds.

I didn't read it properly because of course it is in free verse and you should glance over it first to get a feel of where the phrases close, which I didn't do. But now it falls into order: "You shake your fingers and the raindrops fall / a confused dream about leaving your wife and child / with bloody leaves dripping off the elm tree / and the weather here gets gloomier / the sky insulated with rough clouds." All right. The first line is manifest. No problem. The second line she closes without punctuation, enjambing on the word "with" to let the strong word "bloody" kick off the following line. You see, the typography of free verse tends to accent the start of the line, whereas metrical verse accents the end where the rhyme sounds. That's why we get so much enjambment, and floating or suspended endings, mostly to get the strong word ahead for the impending jump off. That's the visual or typographical aspect. But the underlying feeling is evolving through the rhythmic concatention of syllable, word, and phrase, with the sentence wrapping up the thought.

STALKER: Let me ask you specifically about a couple of your poems if I could, in particular "Chainsaw" and "The Visitation," because their focuses are in some ways about the same thing. In "Chainsaw" you have visually short lines and in "The Visitation" you have visually quite long lines. Are they aurally the same?

EVERSON: Yes, the aural line, the diction line is the same.

STALKER: The only difference is the way it's printed?

EVERSON: Yes.

STALKER: But what do you gain by printing them differently? Why is "Chainsaw" printed in short lines and why is "The Visitation" printed in long lines?

EVERSON: I haven't thought about why I printed "Chainsaw" in short lines. Ideally it is a choice determined in the initial blaze of creative intuition shown in the earliest drafts. That's when the eye and ear are unified in a psychic fusion that betokens no less an analogy than orgasm. But it is not an absolute. I once undertook to print an edition of my poems wholly given over to Whitman's practice which seems to suggest that the sentence constitutes the line, only the language does not oblige. There were some gains, chiefly in that famous "buffalo strength" of Whitman, but ultimately it proved too simplistic, and I abandoned the project. Earlier in my printing of *The Crooked Lines of God* in 1959, at the height of the Beat wave, as a salute to that revolution I adopted a horizontal format and let the lines of certain poems hang out. But thereafter the use of enjambment proved too compelling, and I returned to a shorter measure.

STALKER: Whitman never used enjambment?

EVERSON: None that I ever found. He seems never to have been intrigued with it, which is strange, given Milton's powerful use of it in *Samson Agonistes*. When I transposed the Preface of the 1855 edition of *Leaves* from prose to verse, I adopted a bit of enjambment out of deference to modern tastes, but very sparingly. It could have stood a lot more, but it just wasn't Whitman's way. I can only surmise that his model was not derived from the literary tradition but sprang from the Bible, perhaps the psalms and the canticles of the prophets. Even so, Robert Peters proposed an edition of *Leaves of Grass* printed as severely enjambed as any Objectivist ever came up with. It wouldn't have worked though; too nervous. But these instances support my contention that the aural line and the typographical line are approximate, not conjugate. I do concede, though, in fact insist, that every poem has an optimum configuration, and it is up to the poet to find it. Whitman's failure to do so with the 1855 Preface deprived the world of a great poem for a hundred and twenty-five years, and consigned a thousand scholars to life at hard labor in trying to make sense of it as prose.

STALKER: Returning to "Chainsaw" with these clarifications, could you explain why you thought a shorter line more appropriate for this poem?

EVERSON: Let me see if I can put my finger on it. Yes, it's printed in shorter lines that I usually work with today. Generally when I print a poem in short lines, I'm trying for terseness, severe torque, high tension. Modernists take it as axiomatic that the shorter the line, the tighter the tension. That's why we see so many skinny poems around today. By the same token, the longer the line, the more slack the tension. That's a good modernist precept, right? Yet Whitman disproved that. He wrote lines of great length so high in tension that your flesh creeps reading them [as in the following, from "Song of Myself"]: "You there, impotent, loose in the knees, open your scarfed chops till I blow grit within you." In any case, "Chainsaw" is highly tensed so that apparently I felt that I could handle the movement within a more quickly pivotal, angular, and staccato-like emphasis. It was not a meditative moment that I wrote of, but hinges on the graze of incipient catastrophe.

STALKER: Would you say that the shorter lines in "Chainsaw" are visual representations of the sounds of the chainsaw engine, that staccato?

EVERSON: Well, I wasn't trying for that. And if onomatopoeia is there, it too was unconscious. I think it has to do more with intensity, the ominous approach of the actual, near-disastrous experience:

> I bring the blade,
> Wiping it,
> Handling it gingerly.
>
> Scythes and axes I understand,
> But the chainsaw?
> What governs it?
>
> The mechanistic fury.
> The annihilate god.
>
> I hear him moaning there,
> Drawing the lovely alders down,
> Calling them.
>
> I feel the hunger of death
> Pulse in his loins,
> Tremble in his thews.
>
> I smell his breath.

It's open. The experience is much more open in those short lines and especially by the prevalence of the double spaces. That exposure, plus the ingredient of short pulsation, has something to do with the tentative threat of the experience it's dealing with. Something ominous is stalking there.

STALKER: I notice as we look at it that each of the stanzas is either a single sentence or two sentences, so that a phrase in this poem becomes a sentence.

EVERSON: Yes, that's true. I think it could well happen, but mostly it's the quality of the experience that's trying to be approximated visually. In terms of the aural, there really isn't any difference.

STALKER: Would you read the first stanza or two of "The Visitation"?

EVERSON: Yes. Let me glance over it first for a moment. Now:

> Midsummer hush: warm light, inert windless air
> Smoothing for sundown. We linger at table, sip wine,
> Idly talking, the casual things of the day's dimension,
> Our thought settling toward dusk.

This far I wanted a much more relaxed feeling, and I sealed it with my first break.

> Suddenly in the vast
> Calm of the canyon, an ominous crack, a break and snapping.
> We look up alarmed. Something in the sound
> Wrings our sense, flings us to our feet,
> Slamming back chairs.

The energy is churning out now, gaining momentum, seeking an out.

> Then the crackling
> Begins to rip, something going down out there
> Tearing its guts out in an awful fall,
> Hauled down out of life, the shrill
> Maniacal whine of fibers at last letting go,
> The whoosh of a great weight falling, twisting as it drops,
> Plunging toward chaos.

I think the reason I didn't open it up more is that I wanted the massive brunt of the thing to come through, and also the sense of resistance groined in the stanzaic empaction. The texture tends more toward toughness, to get at the actuality there, than does "Chainsaw," which is more wheeling and dealing.

STALKER: Let me ask you in the next stanza down. "And then the crash . . ."

> And then the crash,
> The clobbering force of that smash as it hits,
> The boom sweeping over like dynamite blast.
> We gaze at each other, thunderstruck,
> Utterly aghast—what in God's name!—

> The terrible question in each other's eyes,
> What skeletons toppling out of what
> Unacknowledged closets, nakedly asprawl—

Why did you break the line after the "what"?

EVERSON: Because there's a lurking caesura there between "what" and "unacknowledged." There's a hitch in pulsation there, and I moved to turn that liability into an asset. Also, the two "whats" sound repetitious, being so close together, but hanging the second one out it takes the endline emphasis and is subtly colored by its position, which would not have occurred if buried in the line.

STALKER: So that break in a sense is an aid to the reader?

EVERSON: Yes. And it's the enjambment. The sense of hovering at "what" works because it is an intrinsically suspensive word. Then the heavy word "unacknowledged," with all its guilt associations, drops right back down to start the new line before you can evade its implications.

This discussion brings to mind another interesting instance of a line-change made to help the reader. When the book was first published, a reviewer, after praising the vitality of this poem, censured my recourse to expatiation in the tenth stanza. I dismissed the objection in my own mind because I felt the need of a generalizing emotion following the pyrotechnics of the tree-fall:

> Suddenly emerging,
> Out of the long anonymity of its dream in the massed forest,
> Expending its whole potential of life-force
> In the apotheosis of its collapse. . . .

But discussing it with a friend, as he read the passage aloud, I noticed he stumbled over the line "Out of the long anonymity of its dream." It was the caesura between "long" and "anonymity" that tripped him up. This is the identical situation I had avoided in the line we were discussing, the caesura between "what" and "unacknowledged," by recourse to enjambment. So I decided that when reprinting I will alter the typography by changing the approach in preparation for the enjambment.

> Suddenly emerging, out of the long
> Anonymity of its dream in the massed forest.

Also, this is another example of how the aural line persists despite the typographical machinations.

STALKER: Very interesting.

EVERSON: The beautiful thing about enjambment is that you can do in the typography of a poem what you can never do in the typography of prose. It gives you another option in restoring creative tension when things start to go slack, gaining great versatility in exploiting the common language. It helps densen the syllabic content itself and at the same time helps determine the typographical construct, so you can wrench the poem back and forth between its feeling states and latent paraphrasable content, exposing or opening up, making visible its latent meaning in a way that prose simply can't do. People are beginning to write prose poems, and I think they are a mistake. They forfeit exactly these strengths.

STALKER: It has to because you lose the line in the prose poem. Retain the phrase and lose the line, and in losing the line you are losing that tension you're talking about. Let's take a different tack for just a moment. When you talk about densening the syllables, can you elaborate on that at all?

EVERSON: It's accenting the rhythm in order to intensify the feeling content, compress the feeling-quotient to increase value. Let's look at "The Visitation" again, reading it syllabically as if it were a metrical poem: "Midsummer hush # warm light # inert windless air # smoothing for sundown." See, there's that Everson anapest again. I wrote for seven years before I realized I was an anapestic poet. Somebody had to tell me! In my book on Jeffers, I spoke of it as the accent of slaking desire. "We linger at table. . . ." But the anapest can be excessively lulling, so I check it with a spondee: "sip wine" then "idly talking # the casual things of the day's dimension # our thought settling toward dusk #." Now a stanza break. "Suddenly, in the vast calm of the canyon **#** an ominous crack **#** a break and snapping **#**." To me the resolving element—we touched on those two factors earlier, inception and resolution—the resolving element is always ingrediential in the syllables, and I try to sustain it. You have to hurt, you know, if you're going to effect any changes at all. But you have to heal as well. So my poetry, even at the syllabic level, is always jabbing and resolving, hurting and healing.

STALKER: Let's take the second line. "We linger at table" is soothing, healing, "sip wine" is the jab, and that's where you densen the line.

EVERSON: Yes, right. "Idly talking, the casual things of the day's dimension." I was wanting the peace at the end of day in the approach of evening, the twilight. Your nerves are relaxed, and you're just settling down to some serious drinking. So I jab there, but it's not a hurting; it's more a stimulus. But you grasped the idea.

STALKER: And if we compare the beginning of the third stanza, "Then the crackling" with the fourth, "And then the crash," the first would be the opening up of the line or the healing, as you call it. "And then the crash" would be the jab.

EVERSON: I don't know if it would. I think of them both as jabbing. "Something going down out there tearing its guts out in an awful fall." When I read the line aloud and realize what it's saying, I tend to voice it more urgently and intensify it. "The air slashed by the shrieked," and start hitting those verbs and adverbs, "Agony of a form hauled down out of life **#** the shrill maniacal whine of fibers at last letting go, **#** The whoosh of a great weight falling, twisting as it drops **#** plunging toward chaos." But at the same time, all through there the slaking also, because I never let it get far from that.

STALKER: Part of what you as a poet are doing is setting up tensions that you then resolve. The tension of the printed lines against the aural line. There's a tension there that you work with and use to advantage to tell the reader what to do, or where you want him to go, the tension between syllables that are more relaxed and syllables that are denser. What the line does is allow you to set these tensions up and then resolve them.

EVERSON: Exactly.

STALKER: How does your sense of the line square with Charles Olson's theory of Projective Verse, for a time the most ambitious and widely practiced contemporary American theory of versification?

EVERSON: Not very well, I'm afraid. Olson's theory stems from William Carlos Williams's old Objectivist program from the early thirties, which I never cottoned to because of its positivistic assumptions: "No ideas but in things." This was consonant with Newtonian scientific theory at the time of Modernism's emergence at the turn of the century, but by the time Williams enunciated it, Einstein had rendered it untenable. As a derivation from Imagism, Objectivism clung to the short, idio-syncratic line, but when Olson launched Projective verse in 1950, he stressed a feature Objectivism had not fully explored. This was the theory of breath as the determinant of the measure, the unity that constitutes the poetic line. The insight was Williams's, but it was Olson who codified it. I believe that Williams and Olson were wholly in error when they theorized that the breath should determine the length of the line. It's an appealing idea, but the breath, as a matter of fact, has nothing to do with the way poetry is written, and very little to do with the way it is read. How long is a breath? What is it? You can read an entire poem in a single breath. Poetry is of the mind: it is produced by inspiration, not respiration—a cheap shot, you may say, but suggestive.

Birth of a Poet

STEPHEN HENRY MADOFF: You just said that one of the problems you're dealing with now is that eleven years after the renunciation of your vows, you are still thought of as Brother Antoninus. Could you talk about that?

WILLIAM EVERSON: Well, it's difficult because, just on a rudimentary public level, the PR people say that the hardest task they have is to change a celebrity's image in mid-career. They can promote an unknown, but once the public has a fix on a figure, once a certain image is established there, it's extremely difficult to alter it. And this is disconcerting in your performing capacity because you've left that phase of your life behind you and there's no way you can take it forward. Your relation to your present work is seriously compromised, even if it's no more than an anxiety stress.

Leaving the Order was one of the hardest things I've ever had to do. I worked hard to establish myself as Brother Antoninus, and once I had succeeded I was extremely reluctant to forego it. I loved monasticism as a solution to the problem of a way of life and, most crucially, I knew that when I left the Order, I'd be stepping out of the Sacraments, which I certainly regretted doing. After twenty-two years as a daily communicant, what was going to take its place? I was in no disillusionment with either the Order or the Church. It was just that I wasn't living my vows. I realized that I was going to have to correct my life, even though it meant a stepping down.

MADOFF: Why a stepping down?

EVERSON: Good question! But the ideal is so exalted in monastic life. You see, in Catholicism the secular life is considered the way of sal-

Conducted by Stephen Henry Madoff in 1983. Previously unpublished.

vation; the religious life is considered the way of perfection. To think of leaving after so many years as anything other than a stepping down would mean that two decades of life were wasted. I still dream about the Order, still find myself back there, wandering around, unable to find my place in choir or make my way to my cell.

MADOFF: Well, how has the change affected your writing?

EVERSON: I went through an adjustment period, which is covered in *Man-Fate*. After that, once I came here to Santa Cruz, academia absorbed a lot of energy. It was hard for me to break into becoming a teacher in a university: the teaching itself wasn't hard because I'd been on the platform enough in and out of university life for ten years. But other aspects, the *system*, evaluations, the relationship to the institution, the paperwork, all that was difficult for me. I broke into it very slowly, but I did survive it.

MADOFF: There are an incredible number of poets in academia nowadays. It seems almost an automatic reflex for poets to go into teaching. Would you say it's the answer for you?

EVERSON: No, no. Certainly it was a challenge. I couldn't have entered it much earlier than I did. The structure of my psyche was too opposed to it. You see, I had only three semesters of college. I'd dropped out to go back to the land and take up my vocation as a poet. I've always preferred earthly skills of that kind, making my living as a laborer, rather than going into journalism or academic life. I wanted to keep my interior faculties free. Most poets don't have to do that; they make their adaptation to academic life early. As you say, it's standard process. I no longer fight it or quarrel with it as I used to in the Beat days when we challenged it, when it was Beats versus Academics. Now most of those Beat poets are themselves. . .

MADOFF: Academics, right. Does that have something to do with the kind of fundamental opposites which you've spoken so much about, the Dionysian and the Apollonian, the charismatic and the institutional, their relation to the archetype? But maybe you ought to explain those terms a bit first.

EVERSON: I use them intuitively, without hard and fast definitions. Actually I first encountered them in Nietzsche, *The Birth of Tragedy*, but I vary them somewhat from his use, especially the Apollonian. For me, the Apollonian implies control, control implies a plan, following the plan, executing it. The Apollonian will specify in order to execute and enforce. That kind of conscious control, that sense of being in command of the faculties. Dionysian, of course, relies more on the sweep and flow of feeling, of impulse and intuition. Both can be passionate, but there's a difference in quality between Apollonian and Dionysian passion.

As I've grown older, I've become more Apollonian. When I entered the Church I was thirty-six years old, ready for an intellectual conversion as well as a religious one, and I suddenly began to think, as one who has awakened. After I entered the Dominicans, a highly speculative institute, I began to devour all branches of religious learning, theology, and mysticism, and it was then that I began to acquire the frame of reference to begin to link things in terms of polarities. I realized instantly that I am by temperament a Dionysian, that I had entered an Apollonian Order, and that it was the wisest thing I could have done. It gave me what I needed most, what I had never developed. I've learned to think much more constructively. I believe the process of growth does involve starting from one polarity and gradually, across the shape of your life, accommodating to the opposite principle. Otherwise, there's no real advance.

MADOFF: But it seems to me that you can't be simply Dionysian or Apollonian; there's always some kind of falling over into the other camp and some kind of return as well. In your earliest poetry you deal with the land in a certain way, and now, in *The Masks of Drought* you come back to the land with a simpler touch. A quieter way, it seems. More Apollonian, as you say. And yet, it's a return.

EVERSON: Yes, the poems in *The Masks of Drought* are more highly structured than those I've written before. My religious verse tended to accent the Dionysian. Actually, I think of it as more Dionysian than my earlier pantheistic work. You'd expect it to be the other way around, especially with a highly structured religion like Catholicism. But that wasn't the way it was for me. Catholicism gave me the mystical goal, the centering to touch the ecstasy. In pantheism there wasn't really enough focus to get that much ecstasy out of it.

MADOFF: Did you need that highly structured environment in order to realize the need to break through?

EVERSON: Certainly that was its component function. I often defend that move by calling it the barrel of the gun, the telescopic sight. The problem of pantheistic mysticism is its diffuseness.

MADOFF: Let's get back to a biographical point. You said that the difficulty partly for you in entering academia was that you hadn't much formal education yourself: three semesters at Fresno State. Is that where you first wrote poetry?

EVERSON: I'd been writing before that, starting in high school, but without an adequate model. It was at State that I discovered Robinson Jeffers. He just wrapped me up in his slip-stream and sucked me forward into a whole new territory. And it was in this encounter that my vocation took. From that point on I began to write substantive verse. Find it right there opening *The Residual Years*. Work that's still being anthologized. It was simply an instantaneous take, that encounter with my master.

MADOFF: Was there anyone in particular who nurtured your poetry at the beginning?

EVERSON: Well, only my peer group at State; none of the professors there. In college you learn more from your peers than you do from your teachers. The teachers have to be there to define the field for you, but you and your peers carry the vibration of the future, picking up on each other's challenge to create the new wave. The verification that I received from those three or four people who were my peers sealed my vocation.

MADOFF: Considering how brief your education was, do you think your writing would be different if you'd been impressed with the academic literary canon?

EVERSON: No, I don't think it would have made much difference. The model there would be Thomas Wolfe, who went through the whole academic circuit, became a professor at New York University, and yet all that academic saturation had almost no effect on his literary approach, the reason he wrote. Same for me. In fact, as soon as I started to write, I began to read the New Critics, who where just then coming in. But all the while I was writing along on a quite different level— the assuagement of an inner hunger, the slaking.

MADOFF: What happened after Fresno State?

EVERSON: I went back to the land. Got married. Planted a vineyard. Wrote my books and waited for World War II, which was the cleaver stroke that cut the dream off at the root. I opted for conscientious objection and was sent to a camp at Waldport, Oregon where I was stationed for three years. The marriage came apart. We gave up the vineyard. But once again I found my peer group; one of the most formative periods of my life, that interval with the objectors. Got there in January, 1943; came out much more shaped as a man but also much more stripped down and bleeding. The failure of the marriage was the most devastating thing that had happened to me. But all the time I was writing my way through it. I became a confessional poet long before the term was coined. Later, when they'd speak of Lowell as a confessional poet, I'd say, "I was writing confessional poetry twenty years before that!"

MADOFF: But it's not the same kind of confessionalism, wouldn't you say, as M. L. Rosenthal was talking about?

EVERSON: No, it's the same. What he wrote was, "To build a great poem out of the predicament and horror of the lost Self has been the recurrent effort of the most ambitious poetry of the last century." From that point of view, *The Waste Land* is a confessional poem. But because the term was so identified with Lowell and Plath and Sexton and Snodgrass, it began to have coterie implications that made it objectionable. Nevertheless, it was that notion of Rosenthal's about the drama of the Self in the chaos of the world as the abiding theme of modern poetry which made me realize where my relevance lay. The point is important because my religious verse is sometimes dismissed as being outside the mainstream of contemporary poetry. But if the travail of the Self is the term of relevancy, then I'm relevant to my time. It has been the theme and the subject of all my verse.

MADOFF: This travail, is that what attracted you to Jeffers?

EVERSON: Well, *The Women at Point Sur* addressed itself as directly to the travail of contemporary consciousness as did *The Waste Land*. Jeffers sees humanity against the backdrop of the cosmos, which he called God. He sees a deficiency in man and aspires to tear the veil from man's eyes, to break up the process of introversion. It's just that Jeffers, like Whitman, took an affirmative stance towards an Absolute, whereas the early Eliot and the later Lowell were skeptical and dubious. But strictly speaking, Jeffers is not a confessional poet. His concern isn't with the lost Self, but with the lost race, and he wrote not to express that lostness but to rebuke it. It was World War II that wrenched me from Jeffers's solutions and threw me towards the confessional mode.

MADOFF: And that was focused during the years at Waldport?

EVERSON: That's when I moved; when the travail of the Self became the central problem of my life. At the time I arrived, there was a camp paper called *The Tide*, and then there was a little radical underground sheet that called itself *Untide*—"what is not *Tide* is *Untide*"—it's a glib pun like that. I began to publish anti-war poems in that little paper. Later we gathered those loose sheets together and made our first publication of it, our first book. And from that point on we acquired a press and began to do serious work. Then I became head of the Fine Arts Group, an officially sponsored enterprise to which men in other camps could transfer in order to participate in the program.

MADOFF: Was that your first experience with press work?

EVERSON: No. My father was a printer, so I had very early training in printing. The first thing I learned to do after school around the shop was to set type. But my relationship with my father was so difficult I got out of there as soon as I could. I had no real interest in printing until I became a poet and realized my lost opportunity.

At Waldport we printed four books of mine: *War Elegies, Waldport Poems, The Residual Years,* and *Poems MCMXLII.* Then we printed the work of a C.O. named Jacob Sloan from another camp, *Generation of Journey,* a good poet who never followed through after the war, and we did a book by Kenneth Patchen, *An Astonished Eye Looks Out of the Air.* We were blessed in that our work sold readily. Suddenly I'd found an audience, and for the first time. When I began down in the San Joaquin Valley, I was simply a regionalist, but the pacifist movement gave me a positive group identification. It gave me a following of people who were interested in my work for the subject matter, what the poetry was *about.* And that led to my first national publication with New Directions.

MADOFF: After you were released, what happened?

EVERSON: I went to San Francisco and joined the group around Kenneth Rexroth.

MADOFF: And what was that like?

EVERSON: Well, we started out fine. We were filled with zeal and energy, but pretty soon the personality problems began to erupt, and the early phase of the San Francisco Renaissance blew sky high. By the end of the decade some of us weren't talking to each other. It was painful.

MADOFF: Who were the writers involved?

EVERSON: That would principally be Rexroth, Duncan, Lamantia, Broughton, Parkinson, and myself. Others of good promise too, but their names are unfamiliar now. Jack Spicer was on hand but stood apart from us. Sanders Russell, the friend of Duncan, was also involved.

MADOFF: Would you say that the group broke up because everyone was, in your terms, Dionysian, that it was the major spiritual mode there and simply couldn't tolerate its own power?

EVERSON: Perhaps. But with me it was mainly the woman problem.

MADOFF: The woman problem?

EVERSON: When I met Mary Fabilli. You see, Rexroth thought I should get back together with my first wife, Edwa. In the course of her wanderings, they met; and he was enchanted with her. But I didn't go back to Edwa after the war because she was involved with this other man. Rather I moved towards Mary Fabilli, and Rexroth didn't like it at all. In time he insulted Mary, who is a very proud person, and it meant that I was put in the position of having to choose between them, my mentor or my lover. There's often a dispute between the woman in your life and your mentor. Your mentor can see your career in its political ramifications and tell you what you should do, direct you. But your woman may be feeling these directions as a threat, and they clash. And the woman's going to win because her grip is lower down in your anatomy.

After the split with Kenneth, the group tended to concentrate in Berkeley, mostly under the sponsorship of Duncan. There was a great deal of literary exchange. I mean, the exacting poring over manuscripts. You know, talking poems out, talking craft and the problem of values, literary values generally, but also psychological and ethical ones. We were markedly Reichian then.

MADOFF: You were getting involved more and more with handpress activity at this time—leaving the Untide Press and starting the Equinox Press, is that right?

EVERSON: Right. I began to gravitate towards the handpress because the limitations of the machine press at Waldport emerged as we advanced in technique. And I began to learn a little of the lore and mystique of the handpress there. When I left the camp, left conscription, I bought a handpress in San Francisco and first set it up near Sebastopol. Then when I came back down to Berkeley to live with Mary Fabilli, I brought it with me and put it in a pressroom that I made at the back of the house. I got a job as a janitor at the University of California Press, which was about the best thing that could have happened to me because it put me right in the center of a marvelous typographical world. I began to read in earnest then and perfect my printing, perfect my typographical taste by exposure to fine printing in the libraries.

MADOFF: As a janitor you were able to get around through the pressroom?

EVERSON: Yes. I was on the night shift, and I could talk with the craftsmen, the printers as they worked. So I had this literary life on the outside going, but I also had this typographical life during my work hours. So that was the emergence of my second big dream: to found my press, write my poems, and print my books. And where before in the vineyard I was going to be the poet laureate of the San Joaquin Valley, now I was going to be the Bay Area anarcho-pacifist poet and craftsman, printing my books as I went along, and making a living at it.

For the poet, the book is the principle of immortality. He seeks permanence in its pages because instinctively every poet writes for posterity more than he does for his own time. This is dictated by the nature of poetry itself. Its function is to stabilize mankind through the processes of change by reassuring it of the significance of its past, not through nostalgic recovery, but by making the present comprehensible to the future. The poet addresses his own time, indeed, but only in terms posterity can fully understand, for his time is deaf. Being of the noumenon, the poem can't compete with the clamor of the phenomenal world, so it is driven underground. It sinks into the collective substrata until the cultural sorting out is completed and then emerges in its irreducible essence, a gold nugget panned from the river of time. As a printer you make the book permanent and beautiful, so that it will be valued and physically survive, until the poem can be recognized for what it is, come into its own, and complete its destiny.

Of course, you understand that it was the ambiance of Mary Fabilli that stood behind this vision of the poet-printer, just as it was that of Edwa that stood behind the poet-vineyardist. But the religious break-through erupted in the midst of it, as the war had done the other, and once again the dream was broken. Mary led me into the Church, gave my religious impulse the focus it needed. I had no idea how much religious intensity I was carrying inside me until I found the place where it could be focused. But then we had to part because we both had valid marriages. So in 1949 we separated, I to become baptized into the Catholic Church, she to return to the Sacraments. On the basis of *The Residual Years* of 1948, I applied for a Guggenheim, and it came through. So that following year I was writing on the Guggenheim and also breaking into Catholicism.

MADOFF: Then did you see some fundamental change taking place in your poetry?

EVERSON: I used the same landscape, but the subject matter changed abruptly. I was able to draw on a deeper and more rich tradition so that my verse gained in associations. Before, the nature poetry had tended to be rather confined. The Church gave me a universality that became instantly manifest in the work. The shift is almost like night and day. When you finish *The Residual Years* and pick up *The Veritable Years*, you've entered another world. The only comparable event was when I first became a poet under the influence of Jeffers. There was that night and day break-in-plane between the old and new. And, yes, once again when I moved out of the Order to go back towards the earth, it had that same sharp definition. To read "Tendril in the Mesh" after *The Rose of Solitude* is mind-boggling.

MADOFF: I'm struck by the poem "The Mate-Flight of Eagles," written in '53—particularly by the emphasis on the determinacy of the Divine order, a kind of holy inevitability. The passage, for example, when you speak about Christ lanced on the cross and exclaim, "When the Christ-love and the Christ-death find the love-death of the cross."

EVERSON: Well, when I call that factor to mind, I think of it as *providential*, a religious term actually, rather than, say, destiny or fatality. It's a sense of participating in a movement of God, of participation in the directed purpose of things, the flow of events even when they're painful, being supported by them and sustained by them. This gives an intensity the earlier work lacked. In registering that sense, the craft, I suppose, does contribute. I daresay that's the chief stylistic difference between myself and Jeffers: the increase in density at the syllabic level. My rhythmic units are much more closely moulded than his. He can tolerate a more relaxed line because he's dealing with more phenomena. Going back and down to the drama of the Self, I build up rhythmic intensity in order to get the emotive urgency across, the travail of experience, to register the ordeal. And so the line becomes shorter, a lot more enjambment. Yes, jump the line back to the opening, stress the kick-off, put the operative word at the beginning of the line. You see the same thing in Hopkins and Donne. There is a closeness of figuration that makes for intensity. It's not really meant to be an innovative, experimental element so much as it is a cumulative and intensifying factor.

MADOFF: It seems to me you've always combined religious ecstasy and sexual ecstasy to create that kind of intensity.

EVERSON: Yes, it began when I first read *Lady Chatterley's Lover*. It was a forbidden book at that time, and some friends down in the Valley got a copy in Paris. They put it in my hands. It was one of the transforming books in my life.

MADOFF: When was that?

EVERSON: That would be 1937. Up to that point I had no sense of erotic mystique. I knew sex as a peak experience all right, but I had no sense of its mystical aspect. But then that book came into my hands and suddenly sexuality assumed a religious dimension. It was acquired directly from Lawrence. Then when I became a Catholic, not surprisingly, sex became divinized at a different level than it had been under Lawrence and the pantheistic aegis. As a pantheist, [I perceived that] sex was mostly instinctual and therefore closest to nature. It got its religious mode from that. But later on as a Catholic, it emerged in its incarnational aspects. Traditionally, it has served as a metaphor of the love between God and man, as canonized in the Song of Songs, from Scripture. And for the most part, my program of erotic mysticism followed that vision. But then I brought the two strains together in *River-Root*, probably my most important and revolutionary piece of writing. I fused the strains of Lawrence and Solomon together in an attempt to heal a division that has lain like a fracture in the sensibility of the race.

MADOFF: Thinking about the craft, the kind of verse that you're talking about isn't formal in its composition, is it? Take a poem like "The Way of Life and the Way of Death" in *The Rose of Solitude*. You use a kind of incantatory rhetoric that heightens the implications in your lines. And it seems that the rhetorical repetitions of increasing sexual ecstasy and violence replace more formal poetic structures.

EVERSON: Sure. But usually at the end of a confessional sequence, I use rhyme and meter in the interest of a more formal resolution. I launch out through open form or free form, let it all out, and then pull it together by verging back into slower resolving meters and rhymes.

MADOFF: Well, to get back to the biographical . . .

EVERSON: Right. In any case, after my Guggenheim year, I entered the Catholic Worker Movement. They had just started a house in West Oakland. I'd run across *The Catholic Worker* in camp, because they were the only pacifists and anarchists in the Church. Actually, it was the existence of the *Worker* that enabled me to become a Catholic. Given my anarchism and pacifism, I doubt if I could ever have made it into the Church without some such platform. But suddenly, just as my Guggenheim expired, there it was, so I found myself involved from the winter of 1950 to the summer of '51. I even moved my press and printed my book, *Triptych for the Living*, there. Changed the name of the press from Equinox to Seraphim. And in June of '51 I finally went into the Dominican Order, brought my handpress later that same year, and began to print the *Psalter*, the Book of Psalms.

MADOFF: Your *Psalter* is considered one of the great works of American printing. How did you get to that level of expertise?

EVERSON: Just did, I guess. Actually, all the expertise necessary to print the *Psalter* was right there in my first broadside from the hand-press, the Equinox Press announcement: the subsumed sense of proportion, the textual intricacy in the monumental scale. For the Dionysian it is given with the vocation, from the beginning. The Modernists, who extol the technique but minimize the subject, paralyze you with their insistence on the years of conscious acquisition of the craft, that Apollonian bullshit. But vocation is mythic and archetypal, like King Arthur easing the sword from the rock or David slaying Goliath. The preparation is all internal, a brooding gestation, a mysterious hatching, the smouldering evolution of your relation to the subject. And when the moment of the Call comes around, then breakthrough! The power in the heart flows down the arms and into the hands. That's the way it's always been for me. I told you how my first true poems struck through; still in print after forty-five years. It happened again with the handpress. It happened with the monastic life. So when I came to print the *Psalter*, the work was blessed. The elements flowed together. The sheets began to come off the press with perfect register and perfect printing. It proved to be one of those converging points again where every thing coalesces in a sort of epiphany or revelation.

MADOFF: So at the same time your religious life and your printing work were growing incredibly intense. What about your writing?

EVERSON: Well, when I went into the Order, there was a moment of surcease and peace while I made my adjustments—kind of wrapped the walls of the monastery around me. Thus several years with only a poem or two a year. But after a while the Dark Night of the Soul began. After the intensity of your interior life starts to burn out, this phase begins. And a good deal of my monastic poetry is taken up with that. For instance, the book called *The Hazards of Holiness*, which was highly confessional. And I then moved into *The Rose of Solitude*, which I consider confessional too.

MADOFF: And this period you talk about in which the dedication begins to burn out, how long did it take for that to happen? How long were you in the Order?

EVERSON: Eighteen-and-a-half years. But that isn't why I left the Order, not because of the burnout. I left because I fell in love. It was a celibacy problem that necessitated leaving monastic life.

MADOFF: Could you speak a little about the now legendary occasion on which you left the Order?

EVERSON: Yes. After the affair of *The Rose of Solitude*, I was without a relationship for a year there, still in the Order. Then Susanna my present wife came to me for counseling, and it was in the course of this counseling that I fell in love with her. In *The Rose of Solitude* the celibacy problem, despite a lapse, was largely contained. But when Susanna came into the picture, I just fell into her arms, went right down into, as my title says, the "tendril in the mesh."

Now, Susanna wanted to marry, but I wasn't ready to give up my monastic vocation. I loved the life. I'd fought so hard to achieve the place I had in terms of my career. Also I didn't want to leave the Sacraments, which I knew I must, since I couldn't marry her formally in the Church. I fled to Europe that summer (this is now 1969 we're talking about), but when I returned in the fall nothing was different, and I made my autumn East Coast reading tour. When I finally got back, I realized that things just weren't going to change, that I was going to have to pull my life together. I couldn't go on violating my vows. So I asked Sue to marry me, and she accepted. My last scheduled appearance was at the University of California at Davis, December 7, 1969. I read "Tendril in the Mesh" for the first time, and at the conclusion I pulled my habit off—just took it off right there and fled the platform. I saw it as a public divestment-ritual complementary to the public investiture-ceremony in which the habit was received.

MADOFF: And you never returned to the Order?

EVERSON: No, that night I left, joined Susanna at Stinson Beach. But the facts of my nature are just as irreconcilable. The monk is still there; the celibate and the lover are still in a state of contention within me, but I have more peace in it.

MADOFF: In your most recent poetry, there does seem to be a certain degree of relaxation. In Albert Gelpi's review of your last book, *The Masks of Drought,* he says it seems as if God is no longer in your landscape. But then, as the poems mount, the religious aspect becomes apparent, but transformed. When you left the Order, what changes took place in the verse?

EVERSON: Mostly there's been a higher degree of self-acceptance than anything experienced in the religious life. Maybe it's just growing older, but I think it's more than that. I like to think that some of the lessons of the religious life are finally being learned. That's to say, not to have to struggle so ferociously every step of the way, as I felt it necessary to do before, to "bear off a point or two," as Susanna would say. I don't know what the future's going to hold in terms of my themes, though my craft was never more finely honed than it is now. I mean, it's at my fingertips in a way I never knew before. And yet at the same time there's a decline in high energy. Acceptance has meant some decline in high purpose. There's not the insistent begging for relief, but at the same time neither is there as much curiosity.

MADOFF: You say that the craft has never been so much at your fingertips as it is now. As a writer's work evolves, it seems that the language usually drops its ornate design for a simpler expression that comes with practice, mastery, experience. It seems to me that your first move into simpler expression came in the late forties with *A Privacy of Speech.* What brought the change at that time, do you think?

EVERSON: It was the burnout following "Chronicle of Division" and the rupture of divorce. See, I was still in camp when I wrote *A Privacy of Speech,* and it was pure pain that had cauterized that area and given that paring down of diction. It surprised even me at the time. It was written just after the "Sea" section at the close of "Chronicle," the highwater mark of what I'd done up to that time. I was in that high revelatory illumination that great pain bestows, and I moved right into "Privacy" from that. Although not confessional work, being more objective, it profited from the confessional ordeal that preceded it.

MADOFF: But now you say that even with mastery some of the verve of curiosity has ebbed. Yet your curiosity certainly seems to continue in another way. You've written two books of criticism and several essays in recent years. Have you found writing criticism helpful to writing poetry?

EVERSON: No, I've found writing poetry helpful to the criticism. I mean the actual writing of poetry substantiates your taste so that you're able to speak with more assurance, more authority.

MADOFF: What were you attempting to do in the book on Jeffers [*Fragments of an Older Fury*]?

EVERSON: I wrote the book at the low point of Jeffers's critical reputation and I was moved by a revisionist tactic. My whole work on Jeffers has been to bring him into sharper focus for the literate intelligence of the nation—the feeling being that until this is done, the course of poetry, and hence of consciousness, cannot go forward. My belief is that the mainstream of American poetry flows between Whitman and Jeffers, both Emersonians, whereas Modernism, generally taken to be the mainstream, is a detour from the channel. Modernism is a European derivative—elitist, skeptical, ironic, arcane. It's the antithesis of all the American singularities come down to us through Whitman and the Emersonian tradition. I believe Jeffers is one of the pylons of that line, though he presents its negative face, as does Thoreau. Of course, it's my own problem too. I can't deny that. Until Jeffers is received, I can't be either. Of course, I now distinguish myself from him in many ways: stylistically, I don't write like him; theologically, I don't share his religious views; philosophically, I have a different view of the human situation; psychologically, I represent a differing attitude. But I began with him, and if I've evolved in another way, the stamp of origin remains with me. Moreover, as the link between Whitman and Jeffers, I must keep my hands on them both.

MADOFF: You're suggesting the nationalistic character of poetry. Is poetry a political act?

EVERSON: The way literature goes is the way consciousness will go, and to see consciousness going in a wrong way is distressing. My whole sense of truth, the rightness of things and the religiousness of reality, is violated when I see the skeptical spirit in the triumphant mode.

MADOFF: I wonder if that attitude has anything to do with the regionalism of your work. You've talked about the way Steinbeck and Roethke, for instance, were drawn by the notion of the Eastern literary establishment's certification of their writing. They lost their edge when they lost their regional incentive. Is the literary establishment anathema to you, or is it just the dislocation of the author that's the problem?

EVERSON: Well, the idea of a literary establishment per se isn't really anathema to me. It's just that in America the establishment, by virtue of its colonial origins, is looking chiefly overseas. The establishment doesn't have too much to do with what is actually written; the South and the West and the Midwest follow their own regional incentives. But it has a lot to do with what's being validated, with where the giants go, who gets the awards, and who is studied in school. In every culture, the people look to the values of the intelligentsia, the critics, the journalists, the editors, for their guidelines. The great thing about Pound was his mission to purify the language so that it could bring coherence back into public life. In spite of his Europeanism, I have only respect for that motive.

MADOFF: But it's not the task you've taken on, your prophetic task?

EVERSON: My view of the Dionysian is that you gain more through a certain quality of imprecision, not the cynical political imprecision that Pound attacked, or the cunning imprecision of false advertising, the depravity of the breakdown of language that comes through politics and merchandising. But rather the imprecision that comes through a certain openness or vulnerability to sensation. In this I'm quite Lawrentian—Lawrence's insight into the primacy of libido and the passions as purifying agents of speech. Language is refreshed through this immersion in spiritual and instinctual passion rather than through the arcane skills of an Apollonian precisionism.

MADOFF: Given your precisionist antipathy, how have the critics affected your work? Does it come into your writing? Do you read your critics?

EVERSON: Criticism certainly affects me. I mean, I'm not above it like Jeffers was. I read it, and when I get a devastating review, I suffer. I suffer with it maybe for days. And I'm outraged and affronted by any kind of willful misunderstanding. I know it has to be that way, because when you're deeply and powerfully moved, you upset people. There are certain sensibilities that are going to be as upset by my passion as I'm going to be by their urbanity. And I'm wise enough to know that it's going to be that way; but still, I've never been able to resolve this.

MADOFF: Is this the reason why you publish most of your work with small presses?

EVERSON: My career would be miles ahead if I had been able first to publish in the magazines and then go to the trade book, which is of course the way poets generally proceed. I haven't done it because I'm too distracted by the rejection slips. They impinge on the creative process, disturb the fragility of psychic gestation. So early on I began to resist placing them. Instead of publishing in the magazines, I like to publish in limited editions and then go to the trade books. And these limited editions come from the smaller presses. Also there's a richness and satisfaction about them, a whole other angle involving collectors, those preservers of our culture. It's a different world, the world of the rare book, a different audience than the world of the magazine. I'm collected heavily by the collectors of limited editions, whereas I'm not sought by the editors of magazines. I mean they don't even know they miss me!

MADOFF: And yet you're well known throughout the country. I suppose that's because of the proliferation of these small press editions.

EVERSON: Well, I think that has more to do with my public readings. As Brother Antoninus I read all around the country to large audiences.

MADOFF: What about these readings? Could you describe the importance of what you call the "participation mystique" to your work?

EVERSON: It has to do with the expressive side. As an introvert, the readings enable me to overcome my deficient extroversion, my "inferior function" as the Jungians say, which is usually the point of limitation, the thing that hems you in. The readings give me a chance to cross that barrier, go out and make a living relationship in a way that no other activity affords. I can bring power, intensity, and passion to bear more movingly on that collective level, on the platform, than through any other activity that I know. I love it as a way of life for me. It's a constant challenge and a constant refreshment. I think the poet as prophet, the poet as *shaman*, comes out in the platform work more than any other dimension: a prophetic sense of encounter, to change the disposition of prevailing consciousness, to change lives and affect your time through your presence and passion.

Besides that, a poet today, you know, lives on the platform. You reach far more people on platform than you do with your books. In fact, if you don't keep reading, the public loses interest in your published work and your sales decline. For the poet that's one of the great . . .

MADOFF: Poetry and the world of television!

EVERSON: Television has yet to awaken to the power of poetry, and it's just as well. One of the great dangers for poetry today, on the other hand, is it's so much on platform that often the real literary skills go by the board. You should perfect your powers for a long time before you go on platform. You should integrate your powers till you know you have total possession of your craft. Then you can start to perform.

MADOFF: The readings throughout the country were a hallmark of the Beats.

EVERSON: Yes. That was part of the program, the pitch. We could draw in one night more than an edition of five hundred copies could reach in years. We imbued life into that format. Poets had been reading for a long time, of course, but the reading had a coterie quality about it, a small cultural enclave. You know, stand up, read the poem, polite applause, sit down, pleased to meet you. Well, the Beats changed all that, changed the reading from recitation to encounter, made it a living event. We began to draw a whole range of people, especially from an age bracket not particularly interested in poetry but who wanted to see what this phenomenon was all about.

MADOFF: And you're still doing that.

EVERSON: Yes. My Parkinson's disease has inhibited me some, but I haven't let that throw me. I seem to be able to use it like any other prop on the platform.

MADOFF: I remember you said in a reading last winter at Stanford that your affliction had become a blessing; it had become a part of your work. What did you mean?

EVERSON: Well, I'd just been reading Unamuno's *Tragic Sense of Life* in which he takes the proposition that "consciousness is a disease," the imbalance in man's nature having made him more highly conscious than the other animals in the evolutionary span. Affliction has made me more humble in relation to my audience. I'm more at their mercy instead of having them at mine.

MADOFF: Has that consciousness crept into your writing?

EVERSON: Only vaguely so, but it's going to have to come more and more. I haven't been able to write about the Parkinson's. It's hard to give it any kind of universal perspective.

MADOFF: But it luckily doesn't interfere with your livelihood at this point as a teacher. I'm wondering if the need to support yourself has ever much interfered with your writing.

EVERSON: Distraction only. God has always taken care of me. God and the women in my life, bless them! You see, the great thing about the Order was that, after the first few years, it gave me total time to read, write, lecture, and perform. And I knew I was giving that up when I left. I travelled more from the monastery than I did before or after. It was a beautiful, blessed life for the artist. For me it was perfect— except that there were no women! Or maybe it was just a phase. My confessor said it was. "Don't go, Antoninus. You're in the male menopause!" "Don't blow it for an erotic episode!" But after a while I realized that it was something too powerful and prolonged for me to deny. So I left.

MADOFF: There's something that strikes me about your work, or should I say something that doesn't seem to be there. It's characteristic of religious poets to create complete universes in their work, presenting a complex diagram of God's order. Dante is an obvious case. Milton, Blake, in our time, Eliot. But there doesn't seem to be that kind of epic ambition in your work. Has it ever crossed your mind to take on a task like that?

EVERSON: Years ago I read E. M. W. Tillyard's *The English Epic and its Background* and was immensely stirred by it. "There is nothing so exciting and so awe-inspiring in the world of letters as the spectacle of a great spirit daring to risk everything on one great venture and knowing that in its execution he will be taxed to the limit of what a man can endure." Inspired by these words, I determined to write an autobiographical epic using Teilhard de Chardin's *The Phenomenon of Man* as the model of a contemporary Christian cosmology. Nothing came of it in that way.

But I believe in the autobiographical sequence. I've handled almost all the crises in my life by reverting to that mode. I think my whole work will emerge as that epic. Shakespeare's sonnets are the most famous sequence in this mode. Another great one, you know, is Meredith's *Modern Love*. Beautiful sense of the travail of a soul. Step by step. That was a sonnet sequence, too. I think the confessional sequence is probably the optimum form in this period. I think if you can handle the sequence, and I've put some of the best years of my life into it, you have the power of integration and in the end it can assume its own epic dimensions.

MADOFF: The breadth of that kind of epic makes me think of the narrative aspect of your writing, and I wonder if you've been influenced by anyone's prose.

EVERSON: Well, Lawrence's fictional and descriptive prose was, as I said, vastly important to me. But I wasn't aware of any stylistic influence. His impact was in the liberation of the erotic element that Jeffers had left untouched. Jeffers is highly sexual in his own imagination, of course, but the tenderness of Eros is something he doesn't pay much attention to. Sex is a disruptive force for him rather than a fulfilling one. But in terms of a continuous narrative intensity, I can't really say where that came from. Its purpose is to modify the obsessive self-preoccupation of the confessional sequences. Though the narrative element carries the objective, intensity is the signature of the confessional preoccupation.

MADOFF: How about poets—besides Jeffers, of course? Are there poets particularly strong for you, European as well as American?

EVERSON: As far as Europe goes, the names that come to mind are Rilke, Yeats, and Lorca. But they're not so much stylistic influences as ones revelatory of the capability of poetic expression, lodestones of literary consciousness. Stylistically, Hopkins was useful in the religious, tends to be overplayed. I've never discounted stylistic influence, but made it do a different thing than the original. For instance, Hopkins never used his innovations in the erotic domain, which is precisely where I took it.

MADOFF: The powerful sexual drive that's part of your religious belief, that we've touched upon, I've wondered about that. In your unpublished autobiographical fragment, *Prodigious Thrust,* you wrote, "Out of the psychic rib of man was woman made, and now she is returned, and in his self is formed again, fused in the forked loins and in the inter-listening blood—all that he lost then through that division, the separation struck in himself by that subtraction, restored, restored to him, brought back to him, fused into him, and she fuses into his side, and is made his, and he hers, and they are." Now this view seems to give us an idea about women typical in your writing. Basically that woman is subservient: an object of male creation, taking on the unfortunate status of a vessel. Her autonomy is secondary. Would you say this is an inaccurate summary?

EVERSON: As a matter of fact, I do. In fact, I'm a little disconcerted by your lifting a quotation like that from an unpublished work as representative of my attitude. That was written in the early conversion period when I was trying to work within the frame of the Christian myth of creation, adapted into psychological perspective. The opening part of *In the Fictive Wish* projects the idea of woman as passive, but that was written in the anguish of divorce, and even there it was repudiated before the sequence was done. I still get a lot of flack from feminists in my classes about this. Otherwise, I doubt if any poet has exalted woman as the active principle more than I have. *The Rose of Solitude* is astounding in extolling a given woman for her transformative power. I think my life is witness to the opposite error—placing too much directive power in the hands of women rather than reducing them to the yielding vessel status.

MADOFF: With this kind of intensity you've been talking about, have you ever found writing a chore?

EVERSON: It's never been, except in the case of a long, arduous work that has to be hammered into shape in a relatively short time—then you have to make it jell, have to keep plugging at it, but that's abnormal. Usually I don't work until I'm moved, and then it's not a chore, it's a creative release.

MADOFF: You said earlier that your own critical writing hasn't had much to do with poetry you write. How about your teaching?

EVERSON: No, neither one.

MADOFF: What are you teaching now?

EVERSON: It's a course called "Birth of a Poet"—not how to write poetry, but what a poet is. It's essentially a course in charismatic vocation—the problems and the ordeal of a visionary calling. I teach what the lifestyle entails, how you survive in terms of living the life, rather than, you know, the literary model. Probably that's the only way I can teach. I don't do workshops, never have.

MADOFF: You don't believe that workshops can help a poet?

EVERSON: I think they can, but I don't think they should. I mean, they've moved too fast along certain lines. It's better to find those things out through trial and error than it is to have them inculcated by your teachers.

MADOFF: You've written so much. What has driven you?

EVERSON: Slake, slake, the slaking of need! I treat that in the Foreword to *The Hazards of Holiness*, where I quote Eliot on the three voices of poetry. There's also an element of ambition there that can't be overlooked. The need to excel. That's what keeps me focused on career, sometimes even at the risk of vocation. Sometimes you can concentrate so much on career that you stop writing. You know what I mean? Which is the jeopardy. The vocation comes into jeopardy at that point. I've never pushed it that far, but I've certainly risked it, simply because in some way that's part of the motivating, what the recognition means.

It would be a lot easier to dismiss competition as an incentive to write, but it wouldn't be truthful. I mean, it would be more prudent, more humble, to say that ambition, the need for recognition, has nothing to do with your motivation, but I couldn't say that. It takes me on platform, for instance, and makes me confront the audience the way I do: shock them into recognition, stop them in their tracks, make them respond. It's hard to say precisely what it is. It's complex but compelling. And it's basically healthy. If the poet isn't recognized, it means his work isn't operative. So he fights for recognition as hard as he struggles for expression.

MADOFF: But then he comes up against the institution. He confronts his opposite, because when his recognition comes, he becomes part of the institution. Do you think that's been a danger for you?

EVERSON: No. For one thing, it's come late enough in my life to be beyond the vulnerability of youth. For another thing, I've never been all that famous. Every time fame has approached, some upheaval in my life has prevented its consummation. Either the muse, The White Goddess, has protected me from her rival, The Bitch Goddess Success, or the fear of success has sabotaged my striving at the moment of apotheosis. Either theory could fit. Take your pick.

MADOFF: What kind of advice would you give to young poets?

EVERSON: Joyce said, "Exile, cunning, and silence."

MADOFF: In reviewing your career as it stands now, I'm impressed by the variety of hats you've worn. A poet of prophetic attitude. A conscientious objector. A monastic. A Dionysian, yet also a critic—an Apollonian activity. A teacher. A celebrated printer. And in all this, very much of a regionalist.

EVERSON: Well, they're all responses to various stimuli. The aptitudes have been there within me, latent until expressed. I've lived a long enough life to accommodate to each as its time comes around. They've given variety and richness to my life, but always the primary one has been the poet. The others I consider to be simply adjunct or facets, spin-offs, you might say, of the central one. I've never conceived of any of them, or any combination of them, as displacing the primary one of the poet.

MADOFF: You said it's been about a year since you've written any poetry, following the completion of *The Masks of Drought*. What have you left undone?

EVERSON: Left undone? My God, my life is filled with fragments! There's the completion of *The Integral Years*, the third book of the trilogy I call *The Crooked Lines of God*. *Man-Fate* was an uncertain start, but with *The Masks of Drought* it found its voice. But it waits on the movement of my life as to what I'm going to do now. It all waits on the movement of my life.

On Kenneth Rexroth

LINDA HAMALIAN: You've known Kenneth Rexroth for a long time, haven't you?

WILLIAM EVERSON: Since World War II. That would be 1944 or 1945. I was a conscientious objector in a camp at Waldport, Oregon. I'd known *of* him, of course, but I'd had no contact with him until that time. For one thing, I didn't know he was a pacifist. If I had known, I might well have gotten in touch with him earlier, before I was drafted, just to find a kindred spirit. But since I was unaware of that, it came as a surprise when he wrote to me. He had seen my anti-war poems and was responding to them.

HAMALIAN: What were your first impressions of Rexroth?

EVERSON: When I finally met him, I was utterly charmed. There is this supreme sophistication. No, the first thing you feel is his humanity, his complete lack of pretension. But then the sophistication. And a wonderful sense of humor. It doesn't come through in his writing so much, but he has an extraordinary gift for conversational humor. He delivers his pronouncements with such verve, even aplomb, that you sit there wondering, utterly charmed but rather bedazzled by the pyrotechnics. Basically you have to be around him for a while before the more grave side of his personality begins to show, and you can see where the depths of the man lie. But his sensibility is so acute, so highly keyed, that his relationships are often flanged. He doesn't bear with you very easily if you seem to be deviating from the true path—

The first part of this interview was conducted by Linda Hamalian in 1983 and originally appeared in *The Literary Review* 26 (1983). The second part was conducted by John Tritica and was published in *American Poetry* 7:1 (Fall 1989).

his true path! But after all, everyone has certain reservations of their own that they should be entitled to, right? Actually, over the years he has mellowed rather winningly.

HAMALIAN: Do you see any contradiction between Rexroth's personality and lifestyle, and his poetry? Do you think that there is a great dichotomy between his life and his work?

EVERSON: I never thought of it, which sort of answers your question. As a matter of fact, I think he has made a most impressive synthesis between his life and his work. Given the political aspects of his radicalism, it couldn't have been easy. But he always seems to land on his feet.

Oh, there's been an occasion or two when he's raised my eyebrows. I thought he'd croak before he ever became a columnist for a Hearst newspaper. At the time he defended it by pointing to the great newspapermen, the great journalists; but that sounded like rationalization to me. And after his career of anti-academic bushwhacking I was surprised to see him take that post at the University of California, Santa Barbara. But he emerged from both ordeals intact and untainted, with no evident qualms of conscience, and no loss of stature, no one thinking less of him for it.

More disconcerting to me are his out-and-out reversals. For instance, in his last interview in *Conjunctions*, he dismissed Dylan Thomas, of all people. "Dylan Thomas as a skyrocket that went up and came down faster than any other in the history of literature. Who reads him?" But where does that leave his own memorial to Dylan, "Thou Shalt Not Kill," one of his best known poems? With egg on his face, right? But not to Kenneth. I dare say he could defend his turnabout vehemently.

Mostly, however, his documentation is solid. When he writes in a poem that he is standing by Paper Mill Creek, you can be sure he was actually there. Sometimes I used to think he made too much of his rock-climbing mystique. Like most writers, he seems a fairly sedentary person. But others have assured me that he is an accomplished climber and mountaineer. He learned the literature inside out and then backed it up with experience.

On the other hand, if you get Rexroth on a subject which you happen to know better than he does, you can sense him bulling his way through. This is especially true with Catholicism. He's got marvelous intuition, and a keen researcher's brain as well. But the greatest researcher is, sometime or other, going to have to wing it, skim across the rift in his knowledge as if it does not exist. In this regard, Kenneth is in a class by himself. Sometimes he makes his best shots when he's on shakiest ground. And some of his insights are dead wrong, but you'd never know it from listening to him.

HAMALIAN: Many people describe Rexroth as a religious poet. Do you think he is? Do you see him in the tradition of Hopkins or the later Eliot?

EVERSON: Neither one. But the question gives one pause. He spent time in an Anglican monastery, but we have no poetry to show for it. When people speak of Rexroth as a religious poet, I believe they are addressing themselves to our native American pantheism, which he shares with Emerson and Whitman and Sandburg and Jeffers, and of course scores of lesser voices, including myself.

When I first met Kenneth, he was a nominal Anglican, but the religious dimension has deepened with his movement toward Buddhism in the last decade or so. I shouldn't have been surprised by it. After his last reading here at Santa Cruz, he was asked from the floor if he considered himself a Buddhist. At first he jokingly disclaimed it. "Too many people I can't stand announce themselves as Buddhists!" But then more soberly: "Actually, my life has been moving in that direction for many years. I should no longer equivocate. Yes, I am a Buddhist." My heart sank. He paused, and then said somberly: "In Buddhism there is no God, no soul, and no afterlife."[1]

HAMALIAN: You've mentioned that there are several problems connected to writing a biography of Rexroth. You've touched on some. Are there others?

EVERSON: The most forbidding thing would be to follow Kenneth's mind through its evolution and convolutions. He'll talk about something he knows profoundly with absolute certitude and you accept it. He'll talk about something he knows only superficially, with equal certitude, and you'll accept that. As you learn more, you will see the difference between these positions, although they sound the same. But the persuasive force that validates the one does not validate the other.

HAMALIAN: It's difficult then to distinguish between what he knows and what he doesn't?

EVERSON: That's the real challenge.

HAMALIAN: When I read Rexroth's criticism of other poets, I feel sometimes he is describing his own poetry. I sense that particularly when he is writing about you, when he speaks of the struggle for vision, for reconciliation. Do you agree with that?

EVERSON: It never occurred to me. I suppose it is true. I know he keeps investing great faith in me and I keep letting him down . . . Actually, your question stirs up qualms of conscience in me that I thought I had lived out. Your intuition that what he saw in me was the archetype of what he wished for himself is deeply troubling to me. It means that my failure to live up to what he thought of as my best self deepens my guilt. That characteristic, now that you speak of it, is summed up in the word *autochthonous*. In his introduction to *The Residual Years* he speaks of my early poems: "They were native poems, autochthonous in a way fashionable poems of the day could not manage. Being an autochthon of course is something you don't manage, you are." Aficionados will recognize it as a quintessentially Rexrothian word. As applied to myself, I was never comfortable with it. Among critics, it impugned my powers of conscious control, my craftmanship, though I recognize it as his highest praise. And in the light of your question, something he would have desired for himself. What I regret now is that I couldn't accept it as the supreme attestation he intended. To my shame I even travestied it: "I was to be his Lincolnesque populist pacifist—the "pome-splitter." That must have hurt.

And now it hurts *me*. He lies dying down there in Santa Barbara, and I am filled with thoughts of what we meant to each other, the pain the proof of our mutual esteem. Farewell, old friend and mentor!

JOHN TRITICA: What affinities do you have with the work of Kenneth Rexroth?

WILLIAM EVERSON: Affinities is a good word. My response to his work is actually something apart from the man. He's an experimentalist, and I was never of that tradition myself. He came from a much more esoteric and avant garde background than I did. At first his work was difficult for me. I can't remember which book I came into contact with first, but if I picked up some of his early work now, I couldn't read it. I have a great affinity for his middle period. It's much more comprehensible, much more accessible, much more lyrical. The subject matter is direct, concrete, and sensuous, not abstract. I rank myself as a great aficionado of Rexroth and his work.

TRITICA: What kind of affinities do you have with him?

EVERSON: Father figure. He discovered me, and I owe him a tremendous amount of gratitude for that. He lined me up with New Directions, a national publishing house. He's always praised me in the strongest terms. He never published a qualifying thing about me.

TRITICA: What kind of impact did Rexroth have on your work?

EVERSON: He didn't have much. My work was thoroughly developed by the time I met Rexroth, about '44. He was in San Francisco, and I was in Oregon. People would come up and tell me about this man. I didn't know he was a pacifist himself, or I could have gotten in touch with him earlier.

TRITICA: Erotic mysticism is a key element in Rexroth's work, marital relations primary. Relations with women operate more than just aesthetically. Do women operate as psychic guides in his poetry?

EVERSON: In a way they did, but not near as much as in my work. In my work, I'm almost begging for direction from my guides. The women that figure in his poetry are his wives. His relationships weren't confined to his wives—there are some prostitutes that figure in his poetry. It's hard to tell about that side of Rexroth's poetry, when he praises casual women. It's almost as if he, in his bohemianism, is impatient with the bourgeois world. He ruffles feathers by saying outrageous things that are shocking.

TRITICA: In the introductory note to *The Dragon and the Unicorn*, Rexroth has written that the poet's most important role is prophetic.[2] You have also emphasized the prophetic role of the poet. How would you locate Rexroth in the lineage of prophetic American poets?

EVERSON: How many are there?

TRITICA: Some come to mind: Emerson, Whitman, Crane.

EVERSON: Whitman's the most obvious one. Thoreau. Melville, of course. I'd say Jeffers, but that was one of the big problems between Kenneth and me. But where do we place Rexroth in terms of that continuum? It's not a complete continuum, but there's enough there. You have to put Hart Crane in there too. He would be closer to Rexroth, because he has the same Modernist adhesions and the same native spirit. Rexroth is closer to Hart Crane than he is to Ezra Pound. That's for sure.

   Crane would be the nearest jump off place after that continuum of ascending figures we have there in terms of chronology. I'd say that Crane would be the closest one to Rexroth.

TRITICA: In a related, but slightly different vein, Rexroth commented that in Lawrence's poetry the craft is vision and the vision is craft.[3] I get the sense that he's developing his own poetics here. How is the craft the vision and the vision the craft in Rexroth's work?

EVERSON: I don't know how far you can carry that statement of Kenneth's. It's one of those statements he made that are illuminating in an apocalyptic way. There's a flash of insight there. What I take it to mean is that in a certain type of visionary poet, the craft is subsumed in the vision. The craftsmanship comes out of the vision itself. It's not a studied thing. It's built on connaturality. An identity between subject and object, rather than discursiveness. Craft would be some sort of discursive element. Vision is non-discursive, connatural.

TRITICA: How important is a sense of place in Rexroth's poetry?

EVERSON: You don't think of him as a regionalist, but he made California his own. He's always aware of place. He's like Lawrence in that regard. Lawrence is a regionalist without having one where he could settle down. He keeps hoping to find the perfect region, and keeps wandering over the whole world searching for it. That's not Rexroth. Rexroth doesn't have the hunger to find the perfect region. He has a profound sense of place, and he celebrates it when he's in it. He draws on it. He know where he's at. When he's in Europe, you know where he's at. He draws on the nostalgia of history a great deal to give us the spirit of place—I think a little bit more than Lawrence does.

TRITICA: I think you get that sense when you're reading his long poem *The Dragon and the Unicorn*. Particularly when he's in Provence and Wales, you feel that he's really at home. He knows the people, the way they smell, the fragrances, the landscape.[4]

TRITICA: What kind of role do you think that Rexroth played in the poetry of California?

EVERSON: I think he's the first poet after Jeffers. Politically, he put California on the map. He was the first one to take the Western archetype and make an aesthetic movement out of it and organize it. We had the revolts out there. Kenneth had the political acumen in the historical moment—together, he made it believable so that people could rally around it, and come for miles to participate in it. If hadn't been for him, I don't think there would have been a San Francisco Renaissance, not anything like it was. He's the one who attracted Ginsberg. He liberated Ginsberg, you might say. Ginsberg came from an environment where people like Lionel Trilling, people like that at

Columbia— They weren't radical in any sense. They were politically
liberal, but Kenneth was *radical*. Besides he was bohemian, and those
people were not bohemians.

TRITICA: In the context of performance, you speak of the poet's witness
in relation to his audience.[5] Could you go into the notion of witness
and explain how Rexroth's witness operated in terms of his relation to
his audience?

EVERSON: Witness is like prophecy in the sense that it's based on an
intuition. Prophecy is some form of articulation, whereas witness is
some form of doing. If a poet stands up for his principles, we call that
a form of witness. Prophecy has political dimension, but so does witness. Rexroth's witness would be his pacifism. It would be one area
where his witness would be more powerful than anything he wrote
about it; he didn't write much of anything about pacifism. I never read
it if he did. But his witness was powerful. He adhered to it at his own
cost. He never trimmed his sails.

I never talked to Kenneth much about politics. Anyhow, his witness
is political and ethical. Not so much religious. He didn't seem to need
to take a stand on a religious code. He was pro-Catholic. He accepted
at last baptism and entry into the Church.

TRITICA: You were in the Dominican order almost nineteen years (1951–
1969). Rexroth was also a Catholic. How does Catholicism pervade his
work?

EVERSON: In a sacramental sense more than any other way. In honoring
the sacramental, if not an exact practice of it. It's always there as one
of the fundamental things in his work. In fact, he was the first person
who ever talked to me about the sacraments. I didn't know what he
was talking about. I was coming from a non-religious background. I
was raised as a Christian Scientist, and there's no sacraments in the
Christian Science Church, no baptism.

Kenneth saw me as a sacramental man before I knew I was one.
That was one of the things that was astonishing. I think Kenneth had

far more of a sense of sacrament than Lawrence did. Lawrence might have had a sacramental sense in a pantheistic way, but Rexroth is almost a liturgist.

TRITICA: How do you use the word *sacrament?*

EVERSON: I use the word in two ways. One in specific terms of the sacramental system of the Church. The seven sacraments which we're all aware of. Then in the D. H. Lawrence sense of sex as a sacramental reality. I use it in that sense, just like Kenneth does. He uses it more frequently than I do, and it's looser. I tend to be more conservative in my use of the word than Kenneth. It's just that Rome is a tighter Church than England. They use it more specifically.

It comes to mind that I'm the godfather of his children. I came to their baptism. I wasn't supposed to be there as a Roman Catholic, yet I went anyhow because of my sense of the nature of the sacrament. The definition of a sacrament is a sign that it affects what it signifies. It's the same as an archetype, only an archetype would be in the natural order, whereas the sacrament is in the realm of supernatural grace. I don't hesitate to say that all the sacraments are based on archetypes. Like in marriage, for instance—the Church itself would say that every true marriage is a sacrament whether people realize it or not. The sacramental effect is there. I think sex is a sacrament.

TRITICA: How do you think Rexroth managed to combine the mysticism and the anarchism in his work?

EVERSON: I think the secret in that statement lies in the word vision. Anarchism is a visionary politics. Mysticism is the anarchism of religion. Mystics don't rely on structure.

TRITICA: Why do you think it was so difficult for Rexroth to find community?

EVERSON: I think the psychological factors were so acutely gaged within his personality that he was constantly pitched forward beyond his capacity to sustain a community. This was almost purely in terms of personal relationship. In personal relationships within a communal situation, he constantly tried to reach the sacramental sense of love between men, brothers. At the same time, the fallen human nature is so irascible, including his own. His relations were constantly falling apart, and then he'd pull himself up and try again.

As long as his marriages held together, he was able to sustain community. When those marriages fell apart, I think some kind of nerve broke in him. I think the loss of the mother of his children—I forget her name . . .

TRITICA: Marthe.

EVERSON: Marthe.

TRITICA: The first wife was Andree. She died. Marthe is still alive.

EVERSON: She remarried. She left him. It took him a long time to remarry. I didn't know the first wife, but I knew the other three. The wonderful one there—from the outside, at least—was Marie. She's dead now I guess. Died just recently. She couldn't have children. He wanted children, so he turned to Marthe. But then she had that affair with Creeley. That was a sign of the beginning of the end. I guess he was impossible to live with. It's pretty hard to tell there. I wasn't so close to Kenneth all those years I was in the Order.

TRITICA: What quality of Rexroth's work is most likely to survive?

EVERSON: I think I'd hedge a little on that one between his pantheism— his religious nature of the cosmos, and his celebration of it—and the erotic mysticism. In some ways those come together. They are two distinct strains that come together. His erotic mysticism is very nature oriented. He almost always speaks of it in terms of nature. In element, these are all within the natural order; it's called the wilderness. It depends on what the world wants. I think the world has a growing interest in wilderness, because, as the human race becomes more and more urbanized, the importance of wilderness is going to grow. The world's going to turn to the men who are the celebrators of wilderness for sustenance. The erotic mysticism is another aspect of that same pantheistic celebration. With those two, you've got an unbeatable combination, so fundamental to human nature that even dogs and cats could understand it.

TRITICA: Where do you think Rexroth stands in relation to his contemporaries, people like Eberhart, Roethke, Rukeyser, Zukofsky?

EVERSON: Eberhart honored and respected him, and I'm sure that the others did. He almost made everyone draw lines apart from him. Especially anyone in the establishment. Even on the East Coast, if there wasn't any establishment. He was close to William Carlos Williams and honored him as a prophet. I don't know what Williams ever said about Rexroth. Rexroth's name doesn't occur very often in the index of that big Williams biography.[6] And few of those people you've mentioned acknowledged Williams. Zukofsky was a Williams man too, but he kept his mouth shut about it, whereas Kenneth was a polemicist. In literary politics, he was a genius. Times came to the point where his radical nature and radical program had their historical moment. I don't think we would have heard too much of Kenneth if that hadn't happened. He would have been an isolated figure, a little bit like Williams was. When the times came around there was a crack and so many sparks would fly. People were compelled to listen and consider what he was saying.

TRITICA: What's most memorable to you about Rexroth?

EVERSON: His religion. A synthesis of values that comes from his radical stance and his sacramental sense, erotic mysticism, his Oriental adhesion. It's all subsumed into a cosmic whole, a cosmic vision that had substance and character.

He wasn't exactly a Blake figure; he wasn't as religious as Blake. He wasn't as religious as I am. He was more philosophical. His greatest poem is *The Phoenix and the Tortoise*.

TRITICA: Tom Parkinson agrees.

EVERSON: We were both exposed to it at the same time, Tom and I. That's the thing that took us to Rexroth. I think that's his greatest poem, and that's his best book.

There's one part we haven't talked about, and that's his sense of Classical nostalgia which is in that book. He talks about Catullus and other Roman and Greek figures, he manages to drawn on. He'll locate himself in history by reference to those men in a very persuasive way. If he truly was identified with them, it was something that stood apart from his radicalness—his literary radicalness, his American autochthonism. There's a clear strain there. More than almost anyone I know, he was able to attach that sound Classical sense to the impermanence of human life, to the mystery of love, and to the life of the mind.

You see his radicalness slip in things like that elegy to Dylan Thomas. It enabled him to commemorate artists in his period of time. He lists the names of the people he knew who had come to disaster, because of the twenties and thirties, mostly the period between the Wars. Industrialism and Philistinism was so rampant in the social life of America in this period. But the poem fell apart at the end, I thought. The only way he could save the poem after that wonderful litany was to say. "I killed him." That seething bitter attack at the end: "You son of a bitch in the Brooks Brothers' Suit / You killed him." It would have been better if he would have said, "I killed him."

TRITICA: Did you feel that Rexroth embraced you and your work as an example of someone who was a counterpoint to New Criticism?

EVERSON: Yes, of course he did. That's one of the problems between us. I squirmed, because I didn't want to be so political. I reached a point in my later thirties, and I wanted to begin seeing to the survival of my work and building my reputation. I was willing to take the radical stand, but I wasn't willing to stand still. I accepted the Beat Generation even more than Kenneth did. At the same time, we had kind of a falling out, Kenneth and I. And one of the elements of it was his blurb on the jacket of *The Residual Years*.[7] I thought he pushed me too much into the line of fire. I knew he meant well by that. He never used me politically. I just got a little nervous sometimes.

TRITICA: Were Christianity and Buddhism compatible in Rexroth's life and work?

EVERSON: When it comes to the profane and the sacred, both Buddhism and Christianity are on the side of the angels. This was the basis on which Merton travelled to the east to investigate their monasteries and speak in terms of their religious life and accept their views. There have been several books on Zen Catholicism that find common elements between the two. But it's pretty chilling: ". . . no God, no immortal soul, and no afterlife." Pretty stark for me.

Notes

1. These words were spoken two years before Kenneth Rexroth's death on June 22, 1982. Before he died, at his own request, Rexroth was received into the Roman Catholic Church and given the last rites by Fr. Alberto Huerta, S.J. Officiating at Our Lady of Carmel Church in Monticito, California, Father Huerta also gave the eulogy.

2. Kenneth Rexroth, *The Dragon and the Unicorn* (Norfolk: New Directions, 1952).

3. Kenneth Rexroth, ed., "Introduction," in *Selected Poems* by D. H. Lawrence (Norfolk: New Directions, 1947), p. 15.

4. See Parts I and II of *The Dragon* for Rexroth's detailed observations of the people and the landscape of Wales and Southern France.

5. David Meltzer, ed., *Golden Gate: Interviews with Five San Francisco Poets* (San Francisco: Wingbow Press, 1976), p. 109.

6. Paul Mariani, *William Carlos Williams: A New World Naked* (New York: W.W. Norton, 1981).

7. Kenneth Rexroth, *The Residual Years* (New York: New Directions, 1968).

Talking Poetry

QUESTION: Do you consider yourself a religious poet, both specifically Catholic and in a more general sense?

WILLIAM EVERSON: Yes. The distinction I'd make would be between a religious poet and a nature poet, though. The religious poet would be more generic, the nature poet more specific. I'd also include I suppose the erotic poet, given the emphasis I have on the sexual.

QUESTION: Which of the three is the strongest?

EVERSON: The religious poet. At least it's the most inclusive in that it subsumes the other two.

QUESTION: But by religious you don't necessarily mean Catholic then?

EVERSON: No. I was a religious poet long before I was a Catholic.

QUESTION: How did that change when you entered the Order?

EVERSON: It gained specificity when I became a Catholic. The Order didn't change it all that much—it was my conversion to Catholicism itself. The entry into the Dominicans was simply a further specification, a deepening of focus.

QUESTION: And from the point of conversion you began to work with Catholic subject matter?

This conversation took place in a Writers' Workshop at the University of New Mexico. It appeared originally in Lee Bartlett, ed., *Talking Poetry* (Albuquerque: University of New Mexico Press, 1985).

EVERSON: Yes. I converted to Catholicism in 1949, and the first poem I wrote following that which didn't have a specific Catholic reference point was my elegy for Jeffers, *The Poet is Dead*, in 1962. Everything between those years was specifically Catholic.

QUESTION: Why did you make the shift in 1962?

EVERSON: I didn't want to subsume Jeffers into the Christian hegemony, given his total witness against it all his life. He was my literary master. It was when I found him, at Fresno State College in the fall of 1934, that I discovered my own vocation as a poet. It was one of the great turning points in my life.

QUESTION: Which explains *Fragments of an Older Fury* and the rest of your prose work on Jeffers.

EVERSON: Yes. I didn't really write any prose to speak of before my conversion, but Catholicism gave me a frame of reference. Before that everything was touch and go, highly relative, and I didn't have any orientation point save through the emotional dimension of my poetry. It wasn't until I had the frame of reference which the church gave me, along with its intellectual tradition, that I could begin to work these things out in prose. Also, it was a question of maturation. I converted at age thirty-five, and my mind was just starting to wake up then.

QUESTION: Do you consider yourself a narrative poet?

EVERSON: More and more, especially now that I'm writing *Death Shall Be The Serpent's Food*. It's an autobiographical epic, and almost totally narrative. Actually narrative elements began to creep into my poetry around 1942, when after the death of my mother, I began to ingest more content and narrative appeal in my work. But really the narrative broke through pretty completely when I began to read the Bible seriously. Poems like "The Massacre of the Holy Innocents" in *The Crooked Lines of God* are almost wholly narrative retelling of biblical episodes.

QUESTION: What would the death of your mother have to do with embracing the narrative?

EVERSON: Nothing really. There was just a liberation, a great leap forward towards the intellectual. In a sense there was a deliverance point from the bond of the maternal. That is psychologically one of the great crossover points in the evolution of both the aesthetic and the mystical psyches. In studying other poets, like Jeffers, you can often place their emergence into creative autonomy with the death of the mother. Ginsberg is another very good example of that.

QUESTION: *Masks of Drought* seems thoroughly narrative.

EVERSON: Yes, by that book I've got the narrative at my fingertips. I move towards it instantly when I feel a poem coming.

QUESTION: So you don't feel the approach to be worked out.

EVERSON: Well, the only danger is that it might get a little dry, merely narrative at the expense of the lyrical dimension. I think this is the relevance of *Masks of Drought* in my own evolution as a poet, the constant balancing between those two factors.

QUESTION: What is your plan for the long poem you mentioned?

EVERSON: *Death Shall Be the Serpent's Food?* I begin with the classical epic formula, *in medias res*, the low point in the fortunes of the hero. The plan calls for the use of flashback to explain how he got to that point, as well as his going forward to apotheosis. The first canto begins at the end of World War II in 1945, the death of my father. It should run about ten cantos; I'm writing the second one now. *In Medias Res*, the first canto, has just been published in a limited edition by Adrian Wilson in San Francisco.

QUESTION: So you think of this poem not simply as a long poem, but as an epic?

EVERSON: Yes. It comes out of my teaching a course called "Birth of a Poet" for a decade at the University of California at Santa Cruz. In that course our text was Joseph Campbell's *Hero With A Thousand Faces*, which describes in archetypal outline the journey of the hero as it has come down to us in myth. Through the program I arrived at the necessity for the artist to embrace the classical heroic attitude in order to survive the storms of the charismatic journey. Thus in my course I began to narrate the story of my own life as an introduction to the journey. After a decade of doing that I became so accustomed to saying my life in archetypal terms that I moved naturally towards the writing of epic.

QUESTION: Since you've been working on this longer poem have any shorter poems come?

EVERSON: They've kept coming at their own pace. I've just this last year published another book called *Renegade Christmas* including five poems which are extensions of *The Masks of Drought*. In a sense I had published its poems too soon. A short time earlier I had collected my Catholic poetry into *The Veritable Years*, and I wanted people to know that I wasn't stuck there. But I moved too fast. The five later poems came, and I'm writing another one right now. I can't seem to let go of the theme.

QUESTION: You mentioned teaching. Had you done this in the Order?

EVERSON: Not formally. I was on the reading platform constantly at universities across the country, and I participated in a lot of writing workshops at various conferences. But until Santa Cruz I was not formally connected to a university, which meant that I didn't have to do the work of evaluation, which turns out to be the difficult part. Everyone loves to teach, but evaluations are a pain in the ass.

QUESTION: When did you take the job at Santa Cruz?

EVERSON: After I left the Order and married Susanna, we were almost two years at Stinson Beach, then in 1971 the job opened at U.C.S.C. I retired in 1982.

QUESTION: Did you teach creative writing workshops?

EVERSON: No, I avoided them. They are a solution to a pedagogical problem—How do you teach creative writing?—but I don't cotton to them. Americans are sold on them, and the students pour into the universities demanding to be taught. But in the history of the world it's never been done this way before, and there are a lot of drawbacks. The established poets especially, even the ones who teach in the programs, are starting to take a second look at the whole process. The workshops are getting so good, and the students are all so technically proficient, that it's hard to distinguish between poems. Sometimes I'm asked to judge poetry contests, and when I see a dozen well-crafted student workshop poems before me I just can't tell the difference. A natural or sexual image may strike me, and I'll choose that poem for that reason. But it's got nothing to do with distinguishing between levels of qualities.

QUESTION: So do you see creative writing workshops and programs as being rather dangerous?

EVERSON: Not really. It's not that serious. The direction of poetry will be the direction of genius. The real poets can't be hurt by these programs, unless they become dazzled by the technique of the teachers and start drifting from one university to another. Study with Lowell for a time, then Roethke, and so on. I think that's dangerous for a young poet. The traditional way is to find your master and adhere to him until you outgrow him. You have to watch out for distractions. That's my big problem with Modernism, in fact, that it demeans influence and strives for an impossible and undesirable originality.

QUESTION: So young poets should stay clear of universities?

EVERSON: I didn't say that! I think young writers are drawn to universities, as I was myself. It was at Fresno State College where, as I said, I found Jeffers. But the important thing is to find your peer group, after you find your master. Your master gives you direction and your peer group gives you support.

QUESTION: If "Birth of a Poet" wasn't creative writing what was it?

EVERSON: A course in charismatic vocation, in the necessity to find your vocation. The structure was a series of meditations. As I said, I took Campbell's book for my outline. The notion of vocation came to me both from my own experience with Jeffers and from my years in the Order where vocation was the primary factor. There, it is essential that you discover your vocation before taking final vows, and you've got seven years to do it. The emphasis is on the inner call which carries you forward to your creative destiny. It is natural for religious life, and I simply made the transition over to the aesthetic life.

QUESTION: How many students did you have?

EVERSON: It varied from quarter to quarter, year to year. I threw as broad a net as I could. I wasn't simply interested in writers, but I wanted to establish the general principle of vocation, and thus I drew people from every discipline. In fact, what made the course popular was the assignment of keeping a dream journal, which allowed considerable latitude. This also satisfied the academic requirement for written work. My intuition was to teach the basic concept of vocation during the fall quarter, the American calling in the winter, and the Western calling in the spring. Two years ago Black Sparrow Press published a year's collection of these meditations taken from the mid-seventies. I sometimes had two to three hundred students, though eventually the college made me limit it to one hundred.

QUESTION: Can we shift the topic a little? You were a C.O. during World War II.

EVERSON: Yes.

QUESTION: What was your argument?

EVERSON: It was pretty obscure, actually, the way those predominantly and profoundly attitudinal situations are. Both pacifism and revolution seem more attitudinal than intellectual, which is why both are hard to explain. There are many sources, and your articulation is always limited by your lack of experience. You often get off on idealistic ground which you don't understand until many years later. Thus you often find yourself embarrassed by your most deeply held convictions.

I now realize that there was a lot of the Oedipal complex in my early pacifism. I was simply unable to put my neck on the line for the patriarchy.

QUESTION: Was your father displeased with your stance?

EVERSON: Profoundly.

QUESTION: So it was a rebellion against your father?

EVERSON: There was a good deal of that, but on the other hand there was a deep conviction. I would never have let mere rebellion be the determining factor. I think even at that time I had too much self-knowledge for that. Actually when I was finally drafted I was thirty years old, so I wasn't all that young.

QUESTION: Weren't there many other writers and artists in the camps during the war?

EVERSON: Yes. I was at a camp at Waldport, Oregon, and we got a number of other writers, artists, and musicians to join us there as part of the Fine Arts Program.

QUESTION: The painter Morris Graves?

EVERSON: No. He once visited Waldport, but though he was a pacifist he never went into the C.O. system. He went into the military, refused to put on the uniform, and they threw him in the brig. After a year or two they managed to get rid of him as a mental case. Of course, William Stafford was in a camp.

QUESTION: Did you know him?

EVERSON: Not at the time. He was down at Santa Barbara. I've never asked him why he didn't come up to our Waldport program, but I intend to do it before I die. His beautiful little C.O. journal written during that period has just been reissued. The printer Adrian Wilson was at Waldport; he came as a musician, but he found his printing vocation there. Today he is one of the finest printers in the country.

QUESTION: Are you still a pacifist?

EVERSON: I consider myself one, though I can't honestly say that I retained my pacifist beliefs through my Dominican period. My abandoning of those convictions through the years was a mistake.

QUESTION: Did the Church require it?

EVERSON: No. Somehow it had to do with my identification with the institutional. In political terms it made sense, but it was an error. Reading Guerard's book, *Violence and the Sacred*, illuminated for me the whole point of Christ's "resist not evil," though it's been awhile and I don't think I can be more specific about it. Just that he gave me an insight into the contagious nature of violence. The only thing that can contain it is human specification in terms of law, application of rule. Otherwise, vengeance becomes law, and on the primitive level this is a reflexive disaster. You'd think that would be an argument for the just war, but as I say I am unable to take this any further right now.

QUESTION: What about the role of violence in your work, or Jeffers's?

EVERSON: That's the central problem in life. Look at Shakespeare, Milton, Dante, Homer especially—the work is saturated with violence. It's the obsessional part of human life that is unsolvable save through the religious dimension. I was preoccupied with Old Testament violence, the relation of violence to the sacred. I tried to get through to the heart of it by seeing some of the most violent biblical episodes from a Jungian perspective, the theory of archetypes and mythical structure.

QUESTION: Have you read a lot of Jung?

EVERSON: I don't know anyone who has read all he wrote, but I've pondered on his thought deeply for some years.

QUESTION: How did you come to have an interest in his work?

EVERSON: Through Victor White, the English Dominican priest who was a Jungian. He came to teach for a year at St. Albert's College in Oakland where I was stationed as a lay brother. My friendship with White led me to the whole matter of the unconscious. My emergence into Jung was a way of answering certain problems I was having at the time.

QUESTION: There was no conflict between the Catholic and Jungian system?

EVERSON: Not at all, save for a few technical points like the nature of evil. But that has nothing to do with the therapeutic aspect. In fact, Fr. White did a wonderful job of equating St. Thomas Aquinas, the great Dominican saint and master theologian of the Church, with Jung. I wrote a preface for the recent reissue of his book *God and the Unconscious*, published by the Jungians.

QUESTION: What about Robert Bly, who also speaks of Jung often? Do you have any points of disagreement on Jung?

EVERSON: Not really. We always seem to be fighting, but I'm not sure about what. We have this sense of comradeship based on the fact that we are both Christians, both Norwegians, both poets, both Jungians. That's a pretty strong bond, considering how rare Christianity and Jungianism is in American poetry. But when it comes to poetry itself, he thinks that I'm too rhetorical, while I think he's too surreal. We are like two bulls in a pasture, just butting our heads together and not giving each other his due. He is the best reader on the platform today.

QUESTION: So you've heard him recently?

EVERSON: Yes, not too long ago in Santa Cruz. In fact, the reading has become something of a local legend. I arrived after the hall was fairly full, and Robert and I embraced in front of everyone, an open declaration of brotherhood and amity. I sat down and soon after he began to read. It was a beautiful performance at first, but he had just read Elaine Pagel's book on the Gnostics and soon he was into a thing about them. He is so political that soon he was breathing fire about the suppression of the Gnostics; he began to get warmed up to the subject, and I began to feel uneasy. I was waiting for the intermission so that I could slip out. But finally he declared, "Christianity must renounce the doctrine of the one God!" I just found something grabbing me by the seat of my pants and heading up for the door. He made a great mistake then. He stopped his discourse to call to me, "Are you leaving, Bill?" I had to say something, so I barely paused in my exit and flung over my shoulder: "You'd better believe it!" and kept going. The audience broke up. I heard many reports that at the time he took the whole thing very well. But after a few days he began to steam. I wrote him a letter the next day and sent it along with a book; I told him that I'd looked forward to his appearance and that I regretted what happened. Before he got that, though, he wrote me a savage letter saying that if I differed with him I should have stayed to fight. Further, he said that I stood for the Inquisition, that a few hundred years back I would have reported him to the priests and watched him burn at the stake on the plaza in Santa Cruz. So I immediately wrote back and told him that it wasn't my place to dispute with him at his reading, and closed by telling him that he'd left me only two options, to leave or to punch him out. And I finished by saying that maybe I made the wrong choice!

QUESTION: Have you corresponded since?

EVERSON: Naomi Clark, who runs the Poetry Center in San Jose, got us back together. She and her husband brought Bly and his wife to our house and we had a fine evening together. I have great respect for him.

QUESTION: Any other literary feuds in your seventy years?

EVERSON: Well, there was my confrontation with James Dickey back in the early sixties. He reviewed *The Crooked Lines of God* for the *Sewanee Review*, putting it down very forcefully. It came at a time when I felt that I had to reply, as the Beat Generation was running out of steam. His put-down was actually as much against the Beat Generation as it was against me personally. I can't remember exactly what kind of letter I wrote to the journal, but I left myself open somehow and he swooped in with his reply. I was put in a position where I had to wind up my long right arm and let him have it from the ecclesiastical heights in a second letter. I shouldn't have done it—I stormed with the wrath of God. There was nothing much he could say, but I was really out of order to hit him from the sacred sector.

Later I began to feel guilty, as I did after an earlier controversy with *Poetry*, which was one of the stumbling blocks of my career. I felt remorse, and began to beat my breast. I wrote him a letter and quoted Hardy's poem, saying that like the two soldiers if we had been able to sit down over a beer we'd have had a nice toast together, but as it was we shot at each other. He was in Italy at the time, and eventually he wrote a jubilant letter in reply, which I greatly appreciated. I let matters rest there because I knew there were deep aesthetic divisions between us, as well as cultural and attitudinal differences, but I should have replied. He took my silence amiss, feeling that I had been insincere in my gesture. I just didn't know how to handle the deeper issues, and that was that.

QUESTION: What was the problem with *Poetry?*

EVERSON: The scene in the late thirties was heavily dominated by the Proletarian movement, which might readily translate into the Communist Party. The party was riding very high then. The struggle against fascism was just starting, and the communists seemed to have the only answer to it. They had the bulwark of the Soviets, tremendous prestige, the intellectual elite, and so forth. Many of the great liberal minds who were later disillusioned in those early years were very hopeful.

Communism wasn't the problem for me, but proletarianism was. I wasn't writing proletarian poetry; I was writing nature poetry, as well as trying to find my way into the religious dimension. Before she died,

Harriet Monroe accepted a couple of my poems, but it took years before they were published because of the backlog. When they finally appeared, Morton Zabel was editor; then he left. I started sending in my work, but the poems just kept coming back, as by this time *Poetry* was publishing a lot of proletarian verse. Subject matter seemed to dominate the selection. To prove my hunch was right, I concocted a hoax. I wrote a proletarian-sounding poem, then wrote a cover letter saying I was a fruit worker between Imperial Valley and Yuba City, that I'd drift into cities and see *Poetry* in libraries. I used my mother's maiden name, and scrawled the thing out on a piece of binder paper with a stub pencil. They accepted it! This didn't really prove anything, but it implied so much. I sent another in, and they accepted that also. But as I said, I felt remorse and sent a letter of apology. Needless to say, I never got into the magazine again.

QUESTION: Do you submit unsolicited work to other journals?

EVERSON: Almost never anymore. I should do it, and in fact if I'd done it from the start I'd be further ahead in terms of career. Not vocation, as that has handled itself. I've been far more attuned to vocation than to career, though because career is my weakness I've spent a lot more psychic energy, and ego energy, there than on vocation. It has been so up and down, so erratic, that it's driven me frantic. My introverted relationship to God and women has been harmonious, fruitful, and developed, and I should be content. But I've got this inferiority-complex relationship to the world which is very painful; far too much time worrying about my rank in the poetic pantheon.

QUESTION: Why didn't you send out work early on?

EVERSON: I started that way just like everyone else. I just found out that for me the rejection slips kept interfering with the creative process, so I stopped. It took up far too much time, far too much psychic energy. In fact, when I had a hundred copies of my second book, *San Joaquin*, I simply gave copies to friends rather than sending any out for review. *Poetry* was the only exception. But my advice to younger poets is if you can do it, do it.

QUESTION: Do you read much work by younger poets?

EVERSON: No, not at all. I think it's typical of poets in old age that they only read their contemporaries and show little interest in what's coming from behind. I feel better about my insularity having seen people like Eliot go through the same thing, expressing a profound obliviousness to younger writers' work. It seems pretty natural.

QUESTION: Are there any contemporaries who you think are doing interesting work?

EVERSON: Robert Duncan comes immediately to mind. Also, I was happy that Carol Kizer received the Pulitzer Prize, as she's the second West Coast poet to receive one. We're starting to gain on them! Some of the people in the Bay Area didn't take that as well as they should have. Thomas Parkinson called me up for my signature on a letter trying to get an award for Robert. I'm just glad that a West Coast poet got it.

QUESTION: Though she seems very much part of the East Coast group. She's always at conferences, in *American Poetry Review*, and so on.

EVERSON: Well, yes. And for years she was a wheel in the NEA. Probably Duncan should have won. You know, after the Ekbert Fass biography of Duncan appeared, a lot of questions I'd had about him were answered. I think that the study ensures him a much stronger place in our literature. Somehow when you get a man's life in front of you it makes a profound difference. My own orientation has always been substantially biographical in terms of poetry. I know that's against New Critical precepts. When New Directions published their Poet of the Month series and wanted to include photographs, Randall Jarrell balked at it, which was the Modernist position. It was a reaction against the excessive biographical interest of the Victorians, who let their judgment of the work be swayed by their view of the life. But I know that my life stands behind my work in an archetypal way I can't renounce, and so does Robert's.

QUESTION: Is it important for younger poets to read a lot of poetry?

EVERSON: Can you keep them from it? They read everything that comes out, always trying to relate themselves to it. After a while they get to know, however, and seem to lose that point of curiosity. The attention shifts to your rank with your peers, and this you never get over. Read the biography of Stevens or Williams and watch how they jockey for position right up to the end of their lives.

QUESTION: Why?

EVERSON: I take it to be another archetypal factor, not a blemish. It's part of the creative process, writing to the sense of your time and the sense of the leading voices. The future is blank. The past, however, comes up to a burning point of consciousness, which is you, and you keep looking around to find your level. It's a little bit like a swimming race—you are swimming against both your time and your competition. You see this in the ovum and the sperm. The latter jockeys for position to score with big mama, and it's archetypal in that sense. We are all sperm of God swimming toward the great ovum of the future.

This is important because the way the artist goes determines the direction of consciousness. The artist isn't just in there beating his or her gums, but rather struggling for the potentiality of the whole race as a measure of the future. The artist can't afford to rest just because of the creation of a well rounded work; the drive must keep on to the last inch of being.

QUESTION: So when you write, is it for a particular audience or yourself?

EVERSON: I write for the past. For Shakespeare and Milton, Homer and Dante. For Jeffers. The voices that shape you are the voices you listen to and work for. I don't write for Stevens or Williams. I don't write for Zukofsky or Olson. I write for Duncan, but I don't get his whole attention because he's beating out a different course.

Of all my peers, Robert is probably the closest to me. I don't have the points of contact with him that I've got with Bly—he's neither a Christian nor a Jungian. We are poets, though, and I feel close to him on that level in a way I can't feel close to Bly. I honor Bly, but there is no ring of identity. This is odd in that there are even antipathetical points in our relationship. Duncan is homosexual, and I get no insight from this. Also, there is a rivalry between us which sometimes surfaces. For instance, when my manuscript collection went to the Bancroft Library at U. C. Berkeley, there was a large public celebration and reading at Wheeler Hall on campus. Robert went and he was so jealous it was painful. He sat in the audience with a young gay poet on either side, and at the end of my reading when the audience rose to its feet, Robert didn't budge. He kept the two of them nailed down, too. Afterwards he could hardly speak to me, he was so pissed off. He has given a lot more to Berkeley than I ever have, and he was understandably angry that I should be honored that way, before him.

QUESTION: Duncan is published by New Directions, you were, Snyder is, McClure is, and you are all more or less from the same area. How did that come about?

EVERSON: Through Kenneth Rexroth. He fostered the San Francisco movement which was an entering wedge. He had a strong connection with James Laughlin before we ever met him. My book was published by New Directions in the forties, and I can honestly say Rexroth discovered me. He sold Laughlin on me, and I owe him a great debt for that. Jeffers was my ideal; Rexroth was my mentor, my manager. Eventually, because of a personal problem we had a falling out which never did get squared away properly. It has been painful for me. I was committed to his program, but I couldn't fulfill what he expected of me. I should have taken more care, but it was impossible.

Rexroth saw me as an autochthon, a nativist in the American tradition of Sandburg, Jeffers, Henry Miller. When William Stafford wrote his introduction to *The Achievement of Brother Antoninus*, a kind of brief anthology of my poetry, he tried to place me more in line with the prevailing, antinativist aesthetic, and that made Rexroth very angry. It denied everything he had written about me. When I honored Stafford's introduction, he was upset. But it was more complex than that. His biographer told me that she felt that when Rexroth talked about me he talked about the best he hoped for himself. That's high praise, and in that sense I truly was his son. But like all sons and fathers our relationship was tangled.

QUESTION: Would you say that he was pretty much single-handedly responsible for the San Francisco Renaissance?

EVERSON: Sure. Duncan of course labored hard at it, but he was too young. He just didn't have Rexroth's stature. He was not a polemicist, which was one of Rexroth's greatest strengths. Ginsberg also, whereas both Kerouac and Duncan were the writers. Rexroth got the thing started in San Francisco, then Ginsberg took it back East and sold it to *Time*. Kerouac and his group wrote for ten years before the Beat Generation emerged, and it was Rexroth who made the difference.

QUESTION: Over the years have your work habits changed?

EVERSON: I don't think so.

QUESTION: Do you write on a typewriter?

EVERSON: With a pen for two or three drafts. I generally go to the typewriter when I want to see what the configuration of the poem is going to be. But I have to get the rhythm worked out. I don't see any reason to create poetry on the typewriter; in fact, the whole idea seems ludicrous to me.

QUESTION: And where do you write?

EVERSON: Right in the family. I've got a studio, but I use it for printing or typing. I find that the hatching process is right there in the morning in front of the fireplace.

QUESTION: What about notebooks?

EVERSON: I keep a dream journal. I've been keeping it for a long time, and fairly regularly.

QUESTION: And do you use it in your poetry?

EVERSON: Often. In fact, I think I used it pretty extensively in the *Masks of Drought* poems. Often I'll go into the dream atmosphere in order to get the poem under way.

QUESTION: You mentioned printing. What is the relationship between your printing and your poetry?

EVERSON: It's part of the struggle for consummation. Going back to the analogy of the sperm and the ovum, it's another dimension that the poem goes through in order to achieve apotheosis.

QUESTION: Which means . . .

EVERSON: I'm not satisfied with a poem until I see it perfectly printed. I'm not satisfied until the idea is perfectly articulated, perfectly expressed, and perfectly printed. That's as near to beatitude as I can carry it. When I first got into printing during the war my idea was to write my books, print them, and make a life as a poet-craftsman. I hoped to leave behind me a work of coherence. But when I converted I moved into a different frame of reference and began to worry about my egocentricity. I began to take on printing projects outside my own work, and these turned out to be my "masterpieces." The only thing I do regret is that I couldn't do my own collected poems. I planned the project a few years ago, made a start, but the thing fell through. It was a great disappointment to me.

If I had my life to live over again, I'd develop my artistic capacity more fully in terms of my woodcuts. Then with the hand-press, I'd try for coherence, book by book, section by section. I would establish the folio format from the start, so at the end it could all be bound together. But after all, I didn't even know what I was going to write, let alone the rest of it. Still maybe it gives some idea of my priorities, even if I couldn't accomplish it.

The Place of Poetry in the West

NATHANIEL TARN: I'm very interested in the whole question of whether there is, or not, an "American poetic language" or "American idiom." From Williams on, this has been an important question, though it seems now to be stopped short by the internationalism of a present scene everyone is concerned about, the "Language" community of poetry.

LEE BARTLETT: Bill, have you thought much about the Language poets? Ron Silliman? Barrett Watten? Bruce Andrews? Charles Bernstein?

WILLIAM EVERSON: The names of those particular writers are familiar to me, but I've never gotten into any of their theoretical writing. "Language poets" is an entirely new term to me.

TARN: Well, I wonder if it's even still a live question, "Language" poets aside. The question of an American poetic language.

EVERSON: For me it is. In fact, I'm just getting into it as I write my long autobiographical epic. I find myself resorting to slang, idiomatic expressions that I never would have allowed into my more formal verse. It's as if I'm in a new place, more secular, letting my secular side have a voice. So now I find myself inhabiting the American idiom in a way I never thought necessary for me.

TARN: But that is a personal thing. What does it mean in terms of the overall scene? Is this still a live issue in the culture at large?

This discussion took place at William Everson's home in the Santa Cruz Mountains on June 3, 1986. It was first published in Lee Bartlett, *The Sun Is But a Morning Star: Studies in West Coast Poetry and Poetics* (Albuquerque: University of New Mexico Press, 1989).

EVERSON: I don't think it can be avoided. I think it's going to be around as long as America has any kind of place in the world of thought and letters. We are, after all, infecting the purity of all other idioms on the earth through our media.

BARTLETT: Although interestingly Helen Vendler has a new anthology called *The Harvard Book of Contemporary American Poetry*, which begins with Stevens, yet includes no Pound, Williams, Oppen, H.D., all the way up through no Duncan or Creeley. It's as if for Vendler and Harvard there is a very narrow and peculiar American idiom. Kenneth Rexroth regarded Williams the greatest American prosodist of this century. Can you imagine an anthology of American poetry published in 1986 which includes Stevens but not Williams?

EVERSON: Only for a special purpose. Maybe tracking a trend.

BARTLETT: Yet she includes Ginsberg and Snyder. I can't see either of them coming out of Stevens.

EVERSON: No, neither can I. Stevens was the Matisse of American poetry.

BARTLETT: Nathaniel, you represent an interesting case in this context. Born in Paris, raised and educated more or less in England, and yet you consider yourself now an American poet.
Obviously for you the question of an American idiom must be an open one.

TARN: Well, I try to listen in that way. I am coming, by listening, into speaking that way also. I suppose that, to a certain extent, this involves a theatrical component. It is linguistic *work*. Poets are linguistic *workers*. Actors, for instance, spend a great deal of time perfecting their idioms. I could have gone, I suppose, to an elocution school, except that there is something inauthentic about that. When I die, the telltale voice will have died with me.

BARTLETT: But you and Bill both seem to be thinking of idiom as lexical—que over against line, for example. I'm thinking of it more as, say, cadence.

TARN: It's both. I *certainly* do not think of it as lexical only.

EVERSON: I found Nathaniel's *At the Western Gates* quite American in idiom, and I was very impressed by that. His asking how in the hell do you go about fucking here, in a cabin at the end of the continent.

TARN: When I arrived in America in the late sixties and very early seventies, I was tremendously hopeful because so many of the ethnic voices were coming on strong. It was a linguistic progress that in some ways reminded me of what had happened in England following the war. Although the standard BBC voice had dominated as long as you could remember, after the war, provincial voices came in, so that you began to hear Liverpool, Nottingham, the Angry Young Men, particularly in the theater. England seemed to be listening to itself for the first time. I don't think America was listening to itself for the first time in the sixties and seventies—it had always been more democratic and more populist—but nevertheless it seemed to me a time in which the American language was growing in every possible direction, and the English language was not.

But now, after having lived here fifteen years, and after having gotten through fifteen years of teaching and so on, I've gotten somewhat disappointed with that, lost some of my faith in that. Now, I'm more impressed with the deadening of language which is taking place in the media and in political discourse, a kind of ironing out of the thing into a set of commercial formulae. Bill, as I think I've told you, I think you have five hundred times more faith than anyone else I've ever met, and yet in *Birth of a Poet* you mention this problem only once or twice. You are just far more optimistic than I am. The kids are listening to that stuff more and more, and talking it, and now, instead of expanding, the language is retreating.

EVERSON: Well, my faith on this question is rooted in the archetype. It doesn't have much to do with these more temporal aspects of the problem. It constantly manifests itself in a primal and refreshing way which is inexhaustible; it's the root source of the language per se. My orientation point toward reality is psychological and profoundly symbolic, and for me the poetry lies in the subject matter rather than in the expression. It is the inexhaustible current in the subject of the archetype itself which is the great replenishing factor. The ordeal of the poet is in reconnecting to that, as in prayer.

BARTLETT: This takes us back to the American idiom. You are saying that it's not lexical, not a cadence, but subject matter?

EVERSON: No. The idiom is a matter of expression. I'm not an advocate of the American idiom as Williams was. I employ it because you get vibrations of truth out of it which are relevant to where we find ourselves at any given time. But for me it's not as important as the American idiom, or the Canadian, or the Australian idiom, or the British idiom. The language itself has its own inner dynamic which is the crucial factor.

TARN: It seems to me it has to be *both* expression *and* subject matter, but that expression primes—otherwise why *poetry*? I've got a feeling that this is linked to another question, the mission or function of the poet. Bill, you have a very high regard for the poet as the conservator of language and a healer of the problems of the nations. The poet can only contact solutions through the prophetic function, the shamanistic function. Of course, Ezra Pound had this same kind of high regard for the poet, and it seems to me that one of the primary reasons he was so tragically disappointed late in his life was that his vision really was beginning to encounter the wall of silence he had not wanted to perceive before. So my question here would be rather brutal. Do you think that the coming generations are going to have all that elevated a notion of the poet? My sense of what younger poets are doing today does not imply that prophetic idea of the poet at all.

BARTLETT: I'd agree with that. Certainly I think Michael Palmer would deny a prophetic vocation, as would a poet coming out of Iowa's MFA program.

EVERSON: Poetry goes through changes from primitivism to decadence; we happen to be in a decadent period right now. However, the mythic possibilities are always there, and they'll never be exhausted. If you get a strong enough personality you'll recover those elements. If at a particular time he or she hasn't shown up, then he or she simply hasn't shown up. You must have to wait for the voice that can tap it, and there you'll get the replenishing energy.

BARTLETT: Like Yeats.

EVERSON: Yes, exactly. He was just late enough to be post-Victorian and early enough to be Modernist. And he was able to achieve that vatic voice.

BARTLETT: But Nathaniel, your sense of the poet is in some sense similar to Bill's.

TARN: Well, one of the problems I have had for a while is the nightmare of an incestuous circle: that the consumers of poetry are the producers of poetry and that there is nothing else. It's a self-reinforcing circle in the sense that if none of the poets want that notion of function, then none of the readers will because they are, after all, the poets. I think we have to rediscover the reader, the function in the system of the reader as "other." Without "other" there is no *marriage*. Only incest.

EVERSON: The problem lies in the fact that we are in a new phase of the media and the poets are confused right now among the influx of various alien sources. It's again a matter of waiting for a strong enough voice to emerge in the recovery of taproots. As Emerson insists, if we live in expectation it will happen.

BARTLETT: Although it is always possible that American poetry is finished. It's possible that we've lived through a couple hundred years of a great literature, a great poetry, and now it has worked itself out. Maybe next time it'll emerge in Bangkok, a whole other tradition.

TARN: I doubt that, but at the same I find it hard in the face of all the sociological evidence to have Bill's faith that at some point the voice is going to reemerge. After all, in purely sociological terms, the voice that may be most *listened* to at this moment—a very uneven voice, but the most listened to—is probably somebody like Allen Ginsberg. Does he have this idea?

EVERSON: The oracular incentive. But nobody reads him much these days.

BARTLETT: I don't think Ginsberg is all that popular now. I think that somebody like John Ashbery is far more popular at the moment, at least among people who pay attention in any sustained way to poetry. On the other hand, a poet like Galway Kinnell . . . he read not too long ago in a very large room at the University of New Mexico and we had a standing-room-only crowd. And he's got something close to the religious sense of the poet.

EVERSON: Well, he's a fresh voice for the neoacademics. He's got that traditional dimension which Ginsberg lacks. Ginsberg's idiom is so much looser than Kinnell's. I am not saying that Kinnell is a better poet, not in the ultimate sense of the vocation, for at his top Ginsberg is inimitable. But you can see how new academics would espouse Kinnell—he brings along with him something from the traditional canon.

BARTLETT: Very simply, he writes poems that are in some sense easier to teach in the classroom. There is not all that much you can say about a Ginsberg poem after a certain point. But getting back to your observation, Bill, it's like this voice that's hovering out there waiting to be embodied is the tongue of the race. It doesn't really matter whether it's expressed in 1985 or fifty years from now.

EVERSON: That's my point, though I do take it on faith. It's always happened that way though. Here I am seventy-three years old and I feel it stirring in myself, glowing and burning, whispering, imploring, pleading.

BARTLETT: But as an anthropologist Nathaniel would be forced to see this as a wonderful romantic fiction.

TARN: Yes, as an anthropologist I'd have to see it that way, but as a poet—well, there is that terrible division again which I've suffered through all my life. I am little uneasy about this conversation, playing devil's advocate again. Poets are hard on science—*need* it from Pound to Cage down to now, yet always dump on it. Actually, I'd have a faith at two removes. I'd have the faith that Bill's faith works, or I'd at least try to. But there's something else I'd like to get to. Reading through *Birth of a Poet*, I notice that you say we are passing beyond nationalism. I wish to God this were true. But as we prepare for a third world war, everyone is in the rhetorical posture of a passionate nationalism. The whole social structure of nationalism continues unabated. I don't see Albania shrinking by one jot into something that is not Albania, or the United States growing into something other. All the frontiers seem to be remaining exactly the way they are. I can see that reason and faith are asking for an end to nationalism, but it's just not happening. Look at the number of *new* nations! It is like a plague of locusts. Not that they should not be *free*! But that they should be *nations*?

EVERSON: Everyone knows it's over. Only the inertia of the past is carrying it on. We haven't found the new way yet, but everyone knows in their bones that it's over. We are living in a ghost, waiting for the new forms to emerge.

TARN: I'm just not sure this is so. The poets know this, and the artists, and the environmentalists. But what about the gigantic mass of businessmen, soldiers, technicians?

BARTLETT: I see us as transforming nationalism into something else, but the impulse is the same. Transformation into a religious zeal—"born-again" Christians, for example, who tend to huddle under an American umbrella, but who are obviously Christians before they are Americans, when they can make such a distinction at all. Or corporate executives who'd love to merge Ford with Toyota so that their sense of nationalism is an overarching corporation. You don't necessarily have national borders anymore, but interests and sympathies to which large groups of people adhere. And they are of necessity at odds with one another.

EVERSON: I see the widespread preoccupation with oriental religions as a great sign of the passing of nationalism.

BARTLETT: But do you think that search really has filtered into the general population?

EVERSON: It doesn't matter. The portent is the eye of the fact-to-be. It is already here.

BARTLETT: Maybe in Santa Cruz, but what about San Jose?

EVERSON: It's in the atmosphere. Everything is carrying us into a supranational consciousness. Our technology, the space flights.

BARTLETT: But isn't this just a hypernationalism? Get our flag on the moon first?

EVERSON: The logo, not the cutting edge. The blade is ideology. There will always be nationalism, just as there will always be city pride. But men no longer kill and die for it as they did in the thirteenth century when the city-states supplanted the feudal hegemony, and gave us the Renaissance and Culture. With the sixteenth century came nationalism, which gave us the Enlightenment and Science, between them leveling Culture to Civilization. Now in the twentieth century comes Ideology. World War I was the last great nationalistic war, but it conceived in its violent womb the fountainhead of Ideology, the Russian Revolution, and Fascism arose to match it. True, both Germany and Russia revived nationalism in World War II, for Ideology was not yet strong enough to muster the millions, but that was a death rattle. The terrible spawn of the atomic bomb sealed its doom. The obsolete nations are terrified, shitting their britches. Reagan and Gorbachev embrace each other convulsively, invoking God or destiny that the fearful nationalistic death throes can be contained till Ideology can stop clearing its throat and do its thing. I take secularism and religion to be Ideology's Janus face. So far secularism is winning hands down for the age is linear, but with the rise of the cyclical religion begins to breathe. Look at the environmentalist movement. The call of the prenational.

BARTLETT: But Bill, even there we've seen a tremendous backlash. It's true that James Watt is out, but a popular bumper sticker is "Nuke the Whales," and I think there is very little irony there. A lot of people are just tired of hearing about nuclear power plants and saving whales. I know that you don't spend any time in shopping malls, but if you did I think you'd be a little depressed.

EVERSON: They are just howling in the dark. The future is against them. You've got to go after the new consciousness as the wave of the future.

TARN: Do you think wilderness is still the archetypal American experience?

EVERSON: The archetypal American address, the archetypal American vision, the archetypal American fantasy. And that's the thing that counts. Reality can offer very little to stand against it.

TARN: Well, you have the running dream or ambition of the West which is never reached. It occurs to me that this is a transformed metaphor for immortality, because if you never reach the place where the sun goes down you never die. But in fact when you reach the great ocean you can't move further forward. What then happens? Does the whole thing then retract upon itself? Does it go inward and promote some kind of sickness? I'm wondering about this because you've talked a great deal about violence, and I've never been completely clear on the relationship between reaching the sea and violence. Are you sometimes implying that the violence arises out of the fact that we have reached the last frontier?

EVERSON: No. I don't think that's the source of violence, though thinking about it now, maybe you are right. Maybe each generation feels threatened by this and therefore resorts to violence to restore the new. But generally I think of violence as being an aperture to primal reality, in the sense that the gash is manifestation of dynamic energy. This attempt to get at the dynamic energy that supersedes the form in an attempt to clarify the present and the nature of the future is what the impulse to violence is. I think that, after Christ, it can only have its true resolution in art, where it can be handled in the formal rather than the physical dimension. In a sense, the resort to violence on the material level is a failure of aesthetics. If the aesthetics were properly functioning, violence would transmute into another dimension and the energies could go forward. But there is always a degree of rupture in material forms in nature, which is both closing and opening as a way to the future.

BARTLETT: Are you thinking of violence as personal or institutional?

EVERSON: I think of it as it is in nature first of all, the rupture and disparity between forms and the contingent reality in the process of evolution. The constant subsumption of one form into another. This is a problem for mankind as a spiritual being in the continuum of material forms, of which he is also a part. As a Christian I think this is met first on the cross, then in art.

TARN: You've said Buddhism is a very fine system, but that it doesn't satisfy you because it's not dramatic enough. It doesn't account for any drama in the world.

EVERSON: Well, I don't know too much about it, but my intuition is that it withdraws from the point of violence. The reason I remain a Christian is the drama of the cross. For me that's the point of ultimate reality, ultimate truth. I remain a Christian rather than a Buddhist because of this sense that Buddhism is a deferral, rather than an embracing of violence.

TARN: I'm not really sure that that is so. For instance, in the Zen school of meditation the amount of violence one has to face while sitting still—the violence of trying to remain in the relative world while striving for something else—is amazing. To use your terminology, the violence of having to live in linear time while at the same time trying to transcend it, to get into cyclical time. The amount of violence engendered in the sitting person is tremendous. This tends to be ritualized in those incredible encounters which take place in sesshin. It seems to me that there is certainly a ritual of violence in various forms of Buddhism. The fierce and angry-seeming deities in Tibetan Buddhism are channels for dealing with violence inside us and outside us. It is not just a quietism, which is what you seem to be implying with the word *deferral*.

BARTLETT: But isn't the point of convergence in both Christian violence and Buddhist violence that fact that in each tradition at the moment of violence there is no past and no future, only the here and now? Violence offers the ultimate instance of existential focus.

EVERSON: Well, my further problem with Zen is the notion that reality is an illusion. I don't think it's an illusion at all.

TARN: Again, the illusion thing is tricky. There's the Zen statement that when you go in, the mountains and rivers are there; then the mountains and rivers disappear; when you come out, the mountains and rivers are there once again. This seems to be implying that the question of illusion is complex, to say the least!

EVERSON: A psychological process in any case.

TARN: To come back to the matter of America. I spent three long seasons in Alaska, and I was absolutely fascinated by what was going on there in terms that were usually codified into "this is the last frontier." The huge debate over "what we are going to do with the place." It is, somehow, "our last chance." I was always overwhelmed by the feeling that people wanted to get it over and done with; that they were profoundly uncomfortable with there being an Alaska. Alaska's position on the map is awkward. It is the West's culmination, a grand explosion, yet it feels north rather than west. Most times, it is "off the map": people in the "Lower Forty-eight" prefer to forget it. We had gotten to the Pacific and the book was, we thought, closed. Suddenly we discovered that there was still another state to be developed, and what do we do with the problem now that we've decided that the issue is closed. For Bill, of course, it would never close, but

I still don't see how once we've reached the Pacific we can keep that question open. It loses the force of myth and becomes, say, "folklore." Is that where we want to go?

BARTLETT: So your sense of this is simply as a stage in history, or at least spiritual history.

TARN: Yes, which is why I have a problem with the notion of waiting for the "new" voice.

EVERSON: It's a matter of transmutation to another dimension. That's the function of the artist.

TARN: Will violence remain in this new situation?

EVERSON: It will have to remain.

BARTLETT: What do you mean by "another dimension"? It sounds like something out of science fiction.

EVERSON: I mean the spiritual, or the imaginative—some other dimension of the collective unconscious. It's waiting to be tapped.

BARTLETT: So that the impulse to go West is simply a momentary manifestation in history of the larger psychological process?

EVERSON: If you wish. We are at a great moment, though, in that we have reached the ultimate West. That's why Alaska has a temptation about it as a last frontier, but that's not the problem. The problem is that the line is drawn at the Pacific. And that's the relevance of Jeffers. He made the first great penetration of the post-Pacific spiritual tendency. For his pantheism gave him the map.

BARTLETT: The cynical answer again might be that once you've reached the West, the Pacific, the game is over. Nuclear weapons, AIDS, wholesale starvation . . .

EVERSON: Those signs of impasse will confront us, all kinds of ghoulish threats.

TARN: There is another *realpolitik* take here. We are continuing across the Pacific into Asia which raises the whole issue of the fact that once the inner empire has been built, you move to the outer empire. And God knows that one of the crucial issues of our time is American imperialism. We tried it in Vietnam and it didn't work, though now we are continuing it in Central and South America. Of course, there is the alleged coming of the "Pacific Century." We may have lost the strength for empire by then—too much competition from Japan, Korea, China. Our West should do well though, even if only commercially.

BARTLETT: Why don't you have an interest in the north/south axis? Why simply the east/west?

EVERSON: That's the sun pattern. East is life, West is death. The sun is born and the sun dies. I think of the north–south polarities as stable, fixed. They define the course through which the mobile and changing east–west equation must flow.

TARN: One of the problems I always feel with "archetypal" situations is this: Alaska is in a sense north, but in another way it is very much the continuation of west. If you think of the Rockies as being "archetypally" western, in British Columbia you begin to reach the immense culmination of the West. In a sense, reaching the Pacific Ocean was really a mistake on the ultimacy of the West, which could be continued into the Aleutian archipelago right on to Japan. One of the things that worries me about "archetypal" thinking is that there is very frequently a slippage of categories because the archetype strives to divide the world ruthlessly into its various components. So one finds oneself saying, "Well in this respect it's the West, but in that respect it's North; in some senses it is female, but then it is also male." Symbolically, it's a glorious system, but it seems to me to sometimes negate and drown out the complexity of detail, and my more scientific side begins to rebel.

EVERSON: Yes, it is incorrigibly reductive, but then so are all symbols, all symbolism. All I can say is that the simplicity of the archetypes is so threatening that if it weren't for a little slippage here and there we'd be in a bad way.

TARN: I suppose that fits with your notion of *imprecision*, which of course would drive the scientist crazy. Even when science talks of imprecision (all the way to chaos) it wishes to do it precisely.

BARTLETT: But of course the American continent really stops at the Sierras, and all the coast is really part of a whole other land mass which includes Japan, the Pacific basin.

TARN: Fifteen years or so ago, Robin Blaser had a magazine which was called *Pacific Nation*, and I've always had tremendous sympathy for that idea. One of the things I used to say which made me unpopular in the East was that America was entirely expendable until you got to the Rockies. That's probably one of the reasons I'm in New Mexico right now. I'm a western secessionist at heart. All the rest is still Europe.

BARTLETT: Except that you've told me before that you're a little troubled by Bill's sense of the East Coast/West Coast literary politics scene.

TARN: Well, I do have a question there. Bill, I was surprised when I was reading *Birth of a Poet* to see that you felt that western writers still had to go east to be recognized and blessed. I noticed to my surprise also during the Ezra Pound Conference in San Jose, where Lee and I just spoke, that during one panel Robert Duncan suddenly said that his recent National Poetry Award given by Thomas Parkinson's group was all very fine, but that it really doesn't mean anything because it's an award the West is giving to itself. So what does it mean? By that he seems to be saying that the eastern reputation business still holds. I just don't think it does, and I'm very surprised, Bill, that you and Duncan have that kind of defeatism. It's very typical of you both.

BARTLETT: But again to go back to the Vendler anthology, she includes Snyder and Roethke, but as far as I remember they are the only poets from this side of the country she chooses. That's an interesting situation in 1985. Neither Duncan nor Bill are in the book. No Charles Bukowski. Even someone like Carolyn Kizer, whom you'd otherwise expect . . .

EVERSON: The accumulation of the past lies in the East. And it's on the basis of the accumulation of the past that judgments are made. I just don't think that the East is going to validate the West until the transmutation process which we were discussing earlier is complete. When the Pacific Coast becomes the new East through that process, then we'll have a shift in recognition.

TARN: I believe that demography and economics will soon allow us to recognize that the West is now the living center of the nation's cultural life. The East will have simply dropped away. But you are saying that the archetype still holds, but the West has to become the East for it to be realized.

EVERSON: Yes, exactly.

TARN: That's what I would call an enormous category slippage, and unnecessary!

EVERSON: Isn't it that way with London? The East Coast still feels it needs validation from London. And Paris! Not to mention the lust for the Nobel Prize.

TARN: Sure. I think of New York and the East Coast as the "British ghetto." *The New York Review of Books, The New Yorker,* and the Ivy League are the last remaining possessions of Her Majesty's government in the country. So that the East Coast establishment—which produces a Helen Vendler or, God help us, a Harold Bloom—is still British owned. But that is, in your terms, "a ghost we are living in."

BARTLETT: Why? Bill would see this, I think, as an archetypal situation, but from your point of view what is the reason for this?

TARN: I just had a take on it this summer. I went back to England for the first time since I came to New Mexico, and it had finally stopped getting on my nerves. I began to realize that it was no longer home and that I could begin to enjoy it for the historical and traditional dimensions which it had. It's the history department of the University of the United States. But at the same time I understood why so many people loved it for the history and tradition, so that they then committed the crime of considering that that's where everything came from. It became the great model, thereby perpetually undermining American culture. Until one gets out from under all of that, simply refuses to accept those validations anymore, I don't see that the real new voices can arise.

BARTLETT: But even in university English departments, where people should know better, there is always a sense of American writing as a poor stepchild. But I misunderstood, I think, something you said earlier. You weren't denying Bill's sense of an East/West division, but rather you simply couldn't understand why a western writer would care about it.

TARN: Absolutely. Which is why I was so surprised by Duncan's statement.

EVERSON: But don't you see, the East holds the canon of judgment while the West holds the canon of creativity. We create out here in order to be judged back there. From the impersonal archetypal point of view, to write to the East's proscription would be fatal, a true defeat—the western writer who goes east and goes to pot, like Steinbeck. But having written one must wait for the East to catch up.

BARTLETT: So that getting a Pulitzer Prize would carry more weight than the National Poetry Award.

EVERSON: For a Californian.

TARN: See, I have great trouble with that. I don't see that there is any evidence that the Pulitzer ever meant a damn thing in real terms. Same as, nine times out of ten, the Nobel means very little. I cannot accept "we create out here in order to be judged back there." It's too close to slavery.

BARTLETT: But don't you think in part your attitude derives from the fact that you've already got a British background and an eastern background—both of which you decided to leave behind? You do not have that almost innate sense of lack of worth the Westerner takes in with mother's milk.

TARN: Well, I could see this in terms of old, frozen Europe—say London as opposed to English provincial writers. As I said earlier, after the war the provincial writers took over London (the French are still backward in regard to Paris).

BARTLETT: But that's the point. They *took over* London. Maybe they returned to the countryside, but there was obviously a feeling that they had to capture the capital. Until Bill and Duncan have captured New York—which, in both their cases, publication by New Directions in a sense effects—that transformation cannot be achieved.

TARN: But this is still a *new* country! Bill, I feel that your adherence to the archetype theory is almost compelling you to remain in a defeatist position. If you maintain that the eastern archetype is fixed, then there is no reason why the situation of the western writer should change. But this brings me to another question. I wonder if, in your notion of the shaman, there isn't a confusion of the geographic with the ethnographic. That is to say: we have a tendency to think that the American Indian, who is the primal and prime owner of this land, is somehow the fountainhead of our own tradition because we are in the same place, the same *geography*. So that we mask an *ethnographic* imperialism, with all its attendant murders and massacres, with a geographic adhesion of son to father. We try to claim descent from these people, but they don't accept it. And the fact that they don't accept this seems to me to be absolutely cardinal. You must be familiar with the Indian reaction to Jerome Rothenberg's ethnopoetics.

BARTLETT: Leslie Silko has a scathing essay on Snyder's "white shamanism."

TARN: Yes, exactly. How do you feel about this, Bill? It seems to me that you have a much more deeply rooted view of shamanism in terms of your theoretical background than a number of these other people. I'm drawing attention to this because I think one needs to transcend the whole East/West discussion to solve it.

EVERSON: You speak as an anthropologist, and I respect your concern. Perhaps I do presume too much, as you say; but the truth is I place far more emphasis on the Spirit of Place. It is the numinous force that resolves the apparent confusion between what you call "the geographic and ethnographic spheres." The Spirit of Place is the power that makes the aboriginal shaman and the civilized poet two beads on the same thread. It is the power in the American earth that led me to seek the clue as to how it is properly met, and that clue proves to be the shaman. This place was here eons before the Indians arrived. Both our peoples were engendered somewhere else—his in Asia, mine in Europe. But we were drawn ineluctably by the same force; only his people have a longer tenure on it than mine. Nevertheless, any man with eyes to see, nerves to feel, can receive it. As Jeffers has said of the Greeks: "The Greeks were not the inventors / Of shining clarity and jewel-sharp form and the beauty of God. / He was free with men before the Greeks came: / He is here naked on the shining water. / Every eye that has a man's nerves behind it has known it." As for the shaman, were I to usurp his cult, imitate his rites and practices, he would clearly have the right to object, especially if I had not been received into the tribe, initiated into the mysteries, validated by the elders. It would be as presumptuous and futile as trying to consecrate the eucharist in the Mass without ordination. Poets are sometimes called priests of the world, prophets. But this has become a cliché. It is the shaman's penetration of the unconscious to engage the demonic that causes the poet to turn to him for a model. It is not a case of either Snyder or myself trying to pass ourselves off as bona fide shamans.

BARTLETT: So you don't see this as a question of cultural imperialism?

EVERSON: No, though obviously there are traces of it. Maybe it is cultural imperialism in inception, but it can't end that way. Certainly there are terrible traces of imperialism in our occupation of this land, but we can't let that defeat us.

TARN: I'm with you there, very much so, but we have to get everyone to agree and this will take time. OK. I guess I was looking at another facet of the western lack of independence: looking to the Indian as father, to the European as father, to the Easterner as father. The question of the weight of tradition. Well, this calls to mind another question. Bill, you are obviously a pillar of this evolving western ethos, while at the same time you are strongly involved in Catholicism, which is certainly not a majority religious situation in America. How do you see your Catholicism and your westernism as a nexus? Is there a connection, or is it just a historical accident in your particular situation?

EVERSON: It's an extremely problematic situation for me psychologically. I am archetypally tied into two distinct ideas. First, there is the American pragmatism which everyone here begins with, the Protestant ethic. Second, there is the Catholicism, which ties me to the history of Europe and Western civilization, its origins in Asia Minor. I made a break with my American pragmatism, and for eighteen-and-a-half years lived in a monastery; then I reached a point where in a sense the American pragmatism caught up with me, after Vatican II, when the Church became social action oriented at the expense of mystical contemplation.

BARTLETT: You left the Dominican Order. Not the Church.

EVERSON: Right, though I'm not in the sacraments. But I never left the Church. Once out of the monastery, I attempted to recover my aboriginal roots, to go back beyond the pragmatism and the Catholicism to a recovery of nature. I took the figure of the shaman as the most direct route to that. After all, I came to understand Catholicism through the medieval tradition of the vocation of the monk, and it seemed only natural that I might understand my aboriginal roots through the vocation of the shaman. The shaman is the most crystallized symbolic entity in this context, and so I began to shamanize—which, in a sense, as an artist I'd been doing all along. It was simply that now I could make a conscious attribution through animism back into the instinctual, which is the basis of the archetypal. Jung's theory of the archetypes is the method by which I can relate these three cultural levels. The project isn't complete, though, because I've not yet changed my life enough. But currently I'm writing my autobiographical epic as an attempt to bring these aspects together. Actually, I never realized that until this moment, but I see it clearly. In some way all three levels will come together there, which brings me back to the idea of transmutation. That is the function of the artist in society. Jeffers could stand aloof from whether or not the East Coast validated him, knowing that the future would. I have the same kind of faith that he did, but I can't bring myself to say the hell with you, that I'm putting my stakes on a thousand years from now. I just can't live that conviction of Jeffers's. I feel myself driven to heal the wound in the American psyche, the tension between the East and the West. And until the East validates the West the nation cannot be healed. I just can't let it go.

BARTLETT: Which brings us back to the Pulitzer Prize.

EVERSON: It would go a long way to heal the rift. I agree with Nathaniel that the award itself is not all that distinguished actually, but as symbolic gesture it would mean acceptance.

TARN: Well, what you've just said is very beautiful. I feel it may have some relation to my triad of "vocal," "silence," and "choral." It helps me see how with a certain view of the archetype you might transcend various political realities which seem to run directly counter to it. But after all, I continue to feel that an *American Indian* poet might still question your right or my right to that view. This seems in some ways to raise that spectre of violence again.

BARTLETT: And yet most Indian poets, like Wendy Rose and Simon Ortiz, write in English.

TARN: That's something history has forced them into.

BARTLETT: Of course. But history has forced Bill into his position also. Leslie Silko makes many good points about cultural imperialism, but it's interesting that Bill and Snyder have come to their positions very consciously, while many Indian writers might well dismiss the question of their language by saying simply that history has forced them into it. Which is not a satisfactory answer to a very complex problem. After all, Indian writers who write in English, it might be argued, perpetuate cultural imperialism through their art. That the true Indian artists are those people who stay in the pueblos close to their root languages and traditions, though of course it is more complex than that. But back to what you were asking Bill, Nathaniel, your case is very similar—Judaism combined with your interest in Buddhism.

TARN: In my case, I think it may well be irreconcilable. Bill has found a coherent way of bringing his contradictions together. But I remain in contradictions which sometimes cease to be beautiful. My own situation sometimes causes me abject despair simply because there are so many strands. I've come to believe that the artistic, political, and sociological situation in our time has become so complex that the only thing the artist can do is remain in a state of contradiction and give voice(s) to it, at least until history brings about a transmutation. But the artist is not in the position to effect this: she/he is not history. I have a very high view of Bill's faith in this matter, but in reality I think that, as you say, he can only do this in his head. Unfortunately, your head is not the world out there. I could go into detail on the relation between my Judaism and my Buddhism, but that would lead to autobiography, which isn't really the point of this.

BARTLETT: But obviously, without the vision in your head you can't effect it in the world.

TARN: Sure, and it's that vision, I suppose, which may break us out of the international East/West axis in favor of a more circular view. It got us into space, for example, though what bothers me there is the tremendous deadness of the place. Don't you hanker sometimes for another planet out there, functioning instead of being just a dead mass? I suppose we have to push on further.

EVERSON: Through astrology I know they are not dead masses, they are functioning. It's my link to the dimension we were speaking about before; purely symbolic, but there it is.

TARN: Well, that's another of your beautiful notions that I'm not so sure about. Geez, I feel like a party pooper!

BARTLETT: Is your sense of this functioning as something abstracted from human consciousness?

EVERSON: No. In terms of it. The archetype relates to the instincts, but it is also operating out there. There is always a dichotomy between the subjective and the objective, two beads on the same string. The planet activates a potentiality within us. If it weren't doing it, we wouldn't recognize it at all. There is much out there that we don't recognize because it is not activating any potentiality within the race. When that material comes it will work through the symbolic mode so that we will recognize it. The result is that the symbolic is therefore superior to all other truth. Hard for the scientist to accept.

TARN: I guess I may have more trouble with the way this material is usually handled than with the material itself. Most "New Age" handling seems to me to be the tail end of the weakest side of the "counter culture." It is sentimental, anti-intellectual, gushy, and wretchedly apolitical in every sense.

BARTLETT: Yet look at something as simple as biorhythms, which you see at work in athletes all the time. Some days John McEnroe doesn't give up a point, a whole basketball team shoots seventy percent, or no one can touch Marcus Allen—then other days it all falls apart. Some days we are so in tune with our bodies that it's beyond understanding, wonderfully transcendent; other times the timing or whatever is all off. It seems to me that this shift is not simply psychological, but rather muscular. Now if this is true, the rhythm might as well connect with the planets as anything else.

TARN: You've got a point, and I don't want to deny that, though I don't think "might as well" is very conclusive. It's just that some of the same problems I have with the archetypal theory come into play here. But I'd like to turn to one final point. Again, reading *Birth of a Poet* I came across the following: "Americans cannot create a clerkly caste, not even by joining the university." But isn't that exactly what happened in America? By joining universities haven't poets created a clerkly caste, especially through the artificial production of writers by the MFA machine? All these babies who've done most of their living in test tubes?

BARTLETT: I think Bill was alluding there to Auden's notion that the British writer traditionally thinks of himself as a member of a clerkly caste, while the American writer thinks of himself as an aristocracy of one.

TARN: Not *all* British writers, surely. Auden was class-bound? But are the writing schools a question of an aristocracy of one?

EVERSON: No, which is exactly why I said that.

TARN: I see. So you would argue that while it appears to be happening, in fact it's not successful. It's not going to produce the Great Voice.

EVERSON: But on the other hand, Thomas Wolfe went through the whole system, yet he's considered to be almost the archetypal poet. Certainly nobody would mistake him for an academic, yet Faulkner thought of him as the greatest American novelist.

BARTLETT: And he's not often taught in the universities.

TARN: I didn't know Faulkner felt that way.

EVERSON: In an interview someone asked him to rate American writers. He said Wolfe was first, he himself second, Hemingway third. Someone quoted that to John Berryman in his *Paris Review* interview and he almost fainted. I guess that points to the difference between Berryman and Faulkner. Wolfe was the greatest celebrator we've seen of the American earth.

BARTLETT: But the lack of critical attention takes us back to the question of how much is there to say in a classroom (or in an article) about the great indigenous American writers like Whitman and Wolfe. Emerson, Jeffers, Ginsberg. I gave a paper at U. C. Davis on the Language poets a few days ago, and the first question to be asked was, "This is all fine, but how do you *teach* one of these poems in an introductory literature class?" As if poems were being written to be taught. Obviously, you can say much more in a critical sense—especially if you are drawn to poststructuralism or deconstruction or whatever—about a poem by Stevens than by, say, Williams. And Stevens's sensibility is thoroughly European.

TARN: Yes, I must admit that I often find it hard to read Stevens as an American poet. On the other hand, the hell with exclusions!

BARTLETT: And we don't want to fall into a kind of simplistic Mc-Carthyism—who is the more "American." Yet the question of canon in late twentieth-century America comes down to what and who is taught in the universities. And there it comes down to which poets and fiction writers can give you the most critical mileage, or mileage in the classroom. I just finished two full weeks on Ginsberg in a course I'm teaching, and I have to admit it was a trial. I was constantly reaching outside the work to fill the hour. Going outside is absolutely fine, and in fact to my mind is even preferable to the various New Critical fictions which still have hold on English departments.

TARN: The expectation of exercises. When the whole literary situation is keyed into the university as a canon-creating mechanism, those people who can be taught in class because of a certain complexity will be at the top of the canon. It's a self-perpetuating system. Though let's not forget that there are alternative canons being created all the time. I was looking at *Four Letters on the Archetype*, and what comes out there is the tremendous importance of Lawrence *as an American*. Here we get into the whole problem of the English over against the American canon. Today Lawrence has tremendous difficulty being accepted simply as a poet in England, and yet he is singlehandedly the great alternative to that whole other traditional U.K. canon. When you look at his work you realize that he had made the passage. It's remarkable. But again, the British ghetto in the East conspires with the ghetto in Britain to keep Lawrence out of the whole system. The transmutation has taken place, but the goddamned East will not acknowledge it.

BARTLETT: I don't have your faith in alternative canons, however. Most people, especially adolescents, simply don't read, and if the few university students who do are left in the hands of a few academics who have a very narrow view of what poetry is and should be, then a whole body of work is going to disappear. Publishers won't, or can't, do much about it. Even James Laughlin says that if you don't make it with the "professors" you're as good as dead. The American reading public doesn't keep poetry in print, classes of twenty students do.

TARN: If this is true, even if the great voice arises there may be no one to listen to it.

BARTLETT: And the further complexity here is that as much as we rail against the tunnel vision of universities, they rescued Emily Dickinson and Herman Melville. The reading public could not have cared less.

EVERSON: I began as an antiacademic, but no more. After all, I taught in the university for ten years.

BARTLETT: And Kenneth Rexroth did the same.

EVERSON: As a poet I know I live by it. I agree that there is little poetry read outside it. I know that if I don't make it in the university I will not survive. But I know I will make it there. And I'll make it in America. There we go again—pure faith.

TARN: Faith against the dragon of sociology.

The Regional Imperative

WAYNE HOLDER: You've done more than anyone else that I know of in the last few years to deepen people's awareness of the importance of a sense of place. Now I come from British Columbia where some of us are just beginning to really think seriously about this, and I think what's impressed me most about your work, both the critical writing and the vision that is revealed in the poetry, is that this kind of regionalism is a positive thing. This is an ideal of regionalism that gives you room for development and growth rather than a negative sort of exclusionary thing as it is often taken to be, almost a pejorative.

WILLIAM EVERSON: Yes.

HOLDER: I'm interested in your way of reaching out to a landscape and your way of manifesting your at-homeness, whether in the San Joaquin Valley where you came from, or here on the coast. Do you feel that it's possible without the Christian approach, the Christian religion?

EVERSON: Certainly. I was a regionalist long before I became a Christian. Regionalism had a bad press at that time. It tended to address itself to the abstract rather than to the specific. And this meant that regionalism had to be dismissed as post-romantic baggage called "local color," you know. But actually, now with the passing of Modernism and the rise of the environmental movement, we're getting a much more cyclical mentality that's able to absorb and appreciate the advantages of a profound identification with place.

HOLDER: It was a surprise for many that the Beat/Hippie thing, the Dionysian, seems to have led us back to the land. Is this the way it seems to have come about?

Conducted by Wayne Holder at Kingfisher Flat, 1987. Previously unpublished.

EVERSON: I think that is a valid point. It's right in part that we tend to think of the Beats as vagrants and as an urban movement.

HOLDER: Does that preclude an identification with place?

EVERSON: The thing is an urban movement, but by looking at it closely it is actually place-oriented; in fact, even a great Modernist like William Carlos Williams made his epic out of a city, Paterson, and then there's Olson and his "Maximus Poems." These are celebrations of, and spontaneous identifications with, the power of place.

HOLDER: Yes, that's true. It's not often enough pointed out, I think. Those really are the seminal documents of Modernism and Black Mountain. Bill, you have spoken about the role of Christianity in your work, you have spoken of a focusing, a sort of concentrating, an incarnational quality. Here, I think the difference between you and Jeffers is instructive.

EVERSON: Yes. What would be your clue there?

HOLDER: Well, one thing you've been very explicit on is that some kind of violence must be predicated, namely the role of violence in the creative act. And, what struck me earlier today is that for a pantheist, Jeffers also incorporates violence very successfully. Usually the pantheistic impulse is a Buddhist one and serves as a denial of that element of violence. How would you contrast the efficacy of the Christian view with the Buddhist in finding a sense of place and in dealing with violence?

EVERSON: Well, I think that it goes back to the incarnational advent as a specification of the Divine. The Buddhist scenario seems to involve a withdrawal from tangibility and the concrete—while in the Christian ethos you get a divinization of the concrete, of the specific. Also, I think that the element of violence in the Christian religion that you don't get in Buddhism is the crucifixion and the sense of atonement. It's almost as if to complete the ways of God with man, the incarnation has to have its place there, and this, I think of as a sort of nuclear dynamic, like breaking the atom, or an attempt to get at the principle of existence in the specificity of things. Not making too much sense here.

HOLDER: It does make sense I think. Breaking the atom. It is clear to me that Jeffers, in being a man of the West, managed to take the Native American pantheism and give it a certain impact that it seems to lack in some others.

EVERSON: That's true, and I think that it was his insight into the mystery of violence that made this possible. That's also what I mean when I speak of the American mainstream as running from Whitman to Jeffers, the great difference between Whitman and Jeffers being that Jeffers is more religious in his comprehension of the meaning of violence . . . Whitman lived in a violent period, too, but not as violent as ours. And he had the Civil War to contend with, which was ferocious. He was exposed to it directly in the hospitals, behind the front. He sopped up the human wreckage of war like a sponge but never denounced it in his poetry. It required a prophet like Jeffers to bring that out and complete the American syndrome that Whitman, following Emerson, practically invented.

HOLDER: Whitman was really, to me, a kind of city dweller, looking West but never really going West, as in fact he didn't.

EVERSON: No. He came as far as the Rockies and never got beyond.

HOLDER: As if he was almost not able to pass, like Moses not being allowed into the promised land. Well, Jeffers is certainly very important for anybody on the West Coast as a sort of groundbreaker. I think it would be interesting to think about. I wonder if the impulse were that sort of American pantheism—a bit different than the impulse toward Buddhism. Now you can see what I'm getting at—I'm interested in the role of Buddhism today and maybe a bit critical of that. Do you think the impulse toward whatever kind of native pantheism was distinguishable from what people's impulse now toward Buddhism might be?

EVERSON: Yes, I think it sharply different. I once heard the noted Dominican theologian Victor White say that the twenty-first century would see the impact of Oriental thought on the modern church rivaling the impact of Greek thought on the early church.

HOLDER: The impulse, say, in my generation toward Buddhism has been something of a flight from violence and confrontation, and people finding peace, as it were, and in some ways it seems to have renounced some of the creative potential in the other consciousness.

EVERSON: Yes, but not being Orientals, it's hard for us to adapt on questions that deep and profound. It's almost true that the speculative range of things is less important than the actualities, and this is what we can't really enter into. We study it because—not that I do, but I mean our generation—because it's looking for a point of contrast to its own background. We're in a time of synthesizing now, and in the synthesizing process it's only natural that the specifying mind of the Occident is looking for a release into another dimension of thought and of our existence. So it's to be welcomed, the preoccupation with the Other, if it doesn't go too far.

HOLDER: Speaking of going too far, we have thought before about the Dionysian in art and process, that, say, was reawakened with somebody like Ginsberg and *Howl*. How do you feel about the way it is today?

EVERSON: I think there's been an assimilation and therefore an advance. We're farther, much farther along than when Jeffers wrote in the twenties, say, and even though I began writing in the thirties, the liberation that's come about since then is incredible. Which is all to the good.

HOLDER: But as far as a sense of place, and a sort of turning away from the urban abstractions and pitfalls like that, do you think things are in a good state in terms of poetics in the United States?

EVERSON: No, not in those terms. I think that [poetry's] in a necessarily muffled state that it has to go through now, but neither do I see any rising personalities required to pull another movement into being.

Seems to me that with the triumph of Projective Verse and the Black Mountain group in the sixties after the breakthrough of the Beat Generation the decade before, the triumph of the Projectivist movement meant that while the academic poet, whom the Beats opposed when they succeeded, the only thing they could do is follow the Projectivists, because Olson had a theory that could be discussed, accepted or rejected, where the Beats, the Dionysians, had no theory, almost by definition.

HOLDER: They worked more by example than by explanation.

EVERSON: Yes. The point I am trying to get to through my own convolutions here is the fact that the triumph of the Projectivist movement was so because it had a discipline and a theory which the academic mind could grasp, and so it proliferated in the academy.

HOLDER: And they actually had a school which none of the others had. It lent itself to the founding of an actual institution in a way that nothing else could.

EVERSON: Now that triumph is complete, and that's the problem we're faced with in American poetry today. We're faced with the triumph of Projective Verse that and the waiting for the new talent to emerge, to set a new perspective. We're in that lull between epochs. The seventies saw the triumph, the complete dominance of the Projectivist movement, and now we're waiting for an auspicious birth.

HOLDER: Something new or something past. So in a way you could almost say that the Black Mountain or the Projectivist school has been almost too successful.

EVERSON: I think it was. But I think that's true of any movement. It has to go through these natural phases of examination, insemination, eruption, triumph, and then the dirty word, which is *decadence* but . . .

HOLDER: That's been debased by other applications, hasn't it? Well, I certainly get a good feeling being here, in terms of your poetry and seeing where it comes from and where it leads. It's its own sort of actualization, which is not something you can say about poetry that is spawned in an urban environment. It doesn't seem to have that same kind of organic existence.

EVERSON: Yes.

HOLDER: And yet oddly enough it's the development of an urban culture that leads people to ask the questions and be interested to begin with.

EVERSON: Maybe. It doesn't see what it's grown up with. It takes the outsiders to come in and explain. I suppose that's a truism.

HOLDER: Easily forgotten though, like most truisms. That brings us to an interesting point. I think regionalism has often gotten a negative context because it's used by the native against the immigrant, and yet some of the best of the explorers and developers in regionalism have actually chosen their ground and said, "This is for me—this is what I want," rather than being born to it. That's true of you in ways—of your more recent work.

EVERSON: My range keeps growing to take in all of California. When I wrote *The Residual Years*, the thesis was the San Joaquin; when I wrote *The Veritable Years*, the antithesis was the City, San Francisco, and now here in Santa Cruz it's the synthesis of those two forerunning themes in poetry.

HOLDER: That's an interesting approach. I hadn't thought of that. So one can actually see the regionalist; I mean you've never really renounced or mitigated your commitment to regionalism, but it has somehow managed to encompass ever more.

EVERSON: It's gone through its phases all right. In thinking now, the redemption of the city, to me, occurred in the monastery and also in terms of the woman, *The Rose of Solitude*. That woman took me into the heart of the city, and what had been a profane thing in my isolationism and my mistrust of the patriarchy and the establishment, freed me. That's one reason why I played so deeply on regionalism in the beginning—because that was what caused me to be a poet in the first place. In my search for wholeness, I had to redeem the city and enter it, belong to it. I did that under the aegis of two women—first, Mary Fabilli, my second wife, who brought me into the city after *The Residual Years*, and after I'd been in the monastery, the Rose took me out into the city at a different level, in a different place. And that was much more café society, a factor that was broadening for me to enter and participate in. But then after I left the Order, I've reverted to nature as the sustainer.

HOLDER: That suggests something interesting: leaving the Order and finding again that nature was the sustainer. Was Christianity for you more important as a way of dealing with the urban situation? Did it have less immediacy out here, say, than in San Francisco?

EVERSON: I dare say. I haven't thought much about the role, the weight of Christianity in terms of that movement. I think it had more to do with entering the patriarchy, my identification with nature as the maternal. My hostility to the establishment and the institution was anti-paternal. By entering the Order I entered the patriarchy. One of its greatest meanings for me was entering into the patriarchy, but this was also an entering into institutional life, which is almost characterized by the city in itself—the city being the organization of institutional life, almost by definition. Yet as an archetype the city is maternal, the cornucopia archetype—the burgeoning mother of all good things concentrated in one place like a honeycomb. So I have this as a result of the redemptive phase, too. When I look back on the poems I wrote in *The Hazards of Holiness* which follow that out, was one I called "A Canticle to the Great Mother of God," in which I celebrate the city as maternal. By the same token I approach the Virgin there considering her as a city. So part of the integration process was the balancing and the subtilization and the comprehension of those two principles and an adaptation to them and, as I say, a surrender to each of them in order to know them. And it did remain profoundly regionalist through the whole thing.

HOLDER: And it was a Western city. I suppose—I don't know—I'm just trying to think in terms of the violence epitome. I don't suppose it has any particular relevance to city or outside the city one way or the other. It seems that more than ever we think of the city as something of a violent place where at one time it was sort of the commonwealth and the place where there was the rule of law. Certainly Jeffers's country was a dangerous place, the passions running wild.

EVERSON: Yes. No structuring.

HOLDER: And yet he spurned the city more than anybody that comes to mind.

EVERSON: Even me.

HOLDER: Even more than you.

EVERSON: And D. H. Lawrence wasn't all that anti-city. He was pro-nature, but you don't get a strong polemic in his work against the urban factor, the way you get it in Jeffers.

HOLDER: So we have some strong voices now for advocating various kinds of alternatives to city life. Wendell Berry, [for instance], whose viability of his family farm thing is sort of questionable, but do you have any thoughts on his approach, or do you know much about it?

EVERSON: Well, I've studied it a little bit and I respect it. I think it's right for him to be doing that and doing what he's doing. I think it's an excellent witness and a strong support for his creativity. On the other hand, I went through that phase writing the early parts of *San Joaquin* and the early parts of *The Residual Years*. That was the ideal mode, [to be] the farmer who is also literate and creative.

HOLDER: And you were in fact farming then, weren't you?

EVERSON: Yes. Then, when I went into the monastery, that changed—and different ideals came, but when I [returned] to nature, I couldn't go back to that image that Wendell Berry is postulating . . . I hadn't perfected it and fulfilled it to the degree he had. The war prevented it, and when I came back after the War, I went into the city under the aegis of the feminine ideals that I followed. But when I left the Order, I knew that I couldn't go back to the good farmer or the good yeoman in the English tradition, a founded gentry on the land that had its roots and its heritage there. It's one of the best places, but it's primarily agricultural.

I was more interested in what the new environmental movement was producing in terms of back to the wilderness, and so it was under this movement that I changed my persona from the monastic habit to buckskin. When I started in the monastery my image was established by the Order itself. I was given a habit and a name. And these became my profound identity through the years, the eighteen years that I was there. But then when I had to set aside the persona of the monk, I didn't know what to go back to. I didn't want to go back to the street; I didn't want to go back to the farm. I was more interested in finding out what the Native Americans had learned about living on this continent, and so I went to the mountain man as the image standing between the two cultures, the culture of white civilization and aboriginal primitivism.

HOLDER: Yes, I see, that's interesting. I hadn't thought of it in that way. But the Jungian studies have a lot to do with your pursuits, do they not?

EVERSON: Well, it did seem to many that it confirmed my solipsism. One of the most persistent criticisms of what I've done is that it has been too subjective, that it's too inflational to serve the self to that degree. But under the Jungian aegis that was more or less canonization.

HOLDER: So there's a basic divergence with the kind of critic that would have that objection and the Jungian way of developing something. That impresses me as a very powerful philosophy/aesthetic. And I would think it is not usually applied in the way that you have applied it. Can you say something about how you feel it's helped you to make the transitions from the various stages that we've talked about in terms of the archetype? I mean a personal archetype? And then I guess there's another thing, it's kind of a regional archetype.

EVERSON: Well, I think that a lot of good has happened to me in my own development—to go through this search for wholeness, this holistic movement which has been confirmed by the counter culture we've been talking about here, has been to shift the emphasis from the objective to the subjective. Our scientific civilization is built on the cult of objectivity, and science, with its specialization, tends to reinforce this. It separates in order to know, but it has little power to reconstitute because of its essential skepticism.

HOLDER: So it's alienating.

EVERSON: Yes, and the new movement which is built on holistic principles, or at least holistic ideals, is an attempt to find by working with nature the dimensions of ourselves that we've neglected. And this movement toward a holistic crystallization—that's too sharp a word for the process or too inorganic a word for it—but it was the Jungian movement which confirmed and gave me the strength of my convictions, that I wasn't just being solipsistic and irrelevant to the needs of men around me, as opposed to the cultivation of the . . .

HOLDER: *Aggregation*, like Marxism, I think you were saying . . .

EVERSON: The aggregate as the solution to social problems, whereas the cultivation of the soul and the Self, which is anathema to Marxism, turns out to be the Jungian perspective, not an aberration but the whole point of realization.

HOLDER: People have used the word "romantic" and applied it to you, though it sounds like both what I've seen in your work and the way you're talking now a kind of applied romanticism—I mean it takes romanticism and lifts it out and works with it, you know.

EVERSON: That's true. It's a new Romanticism I suppose. We have post-Modernism followed by neo-Romanticism. I was once hailed as one. The first publication of *The Residual Years* by New Directions in 1948. Leslie Fiedler writing in *Partisan Review* called our movement a new-Romantic one.

HOLDER: And yet it's not altogether unjust. It's just that he uses it as a pejorative.

EVERSON: He dismissed me along with my "fellow traveler in emotional excess," Dylan Thomas.

HOLDER: Was there anything to that? Do you have particular relation to Dylan Thomas?

EVERSON: No, Dylan Thomas first published in this country before the War and the movement was started in England.

HOLDER: Dylan Thomas. Leslie Fiedler compared you to your "fellow traveler, Dylan Thomas." I think that's of interest. You were just starting to explain that he first published before the Second World War.

EVERSON: There was a movement in England in the early thirties called Apocalypse which defined itself as new-Romantic over against the celebrated Auden–Spender groundswell, but I don't think Dylan was a key or central figure, but I believe he got identified with it.

HOLDER: In his emergence as the strongest poet, certainly in the British Isles, at that time, I don't suppose he repudiated anything that might tend to keep the ball rolling, either. He didn't go out of his way to dissociate himself from anything.

EVERSON: No. But the epithet *neo-Romantic* first got pinned on me there, in that review. I do feel I am a new-Romantic. I think it's a valid categorization of where I'm at—the restoration of what the Romantics thought to achieve intellectually at the beginning of the nineteenth century, and to close off from the excessive rationalism of the previous century. After the Elizabethans, it's the greatest period in English literature. And maybe, in some ways, the full coming of age of English literature, because you get Blake and then the big bang, Wordsworth and after him, Coleridge, Shelley and finally Keats, to round out. It's going to take even the Elizabethans some doing to match in specific gravity what was going on there.

HOLDER: That's true. And yet it occurs to me when you name those names in chronological order that there's a muting at work there. We go from Blake, who is more like you in the high ritual, you know, prophetic voice gone to a very beautiful whisper of Keats. That's maybe how those things ran their course, and Thomas was maybe a resurfacing of that impulse in English poetry.

EVERSON: Just as Romanticism began the nineteenth century, so Modernism began the twentieth century. The triumph of science was complete by the end of the nineteenth century, and this triumph forced the movement to accept it, whereas the Romantics revolted against precisionism as it was dawning back then. But with the beginning of the twentieth century, you found the Modernist movement attempting to accept the scientific purview of reality and work with instead of against it.

HOLDER: So stream of consciousness is almost the new psychology in literature, the Freudian, and so on . . .

EVERSON: Exactly.

HOLDER: And as an example of what you're saying?

EVERSON: But you see, along comes Einstein and by the twenties he'd been verified and the scientific purview of the hardcore Newtonian scientism was completely overturned, and it happened at the time of the inception of the Modernist movement.

HOLDER: So the Einsteinian upheaval or sort of revolution, certainly, had its impact.

EVERSON: I think the first of that comes in the neo-Romantic movement with Dylan Thomas and the Apocalyptics. What happened was, in the forties, the triumph of the New Criticism, and this held good toward the middle of the next decade, the fifties. And then the Romantic continuation with the Beat Generation picked up on open form and the other aspects.

HOLDER: And yet Jeffers probably actually came closer to understanding all that scientific development than most poets, didn't he? He was actually a scientifically educated man.

EVERSON: But his views were crystallized before the Einsteinian upheaval.

HOLDER: The theory of relativity and all that. That's instructive, actually it's not to the point, but the only other place I've seen your name linked with Dylan Thomas consistently is that you succeeded him as a great performer of poetry.

EVERSON: As a platform performer.

HOLDER: I wonder if you have any thoughts on the state of that aspect of the art; I don't see anybody around that's doing the kind of thing that you were doing. Wonder why that is—the charismatic, I guess, is probably not as healthy as it once was.

EVERSON: I developed my platform style when I was in the Order, and it was around the image of the monk that I was able to do that, to polarize that much. When I left the Order, I didn't have the same channel, I don't quite know how to say it. Something shifted when I changed persona.

HOLDER: Well, maybe you can get back to that. Still, somehow you explored the very fact of the charismatic role. And Ginsberg I think probably did that too. Maybe that's the most that you have in common in some ways, although his role is obviously more of a Jewish prophetic persona.

EVERSON: I wonder if that's true. I wish it were more so. I rather feel that Buddhism—it seems to me that—maybe there's a dichotomy there that's troubling.

HOLDER: With *Howl* I think, the howl, the *Kaddish*.

EVERSON: His great poems.

HOLDER: And his turn to Buddhism has militated a bit against the charismatic aspect. Now he's more mellow—Allen with the harmonium, who is a wonderful person we all love. And I guess that brings us back to this Buddhism thing. Certainly the back to the land impulse, the Dionysian going through the whole counter culture and all that. And the next thing you knew, everybody was moving out and trying to buy cheap land and learn how to churn their own butter, or whatever, things that I think pretty much everybody was doing. And it seemed that the Buddhism had a lot to do with it and the people and that impulse was in some way involved, certainly for Snyder, who's very successfully finding his place with the Buddhist approach, although his is Zen, is it not?

EVERSON: Yes.

HOLDER: It's quite different. I guess it's a mistake to think of Buddhism as monolithic. There are all stripes.

EVERSON: Right. But we have to talk that way just like we have to about Christianity—we have to understand that there is the generality and its variations.

HOLDER: Well, then let me ask you something else. You to me partly represent what I think of as Catholic California. I mean that California certainly until World War II was essentially a Roman Catholic region, the culture, the learning, the teaching, certainly the institutions and all of that were essentially from a legacy of the Spanish influence. One of the things we see emerging in the seventies is another kind of Christianity which is perhaps worth going into a little bit. The things I hear from Wendell Berry make me a little nervous sometimes, kind of restrictive. What thoughts on that, the born again or the kind of evangelical fundamental, or the various aspects that are emerging?

EVERSON: Is he into that?

HOLDER: Well, he's I think more fundamentalist Christian in more of a Southern, a good tradition, a revered American tradition.

EVERSON: I didn't know that about Berry. I'll read him some more. You spoke of California as being culturally Catholic prior to World War II. That may be true of the coast, but the San Joaquin-Sacramento Valley has been an outpost of the Midwest since the Gold Rush. It's the Bible Belt. I have a friend from Missouri who when he gets homesick makes his visit to Turlock.

The Sainthood of the Poet

WILLIAM EVERSON: What I was particularly impressed with about Duncan's death was the prestige he had accumulated over the last years of his life. This was apparent in the acclaim and homage occasioned by his passing. The front page of the *San Francisco Chronicle*, no less. I hadn't expected that. No matter how much coterie-support we poets can count on, we hardly think of ourselves as front page news.

LEE BARTLETT: How did you regard his reputation?

EVERSON: Well, over the years we were always under a cloud from the establishment—disparaged as bohemians, beatniks, and hippies. What seems to have happened is that with the passing of all the great Modernists, and now with the second generation almost gone, Duncan emerges in prime place, with impeccable credentials, as a forward carrier of consciousness, the bearer of those celebrated values.

BARTLETT: So you place Duncan in the Modernist line.

EVERSON: Emphatically. Following Pound, he was a long-time, banner-bearing member, and so built his career. Then in the Faas interview he reversed himself and claimed Romanticism. I think he was probably disassociating himself from the oppressive Post Modernist sweep, which has become so total it chiefly inspired tedium. The truth probably is that in his head he was a Modernist but in his heart of hearts he was a Romanticist. Actually the position isn't all that uncommon. Al Gelpi's new book, *A Coherent Splendor*, is a masterful study of the prolongation of Romanticist values in the marrow of the Modernist bone. However, if the Augustan age can be thought of as the thesis,

Conducted by Lee Bartlett on March 9, 1988, a few weeks after Robert Duncan's death. It appeared originally in *American Poetry* 6:1 (Fall 1988).

due to the establishment of a selfconscious formal English Literature, and the Romantic revolt taken as the antithesis, then Modernism shapes up in a fairly creditable synthesis. I say "fairly creditable" because Gelpi stresses what pains the Modernist masters took to disparage Romanticism. But it doesn't look like we're headed for another thesis, a new Augustan Age. On the contrary, it looks like Robert's instinct will prove correct: full speed ahead to Neo-Romanticism! And he brings a special proclivity to the synthesis, possessing almost a physical disposition in the upshot. I have in mind the childhood accident to his eyes, which left him cross-eyed, bifurcating his vision, making him more aware of accidentals than of essences, or at least more than people of normal vision.

BARTLETT: Can you explain this a little more fully, how this apples to Modernism over against Romanticism?

EVERSON: The thrust of Romanticism was toward the Sublime but by the century's close it had deteriorated to the Banal, giving the new century, our own, the opportunity to emerge as a quasi-classical hegemony called Modernism, in which intangibles like complexity and abstraction, sophisticated technical invention and spatialized form, take precedence over the substantive rendition of the subject in Romanticism's preoccupation with strong emotional resonance of the ideal. Thus Robert's eye injury with its consequent bifurcation put him in line with the aesthetic abstraction that was Modernism's special characteristic. In the same way an artist hooked on drugs may find his imbalance actually increases his penetration into the rarified intersticies of a disordered world. Actually, Ekbert Faas goes into it in the opening pages of his biography of Duncan, giving Robert's own version of his weird vision and goes on to speculate that the eye defect may well have had its positive side effects for a child who was to face multiple alienation as orphan, sexual deviant, and disreputable bohemian.

BARTLETT: Who were Duncan's primary Modernist precursors?

EVERSON: Ezra Pound and William Carlos Williams.

BARTLETT: And Romantics?

EVERSON: Coleridge, I would assume. He wasn't particularly Wordsworthian.

BARTLETT: But you seem to regard the Modernist impulse to hold the primary position.

EVERSON: Without doubt, over the greater part of his career Robert was a torchbearer for the Modernist movement, a front-runner for an entire field that is passing away. Even its sequel, Postmodernism, is finished. The new Romanticism is emerging not out of literature as yet but out of popular culture—namely, the New Age. The literary movement will surface later when the intellectual elite gets accustomed to it, which will take some time, because the snobs did not discover it themselves, so they stand aloof. But they'll come around. Never forget the three stages of an idea: first, it's false, heresy, a lie; second, it may not be false but it is irrelevant; and three, "But we knew that all the time!"

I think Robert knew in his bones that Postmodernism was finished; it was so widespread, so universally followed that it had become predictable. So he started back to the fountainhead. But he did not live long enough to do much with it, and maybe it's just as well he completes his witness with his Modernist achievement intact. His life is more coherent this way.

BARTLETT: What do you think is his greatest attribute?

EVERSON: His visionary insight into the intangible dimension of phenomena constituting reality, and the imagination to register it in graphic figures and potent speech. He had a marvelous sense of imagery, but went too much by aesthetic theory, which seems the Modernist pitfall. Modernist art becomes too esoteric, too abstract. It eschews the common touch, the physical dimension. Duncan was a seeker. His life, his art was a quest. All his experimentation was a search for the will-o'-the-wisp of significance in the welter of circumstance. His whole life was a record of sojourning in one or another branch of aesthetic speculation. When he was working out one of these phases he often wrote poems that were not very interesting. To him they were vital, because the search was vital, and to many Postmodernists they were ingenious and hence commendable; but as poetry they were too abstract. Then when he had the implications worked out he would stop to catch his breath, and the span of his attention would drop below the speculative level to the old inveterate lizard waiting with primordial patience in the heart of man, or in his plexus, his groin. And it will rouse itself, wake from its long hibernation, and slit its skin lids, and sing. And the libidinous song will find his lips, and its thin reptilian croon run down his arm to his fingerling pen, and the song of salvation is born again, the litany of self-renewal is heard again in the world.

> Negroes, negroes, all those princes
> holding cups of rhinoceros bone, make
> magic with my blood. Where beautiful Marijuana
> towers taller than the eucalyptus, turns
> with the lips of night and falls,
> falls downward where as giant Kings we gathered
> and devourd her burning hands and feet, O Moonbar
> thee and Clarinet! Those talismans
> that quickened in their sheltering leaves like thieves,
> those Negroes, all those princes
> holding cups of rhino bone,
> were there to burn my hands and feet,
> divine the limit of the bone and with their magic
> tie and twist me like a rope. I know
> no other continent of Africa more dark than this
> dark continent of my breast.

Once the theoretical problem was worked out he would return to a more integrative poetry. At that point the mood changed from intellectual quest to visceral recovery, maybe for only a single poem, essentially out of sequence, but fundamental.

BARTLETT: Would he have thought of himself as a vatic poet?

EVERSON: That was his pride, his sense of vocation.

BARTLETT: Why would he be so drawn to H.D.?

EVERSON: Her Modernist sensibility. Actually, he was always attracted to intellectual women. Unlike many homosexuals he was not a misogynist. But he had enough of it in him that he wasn't cowed by militant feminists, as I am. I've thanked my stars for his presence more than once, on some university panel when my sexist poetry of an earlier day was in hot water. Sexism and violence coexist in the masculine unconscious, as they do in the feminine, and to get at them you have to expose them. This is best done through your art.

Duncan understood the function of the violence in what I was doing. He would stop an incensed feminist in her tracks with "Have you ever been raped? No? Well, I have. I didn't enjoy it, but I understood what was happening and why. And it was not without its value." As for H. D., her Modernist credentials were impeccable. She was the first Imagist. That in itself would be enough to quicken Duncan's interest. Actually, Gelpi's book is very convincing on H. D. as a vatic poet in her own right. But Duncan's esteem for latterday Postmodernism male poets is harder for me to understand. They had the vatic impulse but lacked the means.

BARTLETT: What about Charles Olson?

EVERSON: I could never grasp what Robert saw in Olson's versecraft, his technique. I never thought of him as all that much of a poet. In his Faas interview, Gary Snyder said much the same thing: how, when Olson made his appearance on the San Francisco scene, he provoked interest as a commentator or historian, rather than as a poet.

BARTLETT: What do you make of Duncan's following Olson back to Black Mountain?

EVERSON: Don't get me wrong. Olson was a wonderful man, a stimulator and an engenderer. One of the truly big men of our time, mentally as well as physically. His enthusiasms were profound and contagious. In a word he had awesome charisma—"heavy karma," as the hippies used to say. But he was not a great writer, a great poet. And this seriously limited his literary theories. For a theory is only as great as the sensibility that conceived it. As Rexroth said, "Charles was deaf." The result is that "composition by field" is the most disastrous doctrine to afflict the art of poetry since the prose poem. It is the alternative formulation of a poet deficient in ear, the achievement of Duncan with the method notwithstanding.

Thus Duncan's support—a poet endowed with extraordinary ear— proved a blessing to the Olsonites. For Duncan they in turn supplied the accreditation, the expert opinion necessary for elitist credibility in esoteric performance. It doesn't really matter that an old neanderthal like me, recalling our salad days back in the forties, favors only a couple of Duncan poems a decade. That is more than enough to keep his name alive in the anthologies of the future. My outrageousness cannot hurt his cause. As to the reason Duncan followed Olson back to Black Mountain, all we can go by is what he said: that it was because of the *Maximus Poems*. He further said that he had always considered himself sui generis, until he read Levertov, Creeley, and Olson. It was then he realized he was part of a group.

BARTLETT: Did you find it strange that he didn't regard himself more a part of a San Francisco or Bay Area group?

EVERSON: Oh, he certainly did! But that was politics, literary politics. At the level of aesthetic affinity and intellectual discernment he stood apart, feeling rather lonely till he found the Olsonites. But like politics the world over, our movement was composed of several strains of disaffiliated, disaffected memberships who had serious differences among ourselves, but due to the wintery climate prevailing in the literary scene, found ourselves banding together against the literary establishment. The various strains can be identified via their sources. Duncan claimed Pound; Ferlinghetti claimed Reverdy; Rexroth claimed Williams; Snyder and Whalen claimed Williams also; Lamantia claimed the Surrealists; I don't recall who Broughton and McClure pointed to; I claimed Jeffers. As long as we were in struggle with the academics and the publicational monopoly, we stuck together; but once we had surfaced enough to let some fresh air in, the fragmentation began.

BARTLETT: It was Duncan's acceptance of and by the Black Mountain group that marked the turning of his career.

EVERSON: Yes. The San Francisco identity had been too circumscribed by local insular limitations to register effectively on the national consciousness, and the Beat explosion as it erupted in the fifties found him unresponsive to its ethos. But the Black Mountain movement escaped these limitations. Donald Allen's breakthrough anthology, *The New American Poetry*, in 1960, led off with Black Mountain, Duncan in strong second place, and his success was instantaneous. His highly evolved improvisational skills enabled him to assimilate the Black Mountain aesthetic perspective in short order, and his three most celebrated books followed one another in rapid succession across the sixties: *The Opening of the Field* in 1961, *Roots and Branches* in 1964, and *Bending the Bow* in 1968. Moreover, his vehement anti-Vietnam War poems were widely applauded. Then in the seventies the San Francisco gay movement began to amass the political clout to command civic recognition for its own. As Duncan had been one of the first gay intellectuals to emerge from the closet in World War II, he soon became a widely respected local celebrity, accounting for the front page exposure in the metropolitan press on the occasion of his death. As I mentioned before, this surprised me, but apparently no one else.

BARTLETT: Did you read Duncan's later work, *Groundwork I* or *II*?

EVERSON: Not really. I tried the first one a few times, found nothing I could get my teeth into, and put it aside. It's a good example of what I said earlier about the experimental work which got even more so as he aged, not surprisingly.

BARTLETT: What about the earlier poetry?

EVERSON: I favor his early maturity where he balanced the two sensibilities, the head and the heart. I quoted "An African Elegy." It is one of the most forceful of Duncan's achievements. Capable of work like that, I wish he had never heard of Black Mountain.

BARTLETT: You got to know Duncan through his friend and co-editor James Cooney in about 1940.

EVERSON: Yes. I had corresponded with Cooney, who had advertised his journal, *The Phoenix*, as being Lawrentian. When Duncan moved to Woodstock to work with Cooney, he saw my letters and wrote me that he liked my poem "Orion," which I had submitted. This started a pretty intense correspondence. I didn't meet him until about a year later. He was hitch-hiking from Bakersfield to Berkeley, and he stopped by in Selma for an afternoon. We lost contact a little during the war.

BARTLETT: Then your friendship resumed in the Bay Area after the war.

EVERSON: Yes. Mary Fabilli, whom I would marry, had been a friend of Robert's for many years. Earlier he had given me a print she had done, which I had hanging on my wall for a good number of years before I met her. When Mary and I got together, it brought me closer into Robert's circle, though I always felt he was a little threatened by our relationship. It was at this point, about 1947 or '48, that I began to become aware of certain competitive strains between Robert and me that hadn't been there before. We were at our closest during that period. Mary would invite him over for dinner fairly often. Sometimes the situation was a little strained. Mary had moved out of her bohemian phase and was finding him hard to take at times; when he became hysterically entertaining and outrageous, and deliberately so, she would suffer a bit, so that I couldn't enjoy it either.

BARTLETT: Did he show you much work during this time?

EVERSON: Our relationship was mainly social, though he showed me a few things. The aesthetic dimension was taken up by the soiree readings around Berkeley. I've always admired Robert as a poet, even though I can't understand a lot of his poetry. I think that his homosexuality and his problem with his vision are the two things that enabled him to handle the Modernist technique with such authority. These gave him an orientation that normal people don't have.

BARTLETT: So he would necessarily carry over these aspects of his daily life into the life of his writing.

EVERSON: Yes. This takes us back to his concentration on accidentals. He grew up looking between things. One eye focused one place, one another, which made him constantly aware of the correspondence between two things. This correspondence became the field wherein he wrote. It became the relevant area so that his whole vocabulary, his whole intonation, his style were all oriented around the visionary duality. One problem with the tangible is that it becomes banal all too soon, and it is this banality that the Modernist seeks to avoid at all costs. He keeps his subject matter low profile and his affect high.

BARTLETT: When you use the term "tangible" what exactly do you mean?

EVERSON: The concreteness of subject matter.

BARTLETT: In your article on Duncan in *Credences* you mention a few reservations about his work.

EVERSON: I think my reservations are more cogent than my acceptances. I thirst for substances and Robert doesn't press the thrust through to the consequence. I'm an incarnationist and I'm often frustrated by his poems. Even in the best work, which is some of the best our age has produced, I want to see him press further into the archetype. When he rounds a poem out it's because for that particular project he's arrived at a satisfactory equation between being and nonbeing.

BARTLETT: Can you think of a particular example of this?

EVERSON: Well, take a poem like "Persephone." That was a very early poem, one that Robert sent me in an early letter. I was always impressed with his capacity to go for broke sexually; he had the forthrightness to be explicit, which very few people did in those days. I was the same, only from a heterosexual standpoint. We fought the critics off back to back. In "Persephone" he has that wonderful phrase, "Spore-spotted

Onan, baldheaded, trickling with seed, / moved among us . . ." It's so graphic that it sends me. But then he goes off into intangibles again. You can't let an insight like that just go by the board. You have to make something with it.

BARTLETT: What do you think of the Ekbert Faas biography, *Young Robert Duncan?*

EVERSON: Terrific. I thought I knew Robert but I found I hardly knew the first thing about him. His incredible early life carries the account. You find yourself marvelling that he survived at all, then that he emerged with intelligence intact. Some of my friends were put off by the fact that English is not Faas's first language, but in my reading that proved a plus. The Europeans bring a more historical and objective biographical perspective to the individual life which effects a kind of cultural canonization that Robert's heroic courage, intrepid eccentricity, and aesthetic integrity can sustain. The stiff, rather formal diction, detachedly unshockable, puts its painful burden in benign perspective. I predict the book will prove to be one of the cardinal elements in Duncan's posthumous literary reputation.

BARTLETT: How did Duncan regard it?

EVERSON: When I finished reading it I sat down and wrote Robert a letter intensely reaffirming all our friendship had meant to me. He told me later that the letter arrived at a decisive moment for him. The book itself had depressed him (as well it might) and he tended to fault the author for that. But after my letter he took heart, and I know that in his next reading at Davis he brought the book along for sale with his poetry texts. I rank it among the top two or three literary biographies I have read.

BARTLETT: Faas devotes much of his narrative to Duncan's homosexuality. Do you feel his homosexuality influenced his work beyond its specific subject matter and imagery?

EVERSON: Absolutely. The Apollonian tension in the work comes directly out of his homosexuality. I used to regard him as a Dionysian because of the dithyrambic sensibility, yet he points to the prophetic side of Apollo as his archetype, at least in conversation with me. He formalizes his homosexuality through the Apollonian/Dionysian equation, identifying with Apollo and rejecting Dionysus. This is the basis of his work.

BARTLETT: When did you discover he was gay?

EVERSON: It was implicit in the work he sent and confirmed when he was living with Hamilton and Mary Tyler in Berkeley in the 1940s. They were good friends of mine. Either they told me, or maybe it was George Leite, editor of *Circle*.

BARTLETT: Did this change your attitude towards him?

EVERSON: I recognized it soon as I met him, but interestingly I never let it interfere with our friendship. For some reason it didn't threaten me. His disposition is so generous that my masculinity didn't feel compromised. I never needed to make any kind of adjustment. Whoa! Wait a minute. I just remember he made a pass at me once. It was just after my release as a conscientious objector. I was staying a few days with Lee Watkins in Berkeley, before heading for Sonoma and the Tylers. Robert dropped by one afternoon with a poem he was writing. We discussed it at length. The next morning he showed up unannounced and handed me a note. It contained maybe three or four lines of explicit fellatio, and I protested, "Robert, it's too explicit! It will overbear the poem. You've got to come up with something less sensational!" He took the note back and left without saying a word. I then realized it was a pass. Nothing like that ever happened again, but we did have a strange and intense relationship at times.

BARTLETT: Meaning?

EVERSON: As I explained in my *Talking Poetry* interview, for example, when I gave a reading at the Bancroft (or rather at Wheeler Hall *for* the Bancroft) to celebrate their acquisition of my archive, Duncan was in the audience with two young gay poets. I got a standing ovation, but Robert, who was sitting just ahead of me four or five rows back, had been put off by James D. Hart's introduction, which he more or less laughed through. As everyone rose to their feet, Robert declined to stand. I understood this, though I was hurt by it. That was probably the hardest day in our forty-year friendship.

BARTLETT: What did you make of his decision not to publish for fifteen years?

EVERSON: I thought it was suicide, but it turned out that he knew what he was doing. He emerged from that silence increased in prestige and in purpose.

BARTLETT: When was the last time you saw Duncan?

EVERSON: Three years ago. He came down here with our mutual friend Al Gelpi to spend the afternoon. He had already undergone treatment for his kidney problem and had his portable dialysis machine with him. He had never been here before. We really didn't talk about anything consequential, but it was a good and healing visit. Actually, the healing had come several years earlier, at a conference on the San Francisco Renaissance at U. C. San Diego. It was a good conference, with lively exchange during the day sessions, and the night readings well attended by the public—though with the inevitable ego trips and partisan rhetoric. On my night to read my Parkinson affliction was acting up, and I just stood at the lectern to cover my shaking; I read for an hour, just a straight reading with no pyrotechnics. When I had finished, Duncan came up, his face glowing, his crossed eye shining, and said in hushed tones, "My God, Bill, you cut through all the shit!" I am blessed in my life to have had the friendship of a great man.

BARTLETT: In closing can you speak of Duncan's death, how you saw it in terms of his life?

EVERSON: Apparently he died utterly at peace, in the arms of his housemate and longtime companion, Jess Collins, a very edifying death, given the sensationalism of his early years. I think of him as protected by his Muse, living through the great San Francisco AIDS epidemic of the 1980s, untouched by it all. Actually, beauty as a property of divinity is an ancient philosophical tenet of both the East and West traditions, and in our time Nicholas Berdyaev, the great Russian existentialist thinker, made a strong case for the sanctity of the great artist. When I think of Duncan's invincible courage, aesthetic integrity, and purity of vision, the dross falls away and I experience him again in his essential being, his beautiful soul confirmed in the poet's own degree of sainthood.

On Robinson Jeffers:
The Power of the Negative

KEVIN HEARLE: In the appendix of *Archetype West* you have a letter to Robert Hawley in which you say that having read Joaquin Miller's *Life Amongst the Modocs*, you're going to have to revise your notion of what the archetype is, in order to put social reform at the center of the archetype, and that you also need to reconsider Jeffers based on that.

WILLIAM EVERSON: I was thrown by Miller's account—overwhelmed. Having written my own book and then to come on that! It was like a revelation to me then. I thought I'd have to do my work all over again. It hasn't carried quite through that dimension in my years of reflection following. I don't feel the way I expressed it there; although I think that my analysis was true. I think that "on the archetype," as the saying goes the inception point is crucial. What did I call the element that was at the center?

HEARLE: Social reform.

EVERSON: Jeffers is at the center of that in his religion, his Inhumanist philosophy. It would be the same as a prophet of old, an Isaiah, who indicts in order to correct, and so it is with Jeffers.

HEARLE: In *Archetype West* you say that in some cases one is awed before the terrible dehumanization of archetypal power, and you go on to say that Jeffers is sometimes guilty of it when he is angered politically. What things angered him politically?

Conducted by Kevin Hearle for *Quarry West* 27 (1990).

EVERSON: World War II. He was ferocious. He wrote some of the most incredible anti-war poems. In my introduction to *The Double Axe*, I take that up. I think Jeffers is an interesting case because he shows how a poet can be politically active and at the same time true to his art. Usually, if you become involved in political activity, your art suffers, because it's so involving, so tremendously exciting and consequential. Life and death is at stake in politics, and freedom is at stake, security. It becomes titanic, and the poet struggles as in a whirlwind. Jeffers's work suffered from it, but it was good that it happened when it did because he had got his vision established before World War II. He repeated himself so much in his various books that he was beginning to encounter critical objection. So this in a sense was a lifesaver to him. It gave him a subject that he hadn't treated before, and although nobody liked them, I think in the overall view of the man, they're going to be some of the most compelling things that he wrote. His theory had been well worked out, but this gave him application, and he leaped at the chance.

HEARLE: One question that's asked is why he chose to leave some of the poems out of *Double Axe*, or why according to certain accounts, those poems were suppressed by his editor at Random House. Do you have any thoughts on what Jeffers's role might have been in the suppression of poems that were originally a part of that manuscript?

EVERSON: It's hard to say. Nobody has any real angle on Jeffers's taste in regard to his own poetry—what he thought was the best and why he left things out that he did. It could've been prudence, that he thought that he went too far, like that poem we published in UCSC at the Lime Kiln Press, "Tragedy Has Obligation," in which he invokes Hitler to not go down like a bankrupt stockbroker . . . But he never typed that poem up. Usually when he typed a poem, he was satisfied with it, that it had the energy and succinctness to serve the impulse that produced it, which is a convenient way of looking at his own opus. I published that poem even though it didn't exist in typescript. I thought he might have mislaid it, or it got hidden under his other papers or something. It's a fine poem. I didn't have any qualms about publishing it. Some might find it objectionable in that it seems to glorify Hitler in defeat. Maybe he just got it off his chest, and that was enough for him. But I'm glad it survived. His rhetoric is superb.

HEARLE: In *Fragments of an Older Fury*, you specifically devote a chapter to defending Jeffers from the attack of being a fascist, by suggesting that an artist must be allowed that freedom in the aesthetic realm to choose possibilities which in the political realm would be monstrous. What then is the proper relation between art and reality?

EVERSON: The function of the artist is to manifest the possible. He does this by respecting what moves him and honoring it by establishing it in aesthetic form, which is the universal principle. He can take bad political ideas. The reason why it's necessary for him to do this is because culturally it's a trying on of the ideas that are evoked. In one point of view, it's a trying on for size of a given political equation.

HEARLE: Was Barclay in *Women at Point Sur* such a trying on for size? Was he a certain sort of experiment then in the dangers of discipleship, the dangers of a messiah?

EVERSON: Precisely. I think that's one of the best examples I could point to.

HEARLE: Then would you read Barclay as in some sense a sort of prophetic vision of what was to become of the world ten years later? Is this a proto-Hitler sort of figure?

EVERSON: No, Barclay wasn't a politician, but Hitler was a consummate politician. The main thing about Barclay is that although he is Jeffers's version of what his ideas would lead to in the hands of a madman; in the affirmation of his aesthetic, he's saying, this has tremendous appeal, versifying the power of attention. He's honoring it by working it out in his own soul; he was getting that he had talked like a prophet, that he spoke like a prophet, and so he must have been tempted to evangelize and to appeal to cult. And he was horrified of it at the same time, for himself. I think he was compelled to see the way we do when we appeal to any ecstatic technique. When we appeal to an ecstatic technique, we are seeking a transcendent point from things that are disturbing us or moving us, and the best thing about art is its capacity to do that, like the Wagnerian operas. I say in the book you mentioned that Hitler does not invalidate Wagner. Wagner wrote over his own head—he took some mythical source in the Germanic tradition, which is an ecstatic creating device, and he transcends it by elevating it to supradimensions. Lawrence does the same thing in his Mexican novels. I think Jeffers was almost frightened by *Point Sur*. I think he found there elements so strong in himself that he knew he's only recognized dimly before, and repressed because his conscience had chosen life in his religion, his pantheism, and his Inhumanism. Barclay begins to walk, begins to generate power, and Jeffers responds to it. To me, it's his masterpiece. I'm the only one that thinks that.

HEARLE: Although you call it his masterpiece, in *Archetype West*, you say that Jeffers is best in his shorter poems. That's certainly not a short poem.

EVERSON: No, that's his longest one. It seems to be a contradiction, but not really. The lyrics are not as echoing. It's the view of all the critics that the shorter poems are the best. I can say it in one side of my mouth at the same time I can say the other. It is a flawed poem, but it is a masterpiece.

HEARLE: You don't quite believe it.

EVERSON: It's pretty hard to see anything better than his short poems. Some of those short poems have never been equalled by anybody who ever wrote.

HEARLE: Any ones in particular?

EVERSON: "Night," "Continent's End," and some of the *Descent to the Dead* poems. Oh, there are scores of them. I don't say that they're all better than anything else ever written, but they're poems that can compete with any poem ever written or stand up to them without blushing, which is about all you can expect of a poet, isn't it? But in *Point Sur*, he touched the cosmic; he took the ecstasy of it—aesthetic ecstasy—to the breaking point. It's so consummate and erotic. In my new Stanford book on Jeffers as a religious figure, I show he was profoundly preoccupied with sex. We don't know how far he went in his youth, but sex was one of the things that he never really came to terms with. His nature was so passionate.

HEARLE: When you say he never came to terms with sex, do you mean with the sexual act, or with the difference of genders?

EVERSON: The sexual act. It was a disruptive force in his life, and it was so to the end. When his biography is finally written, it will be seen that it was one of the things that nearly came to unseating him and spoiling his whole witness.

HEARLE: Are you referring in part to Una's suicide attempt after his affair in Santa Fe?

EVERSON: Yes, I'm thinking of that. But there were others after that.

HEARLE: And was Una's suicide attempt a disruptive force in his poetry as well as his life?

EVERSON: No. When he said that she was more like a hawk than a human being, he was speaking after that incident. But he never did waver in his adhesion to Una. Even though he had affairs, he never celebrated another woman the way he celebrated her. He has an untitled poem, "Whom should I write for, dear, but for you? Two years have passed, / The wound is bleeding—new and will never heal. / I used to write for you, and give you the poem / When it was written, and wait easily your verdict . . . but now to whom? . . . as for the precious human consciousness, / Yours has been most precious to me, not mine, not theirs." That was an unpublished poem before. It's not one of his best.

HEARLE: At one point in one of your books you use the word "vulturine" to describe mothers in Jeffers's poems. In general, aside from Una, how would you characterize the relationship between women in Jeffers's work and in his life?

EVERSON: That's heavy. Heavy karma. The people reviewing my book on Jeffers as a religious figure have found fault with some of my observations about Jeffers's relation to women. I'm a little bit amazed by this—a little bit bewildered. Jeffers had a fierce anti-feminist side to him. His nature seems so highly engaged towards women, as any poet tends to be; it's the feminine that in the unconscious is the muse. But when it becomes excessive, then it builds up its own hostility, and the gender equation—man's hostility to women. There's a hostility to that which binds him, a fear of it. Jeffers always spoke in extremes. It's a great virtue of his art. He has a capacity to go for broke like nobody else, and he'll master all the resources of his technique, all that he knows about the language, all that he knows about classical literature. You see it in "Tamar." "Tamar" is his first breakthrough poem. I localize it at the death of his mother. His relation to her was so intense. He dealt with incest in "Tamar". His first facing into it. He destroys her, and he has her destroy the family and the house. But once again, just like he would in *Point Sur*, the intensity belies the disapproval. He said he wrote *Point Sur* because some people had taken "Tamar" to be a document of licentiousness or a romantic glamorization of the licentious. So he decided to take the figure of Barclay and strip everything down to the naked brutality of his violations. Just like he did with "Tamar," the aesthetic is saying this is great, although the moral judgement says this is evil, this is wrong.

HEARLE: And the same would be true of California in "Roan Stallion"?

EVERSON: Yes.

HEARLE: And perhaps in *Medea*, at the end of his career.

EVERSON: Yes, he obviously rebelled in that.

HEARLE: Speaking of his moral judgment rebelling, in *Fragments of an Older Fury*, you wrote of Jeffers, "He is surely one of the great poets of original sin." Are there any specific examples you can give of that?

EVERSON: Well, his indictments of humanity. He takes it as a mistake, an error in the evolutionary process, a bad turn taken somewhere along the line which produced a species that was cunning and malignant, that was wretched from the start.

HEARLE: So then the original sin is not in the garden, it was the very occurrence of humanity.

EVERSON: Yes.

HEARLE: And would that be specifically European humanity? After all, Jeffers the pantheist appropriated Native American shamanism in his work. Was his critique of humanity, then, like that of Joaquin Miller, primarily a critique of European humanity?

EVERSON: I think that's a defensible position, because his philosophy, the philosophical shape of his mind, was shaped by European thought. His value judgments were formed in late childhood and early adolescence in Europe by European masters, and when he speaks of Western society as triumphantly evil, he's undoubtedly talking about the society that we are simply the extension of.

HEARLE: How do you think Jeffers uses Carmel and the Big Sur area as a retreat, as a place?

EVERSON: It's like the Garden of Eden before the Fall.

HEARLE: Except that there are people.

EVERSON: Adam and Eve! The thing that the place did for him was that it crystallized his pantheism. It's so extreme in its beauty and titanic scale, in its majesty, that it enabled him to conceive of a humanity-divorcing symbol, a humanity-reducing symbol. It enabled him to conceive of and articulate a God that was greater than any human being had conceived before. It took modern science and what it exposed about the cosmos to formulate a view of God that couldn't have been done earlier.

HEARLE: And yet, in your meditations on Regionalism at U.C. Santa Cruz in 1974, you suggested that there are certain places—Mt. Shasta, Big Sur—that are in some sense too powerful, too intense, and that in a way Jeffers's own work shows this—that he got too close to it, that he was finally possessed by it, and that this in some sense rigidified and limited his vision. In what way was Big Sur, as you say, too much of the sacred?

EVERSON: I couldn't say it any better than you have. But it's important because it makes you understand him. The scale—the factor of scale, of dimension—is so intense, that it does cause a dwarfing, and it's obviously true that it has a limit on his total effect. In the end it was limiting to him if not as a human being, then as an artist.

HEARLE: Is this perhaps especially true because he chose not to have disciples? And is it a failing that he insisted on solitude in the face of such power?

EVERSON: I think it's obvious that one has to suggest that. I don't think he loses stature by it, because it was necessary for him to get out. It was necessary for him in the history of consciousness to articulate the implications of modern science, and especially the sciences of physics and astronomy.

HEARLE: The fact that he was overpowered by the sacred aspect of Big Sur, is that why you praise him for what you call his reduction in his perspective above violence, in poems such as "Apology for Bad Dreams"?

EVERSON: Yes. I say yes to that question.

HEARLE: Yet you criticize John Steinbeck's use of distance. How is Jeffers's distancing different than Steinbeck's?

EVERSON: Steinbeck is one of the Naturalists; he doesn't have the religious sense. In *Tortilla Flat* the violence tends to be anti-social and ethical. In Jeffers, violence was never ethical; it was always religiously sourced. That was why he could be so haphazard with it, lavish with it. He could throw it across the sky like the comets of the galaxy. He could make it burn purer.

HEARLE: You use violence as a term in most of your essays. What exactly do you mean by archetypal violence?

EVERSON: I localize it in nature, in the world of change, in the world of becoming, as opposed to the world of being. In the world of being, everything is proportionate. In the world of becoming, given the material world, things are of a mutual identity but a mutual antagonism, in all entities—and in the process of change, the factor of violence is inevitable. What Jeffers taught me as a poet was that if you go to the heart of the violence, you come to the operating point of change, of evolution. And he taught me to be obsessed by that point, as both he and I are. We solve it in different ways, but I didn't solve it until I became a Christian. I found it on the cross. Jeffers repudiated Christianity. It was easy to do given his phase in modern consciousness. But he was pre-Einsteinian, and Einstein has given us a different view of the cosmos. Einstein had his vision around 1907. It was scientifically verified in 1919, causing D. H. Lawrence to exclaim, "We're very grateful to the professor for changing the model of the universe from a celestial machine to a swarm of bees!" It means that absurdity is opened up again. I call Einstein the patron saint of the occult, and although he doesn't necessarily verify the occult, he certainly renders it possible.

HEARLE: If Jeffers is Newtonian rather than Einsteinian, does that mean in some sense he came too late? How does that change his relationship to our time?

EVERSON: His world was that of nineteenth-century science. That was what he knew. I think it explains a lot about him, his obsolescent view of the cosmos. It enabled him to focus, and to achieve his greatness of expression and the violence that he wrestles with as the operative force in nature and reality. It is that aspect of Jeffers which is easily criticized and which the critics have taken such liberty in doing. What I'm trying to say is that nineteenth-century science is part of his rigidity, his insularity, his contempt. He's always verging into contempt, and then having to apologize. No, not apologize, but to modify.

HEARLE: Do you think that his own rigidity has anything to do with his massive need for violence, or his expression of it?

EVERSON: I think there's a connection there.

HEARLE: In your latest book you refer to Jeffers as a prophet. Is there any particular incident in either his biography or his poetry that you see as the point where he receives his vision?

EVERSON: I think it was the discovery of the galactic system in 1924, because right after that, or not too long after that, Vasquez—Onorio Vasquez—in *The Women at Point Sur* he goes into that vision, into the scale of the cosmos where we look at the sky and see the Milky Way and know that already each one of those is a star. The cosmos themselves, which everyone knows, is a galaxy. This is so stupendous a thing; I think so confirming to his Newtonian sense of scale, and his Newtonian sense of the cosmos as a mechanism instead of as a fluidity.

HEARLE: How much of a role did his brother the astronomer have?

EVERSON: A great deal. He kept him close to astronomy, to the movement as an intellectual discipline. He respected his brother. He himself almost became a scientist when he was at USC. I think it is a blessing the way Jeffers enlarged his scale. He might not have had to do that if he hadn't had his brother the astronomer there to keep him abreast of all those movements.

HEARLE: Well, if his brother was keeping him abreast of all of his movements, wouldn't he have left being Newtonian and become Einsteinian?

EVERSON: No. Cosmic ontology is too complex, too abstract for the immediate transmission of knowledge. All branches of knowledge were stunned by the sudden intrusion of this new occult.[1]

HEARLE: You say that Jeffers was afraid of love. Do you think he was afraid of the occult also?

EVERSON: I think there's a remarkable lack of fear in Jeffers—there's that residual fear there, but nobody who was afraid of the occult could write "Hungerfield." I think it was his religious sense that saw him through that poem—the religious sense that enabled him to posit the occult—to use the occult phenomenon in poems without having to explain it in terms of Newtonian theory.

HEARLE: Going back to Jeffers as a religious poet, you say that Jeffers is the pessimistic negative to Whitman's optimistic. If Jeffers was a pessimist, and felt that humanity was a blight upon the earth, who was he writing for?

EVERSON: He was writing for the religious content of humanity—the universal religious instinct. That's who I write for.

HEARLE: Doesn't the fact of writing to someone, especially if you're going to indict, imply a belief in the possibility of change, or at least in some motion towards the perfectibility of the species?

EVERSON: Yes, that's why he was so eloquent, because he knew that humanity's not going to do it but that it's possible for the individual here and now to do it. "I've done it myself," he said.

HEARLE: Do you think that he succeeded completely in that?

EVERSON: Up to the limits of his vision, I do. I think he was less satisfied that he'd done all he could upon the matter. I think he was waiting there the night the snow came; he woke up in the middle of the night and looked out and saw that snow on the ground which he'd never seen in all the years that he'd been there. I think he said, "This is it, I'm free to go."

HEARLE: Would it be safe of say that you're a more optimistic poet than Jeffers?

EVERSON: Oh, by far. He's more of a cosmic poet than I am. I'm a poet of the interior self. Where he took the outer cosmos for his domain, I took the inner cosmos for mine. I apply some of the principles of his poetics to the subjectivity of the inner spirit. I could become a Christian for that reason, without failure to my spiritual father.

HEARLE: What parts of his poetics were not adaptable?

EVERSON: I think they're all adaptable; it's invested in the language. The clue I got from him was how reality was, a clue to how the problem is solved in the expression. The sense of violence that he saw in the cosmos was celebrated there. I tend to carry that with more authority to the subjective, or maybe back to the subjective. I tend to share his preoccupation with sex and violence from the interior level, where he never writes of it for himself. I don't have any fears of being imitative of Jeffers, though. For the first five years I was imitative of Jeffers, but sooner or later there comes a time when you have to part company with your master. This generally comes when in the course of your life you come upon a problem that he didn't have to solve; then you're forced to go beyond his teaching, and this is the point of pure . . . they speak of jumping through your shadow. This is where you have to do that. He found it in Emerson. I found it in him.

Note

1. Actually, it takes a couple of centuries for a deeply integrated culture to assimilate a major breakthrough in its ontological point of view. Until Copernicus had been absorbed, a Newton could not emerge. And until the Newton had been assimilated, an Einstein could not show. Science focuses

the linear ideation of cause and effect to achieve its objectives, but Einstein broached a universe of vast synchronicity which turns out to be, in spiritual terms, an abyss of total Love. Nor can we evade it by dismissing the occult. Jeffers's antipathy towards twentieth-century relativity ran deep, as shown by a late poem, "To Kill In War Is Not Murder" (*The Beginning and the End* [NY: Random House, 1963], p. 28) in which he argues against asking the weapons-technicians for their reasons, declaring "They know nothing. They would break up in neo-Christian jargon like Einstein."

Talking With Matthew Fox

MATTHEW FOX: Bill, I was struck by what you said when we met—that you didn't think you would live long enough to hear a theologian who would say the things I say. Would you elaborate on your comment that the millennium is bringing us, poet and theologian, together?

WILLIAM EVERSON: I am impressed by the way your purely theological analysis of the transition now underway between the second and third millenniums after the epiphany of Christ corresponds to the astrological model of the transition between the Piscean and Aquarian Ages also underway.

You speak of the first two millennia as being characterized by the spirit of St. Augustine. For the third millennium you propose Eckhart, a harbinger of early Renaissance renewal, whose time has arrived. A corresponding dichotomy is predicated by astrologers in the passage between the Age of Pisces and the Age of Aquarius. Some feel the whole Piscean Age was stained in the monastic vat of the Dark Ages, that penitential nullity engrossed it, that a joylessly intense introversion oppressed it. Pisces is ruled by Neptune who symbolizes the negative aspect of the spirit.

Now we are moving into another time. The expectations are much more hedonistic. Your use of "extrovert meditation" and "realized eschatology"—these are things we can expect to be the mode of the coming millennium.

Of course, as a Catholic, I was born an Augustinian. St. Augustine converted me. I read his *Confessions* and became a great agonizer. When I read *The Coming of the Cosmic Christ* you didn't stress that contra-Augustine pitch. But I next read *Original Blessing* and found it a more

Originally appeared in *Creation* (Spring 1989) as "William Everson: Native Mystic and Poet Prophet."

nuts and bolts book, almost a handbook for Creation-centered Spirituality, whereas the *Cosmic Christ* is more visionary. I ran into the cleavage point when I hit *Original Blessing* and got your views on what we were coming out of: Augustine's original sin and redemption motif. As I say, I began that way, but with my breakthrough in the summer of 1956, I found Meister Eckhart and Carl Jung.

My Augustinian emphasis, the fruit of my conversion, took me into the Dominican Order and held sway for seven years, growing progressively more restrictive. It came to a head in that summer of 1956 when I experienced a breakthrough from the unconscious. This precipitated me back into the realm of instinct and I turned to depth psychology to see my way through, ending up with Jung. It was Jung who turned me on to Meister Eckhart.

This upheaval, or *nikyia* as it's called, coincided with the call to go out from the monastery, where I had immured myself for the past five years, to resume my appearances on the poetry-reading circuit. With the Beat Generation, this was just then coming into vogue nationally, breaking my conventual introversion and compelling me to create an effective platform persona. Eckhart proved invaluable. He rescued me from the inhibitive, guilt-ridden preoccupation of my strait-laced convert's rigor and placed in my hands the weaponry of an enlightened spirituality. I say "weaponry" advisedly, for it served to transform the poetry reading from a set-piece recital to a spiritual encounter. The Eckhartian principle of a "realized eschatology," the existential immediacy of the divine "isness," the superlative preeminence of the unquenchably vital NOW! and the sacredness of silence, which would become my trademark as a speaker—using silence as a spiritual weapon, a living blade. This was not a gimmick. In the Eckhartian realism it became an authentic mode of existence, springing spontaneously into being on the platform. As the preacher is transformed in the pulpit, *by the pulpit*, from the simple servant of the people to the voice of the living God, so the poet on platform, by the platform possessed, is likewise transformed, likewise transported, likewise divinized.

Among the listeners, all were not edified—and not only among the squares. At my first reading in New York the Beat poet Ed Sanders left the hall muttering, "I came to dig this cat's poetry, but I didn't ask him to mess around with my soul." Sorry! The poet on the platform, like the preacher in the pulpit, is helpless before the exigence of God. As Meister Eckhart recognized: "If anyone understood this sermon I wish him well, but even if no listener came I would have had to preach it to the poor box."

FOX: Your art—poetry reading—was becoming your art-as-meditation.

EVERSON: My extroverted side began to develop on platform where I would still remain in my own solitude and introversion, but just bringing the audience to an absolute still point—silence. That's where I learned to use the silence as a contemplative factor. And here is where the Eckhartian "repose" comes in.

FOX: You talk about these experiences as "encounter." Is that another word for that silence?

EVERSON: It's a threshold of it—you "encounter" to reach it. As long as things are normative and quotidian, nothing happens. It has to be confrontation, an encounter. And that's why I'd often use the negative. It tests the audience out. I would say, "There's a positive and negative in this group and I'm going to make a separation. Some of you are coming with me and some of you aren't. You've got to know the difference."

FOX: That's great. Jakob Boehme writes in one of his books, "If you could get anything out of this book, you know, you've got to change your ways, otherwise, don't read the book. It would be bad for you." I sense that your experience of being on the platform was a contemplative/mystical/prophetic act because you were disturbing our whole culture—if they listened to what you say. What is the poet's role in our culture at this time of a millennial change? We can't make it without the poet, can we?

EVERSON: The poet provides the blaze of consciousness. This is the fire that he casts on earth. It's part of the confrontation, the cutting edge. Robert Frost says poetry is a way of taking life by the throat. The poetaster takes it by the finger.

FOX: Why is it that America has birthed a Walt Whitman and a William Everson? What is it about America that insists upon the erotic in mysticism? Have the Europeans lost it?

EVERSON: It inheres in the scale of the American landscape. The tension, the strain in the archetype exposes the unconscious, and the erotic root of the psyche is released from its collective repression and begins to sing. The erotic images spring spontaneously forward to match the equation between the contesting scales of psyche and landscape. The European landscape is more assimilable to cultural recourse, and therefore the erotic is more socially conformist, whereas the American erotic component is more primal, the libido itself more animal oriented. Thus the American Indian modeled his fertility rites on the mating of the beasts he regarded as his ancestors. This elemental libido is more primal in Jeffers than either Whitman or myself.

The fact that the poet can project from the creative unconscious images corresponding to the intuitions of aboriginal predecessors in the same landscape lets us know that we can trust our attributions as clue to the mystery of what we create.

FOX: The theme for this issue of *Creation* is "freeing the imagination." You take up the theme of salvation and its meaning in your writings. Does salvation have something to do with freeing the imagination?

EVERSON: I think so. It's faith that frees the imagination—because it enables you to risk and it gives you the fundamental platform from which you project and imagination lures you. Faith is certitude in existence. I think mysticism proves this. It is the mystic's faith which enables him to transcend quotidian consciousness. We don't think of mystics as being imaginative and that's why it was a little startling when I said that. Being both a poet and a believer, what faith does for mysticism it does for art.

Many aesthetic philosophers think of the aspiration of the artist as secondary to that of the contemplative mystic. They see it in terms of ascending grades, but the artist is closer to the prophet than he is to the mystic—the prophet takes over where the mystic stops. The mystic is ascent; the prophet is descent. Descent is reversal, an about-face. And this is where faith has to come in.

FOX: Coming down from the mountain and disturbing the peace? Rabbi Heschel says the prophet is "one who interferes." You're saying the artist interferes.

EVERSON: Insofar as he is a prophet, yes.

We tend to deny the imagination to the mystic because we think that would confuse him. We think if we can just clear the mind and the imagination until they are blank, the soul and spirit could commune with God without interference from the psyche. But it doesn't work that way. Eckhart's realized eschatology comes in here—the imagination becomes transfused with this revelation and challenges. God is consciousness itself.

FOX: What's the most prophetic thing you've done in your poetry?

EVERSON: *River-Root.*

FOX: Why?

EVERSON: No one had ever done that before. And the reason I say that is because I believe it could not have been written much earlier—the situation of sexual consciousness was too constrictive to permit such explicitness to be evocatively rendered. I think the breakover point culturally was the invention of the Pill in the early 1950s. With this invention, humanity finally recognized that it could come to terms with the sexual problem. Before the Pill the primacy of procreation in the sex life was so overwhelming that it had to be repressed, placed under taboo, strictly confined to the married state with enforced ignorance of its dynamic mechanism, because of the problem of responsibility for the fate of children. The sex act could only be implied in legitimate expression. The explicit was confined to the pornographic and sold under the counter. With the invention of contraception in the modern world the taboo was softened and we began to get fairly explicit renditions, but there was nothing like amnesty. Not until the invention of the Pill was mankind's apprehension sufficiently relaxed to feel safe with spontaneity.

The other thing about *River-Root* is the religious dimension, or rather, the synthesis between sexual explicitness and religious awe, essentially religious chastity. As long as sexual explicitness was confined to the obscene, religious awe was rigorously excluded from its presentation. By the fact that I had undergone conversion seven years before, and had maintained a rigorous chastity for five of those years as a monk in a monastery, I retained the purity of my baptism. But in the breakthrough of the summer of 1956 the unconscious invaded, and sexual licentiousness in all its pornographic explicitness emerged. My instinct was to forge a reconciliation between the two factors. What *River-Root* did was to exercise the mental need for explicitness with religious awe that was the gift of chastity. The Song of Songs was the model historically, but the factor of explicitness was not yet achieved.

The *Song of Songs* is not a descriptive work; it's a chant; whereas *River-Root* is almost clinical in its description, though I set it in a religious context, which protects it from the excoriation of the profane.

FOX: *River-Root* is like a vision or an eschatology of what sexuality *could* be.

EVERSON: Yes, you've got it.

FOX: Why is it important at this time in history that sexuality be recaptured as a source of eschatology?

EVERSON: Because it's the most fulfilling experience. It is the most fulfilling because it centers the entire libido, the very life-drive, which in its highest registration is love, on the core of the soul's quintessence—man and woman, fused in ecstasy, the first magnitude of consciousness.

FOX: What is it that religion offers affirmatively to an erotic mysticism?

EVERSON: Stability of faith.

FOX: So that the imagination can truly be free in that context?

EVERSON: Exactly. That's why casual sex is so destructive. It can't sustain the reality that it promises.

FOX: What I appreciate about *River-Root* is its cosmic sense. You name the context in which real love takes place as nothing less than the cosmos. You keep going back to the river. Again, there is something very American about that. It's how you defined the American experience earlier—this vast landscape divinized.

In your book *Earth Poetry* you write that "the quest for drugs is nothing less that a thirst for unity of being." It seems to me that another way to that is that the quest for drugs is the quest for mysticism.

EVERSON: Traditionally, the great religions deny drugs because there's no preparation for vision. Drugs distract the fundamental process of self-knowledge and seem to offer transcendence. We all want to transcend where we are. This is why we go to God.

FOX: Would you comment on this statement from one of your essays: "The excruciating tension between civilized head and primitive heart is the American heritage."

EVERSON: The problem is endemic to the American because of deficiency in our experience of culture. We have created the most triumphant civilization in the history of man, but you will look a long time before you can put your finger on anything so evocatively intangible as the essence of European or Asiatic culture. Civilization is of the head, but culture is of the heart and there we are unsophisticated, i.e., primitive. It is the source of our forthrightness and our generosity, our candor and our sincerity. But it is purchased at its own price: excruciating tension. Culture is born of another kind of suffering, namely sorrow. America has never been ground under the heel of a conqueror, so we have never endured that national humiliation, the ubiquitous sorrow that curbs the collective pride and sends the nerve of the soul questing down the heart's bleakest realm, to there suffer a sea-change and shimmer into bloom.

Index

Naked Heart has been published in an edition of 2,000 copies. 126 copies have been specially bound in boards, and are signed by the author as follows: 26 lettered A–Z for friends of the press, with the remaining numbered 1–100. Book is set in Garamond #3 with the display set in Weiss initials Series III. Design by Amy Evans.

AMERICAN POETRY *Studies in Twentieth Century Poetry and Poetics*
General Editor: Lee Bartlett

Managing Editor: Uma Kukathas